CORPORATE PEACE

MARY MARTIN

Corporate Peace

How Global Business Shapes a Hostile World

HURST & COMPANY, LONDON

First published in the United Kingdom in 2019 by
C. Hurst & Co. (Publishers) Ltd.,
41 Great Russell Street, London, WC1B 3PL
© Mary Martin, 2019
All rights reserved.
Printed in India

Distributed in the United States, Canada and Latin America by
Oxford University Press, 198 Madison Avenue, New York, NY 10016,
United States of America.

The right of Mary Martin to be identified as the author of
this publication is asserted by her in accordance with the
Copyright, Designs and Patents Act, 1988.

A Cataloguing-in-Publication data record for this book
is available from the British Library.

ISBN: 9781787381278

This book is printed using paper from registered sustainable
and managed sources.

www.hurstpublishers.com

For Robert (1954–2010)

CONTENTS

ACKNOWLEDGEMENTS

When I set out to write this book I did not realise how many journeys would be involved, how many strange places I would find myself in or people I would talk to, and how much time would pass before I felt that the whole story was good enough to tell. It can never be entirely complete, but my thanks go to all those who gave me time, information, wisdom and inspiration from their experiences. Many took risks to help me for which I am particularly grateful. I hope I have done justice to their stories and views, and in many cases given them the voice they hoped for and deserve.

I want to thank LSE colleagues who encouraged me, and gave ideas about how to mix storytelling and analysis, especially Vesna Bojicic-Dzelilovic; Marina Kemp at Ink Academy for her enthusiasm and skill in suggesting editorial changes: without her, this book would still be sitting in my computer; Michael Dwyer at Hurst for believing in my idea, and for his perceptive suggestions for making it better.

Most of all I have to thank my family for tolerating absences of person and mind over several years. I owe a special debt to Sarah for making me carry on at a time when writing was particularly hard, and to James for his company and knowledge on trips to Mexico.

ACKNOWLEDGEMENTS

ABBREVIATIONS

AFPS	Association France-Palestine Solidarité
BDS	Boycott, Divestment and Sanctions campaign
B4P	Business for Peace
BTC	Baku-Tbilisi-Ceyhan pipeline
CDAP	Caspian Development Advisory Panel
CDC	Centers for Disease Control and Prevention
CEO	Chief Executive Officer
CIP	Community Investment Programme
CSR	Corporate Social Responsibility
DRC	Democratic Republic of Congo
EPSMG	Ebola Private Sector Mobilisation Group
ESG	Environmental, Social and Governance standards
EVD	Ebola Virus Disease
FARC	Fuerzas Armardas Revolucionarias de Colombia
FAS	Fiat Automobile Serbia
IA	International Alert
ICISS	International Commission on Intervention and State Sovereignty
IHL	International Humanitarian Law
ISET	International School of Economics at Tbilisi
MSF	Médecins Sans Frontières
OCHA	UN Office for Coordination of Humanitarian Affairs
PLO	Palestine Liberation Organization
PMSCs	Private military and security companies
R2P	Responsibility to Protect

ABBREVIATIONS

SDG	Sustainable Development Goal
TNC	Transnational corporation
TSJ	Todos Somos Juárez (We Are All Juárez)
UNDP	United Nations Development Programme
UNGP	UN Guiding Principles on Business and Human Rights
UNSC	UN Security Council
WCM	World Class Manufacturing
WHO	World Health Organization

CONFLICT AND THE CORPORATION

On a November evening in 2006, a group of businessmen met in a conference room overlooking the River Thames in London. Bankers, mining company executives, financial analysts and management consultants had been invited by a private security company to discuss the commercial and investment possibilities that were about to open up in the Democratic Republic of Congo. The DRC was emerging from five years of civil war and nearly five decades of political and economic turmoil. It was in the middle of holding its first democratic elections for forty years.

Africa's second-largest country, known as Zaire after independence in 1960, and before that as the Belgian Congo, the DRC had a long history of foreign interference coupled with violence. In 1885 King Leopold II of Belgium, craving a slice of 'ce magnifique gateau africain' ('this magnificent African cake')[1] to use as his personal hunting ground, declared it the Free State of Congo; but it was a fiefdom rather than a colony, and far from free. In the next century the hunters were European colonialists and international companies raiding Congo's natural resources, first rubber and then minerals. Immortalised as 'the heart of darkness' in Joseph Conrad's nineteenth-century novel, the Congo has attracted and horrified the West in equal measure. It boasts deposits of some of the most precious and useful minerals on the planet, supplying 10 per cent of the world's copper, more than a third of the cobalt used to manufacture batteries, and 8 per cent of niobium used in alloys to make pipelines and jet engines, as well as uranium for weapons, gold and diamonds.[2] Casseterite, a tin ore mined amidst the beautiful and remote mountain scenery of eastern Congo, became the gold dust for a modern age, used to manufacture mobile phones, game consoles and laptops for consumers thousands of miles away. A boom in consumer electronics caused prices of these metals to rise by 1,000 per cent at the turn of the century. Orders for the latest model of mobile phone and Sony PlayStation drove demand, and helped transform the economics and politics of the DRC. Access to this mineral mecca, for so long off-limits to Western companies, was a glittering prize indeed.[3]

Foreign mining companies and investors have not been the only people keen to exploit the DRC's mineral riches over the years. In 1997 an uprising ousted the dictator Mobutu Sese Seko, who had presided over the Congo for more than three decades. Nigerian playwright Wole Soyinka described the monarchical tyrant as a 'toad king', living in grotesque splendour while his people starved. Under Mobuto the Congo had become, according to the World Bank, 'a structure for individual enrichment and patronage'. A politics of greed prevailed in which natural resources substituted for the national currency. Top government officials pocketed mineral revenues—sometimes simply by taking gem diamonds and arranging for their sale in Antwerp, Europe's diamond capital. As the World Bank describes it, the role of the private sector was as a source of bribes, not a motor of development.[4]

During Mobutu's dictatorship the Congolese state imploded. State-owned mining companies collapsed, many international firms withdrew, and for over a decade mining was carried out mostly by artisan miners, working informally. Using only shovels and barrows they dug deep holes in a pock-marked landscape of red earth, searching for ore. Many of the miners were young people and women, who had been drawn in from the countryside by the lure of employment and who ended up making a precarious living in dangerous conditions.

The civil war that followed Mobutu's fall did not begin with the DRC's mineral wealth, but it soon became one of the prime features of the conflict. Paramilitary groups preyed on the outputs of the artisan mines, extorting payments or stealing the miners' output, selling it to buy weapons. Through the complicity of foreign companies and networks of intermediaries, the DRC's mineral riches ended up in a global system that connected international manufacturers with raw materials, and the swipe functions of smart phones with the earth-laden wheel-barrows of the artisan diggers. Or, as the NGO International Alert described it: 'The miner who earns his living by using his own physical energy to dig up coltan in some forgotten forest in Kivu forms the first link of a global chain, the last link of which is the mobile phone user.'[5]

The DRC became the symbol of a new type of war that had emerged at the end of the twentieth century. The conflict there claimed between 4 and 5 million lives from 1997 to 2004, many from disease and mal-nutrition as a result of the violence.[6] Sometimes referred to as Africa's First World War, because it spread throughout central Africa, consum-ing neighbouring states, and because of the scale of casualties,[7] it was a war not just between rival states, but an internal conflict between people and their rulers, fuelled by a perverse economics of greed and predation. Nearly 2 million people were uprooted from their homes, 71 per cent of the population was undernourished.[8] The peace treaty signed between warring factions would introduce a ceasefire, but the suffering and violence inflicted on the Congolese would go on, and persists today, two decades later.

This devastation echoed an earlier tragedy. The pursuit of rubber and mineral profits by Belgian and other international groups at the end of the nineteenth century had cost an estimated 6–10 million deaths, or up to a third of the population.[9] Belgian industrial conglom-erates, still powerful today, as well as Belgian cities were founded on the back of riches from the Congo.

In the twentieth century, civil war brought the DRC to the attention of a different group of outsiders. International peacekeepers and for-eign aid agencies piled into the country in the wake of an earlier cease-fire agreed in 1999, bringing stabilisation plans and multimillion-dollar aid programmes in an attempt to build a judicial and legal system and create democratic political institutions. The aim was not only to pro-tect the Congolese people, but also to ensure that the DRC's mineral economy could once again attract investors able to rely on the legality of contracts and the safety of their assets.[10]

The United Nations, the European Union (EU), Britain, Belgium, France, the United States and the DRC's neighbours in southern Africa brokered a peace agreement in 2002, including the appointment of an interim government. Congolese queued in extraordinary numbers to claim their right to vote, walking miles, standing for hours and braving intimidation. People who had been victimised and oppressed by dictators and civil war were at last able to choose their leader. The right to vote came in the shape of a plastic voter card issued to those of voting age who were able to demonstrate where they lived. Possession of the card became a sought-after badge of identity, not just for the poor but also for those in jobs with regular incomes. It was more potent than any bank or business card.

In rural villages and settlements that populated the banks of the long Congo River, 17 million Congolese voted for what they hoped would be a new start in history. At the same time, foreign investors also queued, to grab a stake in the economy, as the potential of the DRC's natural resources once more re-entered the imaginations of foreign capitalists.

The investment dream

Another brown river, another capital. In London, overlooking the Thames, drinks and canapés were served, the small talk subsided, and discussions began in earnest. A Canadian banker addressed the audience to explain the opportunities on offer from a peaceful and newly democratic DRC. The new era had ended the civil war, elected a new president, and promised the creation of new political institutions. It had also brought new foreign technologies that made it possible to restart production in Congolese mines. The banker used as an example one particular site that would require less than 10 per cent of its former workforce of 8,000. Cheaper production costs would ensure increased profitability, at a time when demand and prices for the mine's output were both soaring. It was a combination that was irresistible to foreign investors, offsetting the risks of entering a market where there was still uncertainty and conflict.

At this point, I stood up and asked the banker what his clients, a consortium of companies with rights to the mine, planned to do with the thousands of former workers who would no longer be needed at the plant. These workers had not only been caught up in the conflict, but had actively engaged in it. Newly disarmed and returning to their communities, they were in need of jobs, housing and healthcare, which proceeds from the mine could help deliver. But that wouldn't happen. Under the new production scheme the banker outlined, they would remain on the other side of a perimeter fence separating the mine from the local village, cut off from the wealth being generated. Social tensions among communities that had been uprooted and disrupted by the war were still acute, and in the absence of a functioning state there was no one to provide for even the basic needs of the local population, unless it was the company. The banker's answer to my question was as polite as it was brutal: those people were not his problem. They were someone else's responsibility.

It was this response that set me off on a trail to explore the relationship between big business and people, against a backdrop of conflict in Africa, Latin America, the edges of Europe, the brink of Asia and the Middle East. I needed to understand why dealings between companies and communities were often fractious and problematic; what lay behind the banker's throwaway comment rejecting any responsibility for people in the area of the mine; and what global capitalism meant for those living in the middle of chaos, insecurity and life-shaping change. The situation in the DRC showed how much the presence of business mattered in a country emerging from conflict, and the capacity of foreign investors to affect the lives of the poorest and most vulnerable people. More than this, if the DRC was the scene of a new type of war, what was the role of business in resolving that kind of conflict? Was business part of the solution that eluded international peacekeepers and nation-builders in trying to end global instability, or simply part of the problem?

I came back to thinking about the perimeter fences that separate companies from communities. They don't keep trouble out. On the contrary, the artificial line between the protection, safety and wealth that foreign companies enjoy and the everyday experiences of people on the outside is a fragile creation. On both sides of this line, people are motivated by the potential of money and the promise of wealth and a better life. Companies and communities occupy not only a shared physical and geographical space but also a hope and belief in the benefits of foreign investment. The line is breached when those on the wrong side harbour tensions and grievances that fuel unrest. Trouble ripples outwards and affects national, regional and even international prospects for peace. It seemed to me that this space, which was shared by companies and communities, yet at the same time was deeply fractured, was vital to how peace and prosperity are built and sustained. In the modern world of conflicts which begin within states, and which spread across neighbouring countries and whole regions, were these spaces of commerce, investment and global production the ground zero for imagining a way out of conflict, and building a new kind of global security? I wanted to see how business might work with, rather than in spite of, local people, to navigate insecurity and crises. I wanted to find out whether there is really common ground between companies and communities or simply a terrain of confrontation.

Mixed messages

The spread of international companies in difficult and dangerous places is a phenomenon of globalisation. The DRC has been a poster child for the negative effects of globalisation and foreign investment on poor countries with a history of conflict. It is not only mining companies chasing after valuable resources, as in the DRC, that have attracted the attentions of activists and policy-makers, but also makers of consumer brands from toiletries to soft drinks in search of new markets and cheaper production facilities, banks establishing global networks, and software and telecommunications companies spreading webs of connectivity. This expansion of business collides increasingly with zones of insecurity, chaos, humanitarian crisis and conflict around the world. Even if a company itself is not present in a conflict zone, its products and services can, through global supply chains, be linked back to networks of small companies and individual workers who contribute raw materials, finishing or packaging, working in conditions that are shaped by conflict.

The question at the heart of this book is: how should we view this juxtaposition and its implications for our own and others' safety and well-being? As an inconvenience, a threat or perhaps an opportunity to build peace and stability in new ways? As global companies, operating across borders and national jurisdictions, move into once-remote areas of the world whose wars and crises increasingly impact on our own lives, should we be more vigilant about what these companies do and their ability to shape conflicts, development and global security?

What takes place at ground level, where companies come face to face with the reality of everyday deprivation and insecurity, is not what you read in economic accounts of foreign investment, in the brochures or the websites of foreign companies, or even in the reports of activists, vigilant against corporate wrongdoing.

On the one hand, there is scope for abuse and predatory behaviour by companies, living and operating among people with resources but no independent means of exploiting them. On the other, the globalisation wave of foreign investment is capable of generating material prosperity for conflict-ridden countries, and also of addressing the causes of conflict and instability, which lie in bad politics, weak authority and the inability of people to live and work together. Where there is no single cause of crisis and chaos, but a toxic mix of different problems, could business do more than generate profits: could they improve the conditions for peace in fragile places as well?

Greed and grievance

For much of the period since 1989, the focus of policy-makers and analysts has been on the factors that spark armed violence within states, and understanding what drives conflict. As the Cold War ended, wars erupted in countries over ethnic rivalries, where combinations of identity politics and nationalism were deployed to seize power and promote the interests of particular groups of citizens. So-called 'new wars' had a different logic to traditional conflicts. They were not only about identity, but also about economics.[11] Economists such as Jeffrey Sachs and Paul Collier had shown statistically that conflict has powerful economic correlates. It is fed by poverty, the lack of decent livelihoods, high unemployment and particularly youth unemployment. For desperate individuals, the cost of rebellion, delinquency and corruption is relatively low because they have little to lose. Conflict is particularly linked to natural resource abundance, and by competition for scarce resources such as land and water, and often accompanied by environmental abuse and rapid urbanisation.[12]

The label 'greed and grievance' was applied to explain why this new kind of warfare came to dominate international politics and the economic factors that contribute to the outbreak and persistence of violence. Armed rebellions against the status quo were either triggered by deep inequalities between different groups in society—of income, political power, social status—which gave rise to grievances, or because warring factions found there was money to be made through waging war (greed). Often there was a mixture of both. In the greed argument, oil, minerals, wood and commodities served to enrich a powerful elite, and finance predatory and violent behaviour. In the DRC the availability of high-worth minerals led to the plunder of mining areas by militias, and illicit sales through foreign intermediaries enabling combatants to buy weapons and prolong the war. A continuing flow of income from transferring the control of natural resources also provides cover against an underlying truth that economic and political systems do not function or deliver basic goods for the country's people. This is the paradox of plenty, in which abundant riches trap countries in a cycle of conflict. [13]

Resource wars or, as Philippe Le Billon puts it, 'wars in resource rich countries full of poor people', [14] reveal ways in which business and conflict are linked: through financing weapons and fighters, stirring up tensions around mining sites and through making governments overly reliant on a narrow base of resource revenues and the unpredictable fluctuations in commodity prices on world markets. The private sector may conspire openly or tacitly with governments and local political elites, and exploit vulnerability among local populations as part of its business model for working in dangerous neighbourhoods. Even when open warfare ends and peace deals are sealed, economic after-effects continue. Periods of transition and post-conflict reconstruction may last years, suffer many reversals, and produce uncertain outcomes. A feature of contemporary civil wars is that many of them re-ignite, just as the DRC's did after the 2003 peace accords and the 2006 democratic elections.

This type of persistent conflict and chronic underdevelopment has another characteristic of excessive dependency: fragile states dependent on the vagaries of the global economy, societies on foreign intermediaries and impoverished people on powerful private or public institutions. In countries with weak and dysfunctional governments, and few reliable political institutions, the presence of foreign corporations creates another layer of fragile reliance on an outside power. This is not only true of extractive companies in countries such as the DRC. Nor is it just the result of corrosive connections between corporate predators, global commodity markets and underdeveloped economies. It is bigger than just the resource curse. The story of this book is the dependency of desperate communities and vulnerable individuals on the fortunes, strategies and ethical behaviour of global companies, and how politicians, businessmen and communities themselves manage the complex effects of that dependency.

The business and human rights debate

The idea of a perverse relationship between big business and poor people was central to another key debate about conflict, initiated by the United Nations. In 2005 the UN secretary general asked Harvard academic Professor John Ruggie to devise standards that would govern business accountability for human rights. The aim was to define terms such as 'complicity' between companies and governments, and 'sphere of influence', which described the extent of corporate responsibility. Ruggie defined the challenge of business and human rights abuses as not simply an ethical issue, but about the organisation of international society when national borders are superseded by global commerce and communications. Ruggie stated his concern that bad business behaviour did not only threaten individual human rights, but that it pointed to a deep and dangerous gap in managing international affairs, including the possibility that corporate actions might provoke international crises. Rather than falling back on the traditional tactics of appealing to corporations to behave decently or threatening them with legislation and fines, Ruggie produced a set of 'Guiding Principles on Business and Human Rights', which said that companies shared a responsibility with governments to protect and respect human rights.[15]

In conflict areas there was an increased risk of gross human rights abuses, and what Ruggie termed a 'negative symbiotic relationship' between business and conflict, citing the example of mining companies in parts of the DRC.

What Ruggie did was to present business as part of both the problem and the solution. His framework made a connection between

9

individual business actions and the international context, proposing that this global issue had local roots. His answer was to encircle business with safeguards and checks, rather than try to create new laws.[16]

The business and human rights debate was part of a newer, altogether darker view of capitalism, which viewed companies not as part of national and transnational wealth generation, as traditional economic arguments had it, but as global destabilisers. The consequence of this critical attitude was to promote the idea of corporate responsibility, and make it part of semi-legal codes of conduct. Companies also began to be seen not simply as abstract financial entities, but as political and social agents with the will to act—even as 'citizens' with a role and influence in shaping the societies in which they operated.

Something must be done

Greed and grievance, resource curses, conflict traps and business and human rights had drawn attention to the nefarious connections between global business, particularly among extractive companies in mining, oil and other natural resources and civil wars. But this was only one side of a complex and increasingly confused story linking business with global security. The image of predator corporations gained traction in highly public campaigns by international NGOs such as Global Witness that revealed examples of foreign companies exploiting local communities. However, the assumption that conflict and underdevelopment could be resolved in part by supporting more foreign investment continued to drive public policy and how the international community responded to international crises, particularly arguments for external intervention. A view of investment as the key to reform has deep roots in the persuasive power of democracy and free trade to reduce the incidence of war.[17] The assumption that there could be a positive link between foreign capital and stability and growth in fragile countries was part of the 'liberal peace', an idea that gained a new following among scholars and governments in the wake of the Cold War. The liberal peace is based on a belief that democratic states with open economies are inherently peaceful, and that by spreading their values on markets, trade, human rights and representative democracy, they will create vested interests in support of peace. The liberal peace in action consists of 'efforts to create conditions in which violence will not recur'. It is an enterprise on many different fronts, building market economies, Western-style financial systems, political, judicial and social institutions. Policy-makers and NGOs flocked to the international enterprise that became 'post-conflict reconstruction', a worldwide industry of foreign assistance to fix failed and waning states. Critics see it as a project of 'subsidised capitalism', using investment and market forces to pacify querulous locals and generate gains for economic elites.[18] There was certainly growing evidence that interventions caused confrontation between outsiders and locals, as well as among different groups of locals. Moreover, reforms by external peacebuilders were becoming bogged down in a morass of contradictory, competing strategies and policy agendas.[19] Examples of foreign investment fuelling conflicts within communities in already fragile states challenged the presumption that peaceful development and good governance would flow from introducing free-market democracy.[20]

In post-war DRC, saturated by peacekeepers and reforms, President Kabila admitted that there had been mismanagement of the country's natural resources. 'We need to put an end to the paradox which sees huge mining potential, and ever more intense mining activity, but only modest benefits for the state.'[21] African countries published the 'Africa Mining Vision', which aimed to achieve a trickle-down effect from the sale of minerals. Yet the 'Vision' was about gaining the confidence of the business sector rather than changing the way extractive companies operated. It reflected the confused message about business in conflict zones. Policy-makers performed precarious balancing acts between courting investor support and coercing companies into behaving better.

Business for Peace

The United Nations is the prime example of trying to play the presence of the private sector in fragile countries both ways. On the one hand, it had sponsored the growing business and human rights debate. On the other, it took a decisive step to woo the private sector as a partner, one with deep pockets. In 2000 UN secretary general Kofi Annan, speaking at the World Economic Forum in Davos, called on business leaders to

11

join a 'Global Compact' of principles and values in the areas of human rights, labour standards and environmental practices. The Global Compact was formally initiated a year later, creating a worldwide network between businesses, governments and UN agencies. Two decades later this network has big rhetorical power—companies frequently cite their membership of the Global Compact in talking about responsible and sustainable practices, although critics claim that it has produced limited results on the ground.[22]

Kofi Annan's speech was made on his third visit to the Davos gathering of business leaders in two years, itself a sign of increasing efforts to forge public–private partnerships in the areas of development and human rights.

In 2013 the UN Global Compact set up Business for Peace (B4P), a platform for companies and business associations to catalyse actions that promoted peace. Business for Peace starts from a premise that business has a role to play in international efforts to guarantee stability and social development in war-torn parts of the world.[23] There are currently around 12,000 signatories to the B4P platform where companies can learn to become peacebuilders. Detractors claim that it just represents another layer of international rhetoric that does not confront the ethical and practical challenges of business taking on peacebuilding tasks.[24] But hot on the heels of B4P came a much more ambitious move by the UN which would propel the private sector into its biggest role to date in addressing global development and security: the Sustainable Development Goals (SDGs).

In 2018 Hollywood actor Michael Douglas was the star turn at a meeting to promote Agenda 2030 among business leaders. The SDGs consist of seventeen goals on issues ranging from poverty to water, health and education. Goal 16 is peace, justice and strong institutions. Douglas, as a UN Peace Messenger, was deployed to win the backing, and the wallets, of CEOs. Agenda 2030 has an eye-watering bill of an estimated $3–5 trillion per year, to transform development prospects of the world's poorest countries. The UN strategy for achieving the SDGs relies heavily on mobilising businesses to pick up part of this bill. Many have answered the call. An estimated 20,000 have pledged support for Agenda 2030 and in the first five years committed over $7 trillion of investments. Sustainability and resilience became the new buzz-words of corporate reporting and respectability. In many ways, though, the sustainable development agenda, and specifically goal 16 of peace, justice and strong institutions, have simply muddied the question of business roles in global stability. Corporate commitments to the SDGs are voluntary, with companies free to pick and choose which goals they will support, and how. There are few measurements to indicate whether their contributions are doing good, or simply making companies look good, as critics claim.[25]

The peacebuilder paradox: corporations outside 'Peaceland'[26]

Whatever benefits governments and international organisations may see in co-opting private money for public development projects, it is striking how few companies have been part of formal efforts to stabilise and redevelop crisis-affected countries. Although economic reform is intrinsic to the idea of liberal peacebuilding, and companies are a significant presence on the ground in conflict areas, they sit at the margins of peacebuilding interventions. Companies are rarely invited to peace talks, despite often being present through a conflict, and possessing useful local knowledge. Neither is their advice sought in the process of state (re)building, even though they represent a crucial link in transmitting economic reforms into everyday practice.

The reticence is not just on the part of policy-makers. It is rare that companies themselves use terms such as conflict resolution, transitional justice, security and governance reform which are part of the language of international organisations or NGOs. The global corporation remains aloof from the programmes of peacekeepers and state builders. They are passive peacebuilders, 'internalising conflict as an additional operational cost'.[27]

Corporations are the odd ones out: neither part of government, 'civil society' nor the international aid community.[28] They have a different culture, and the profit motive is usually seen as a barrier that risks tainting public endeavours. Why else would they get involved? 'Humanitarians are very nervous about the private sector,' Sir John Holmes, co-chair of the International Rescue Committee UK, said in 2013. 'The humanitarian system and private sector do not know how to talk to each other.'[29]

Private funding of humanitarian interventions nearly doubled between 2006 and 2010, representing nearly a third of the total. There have been high-profile partnerships such as with Microsoft and the Bill and Melinda Gates Foundation to combat malaria. Companies such as Coca-Cola and Nike pick their favourite causes such as helping girls and women to find employment. Aid agencies such as Oxfam and Save the Children work with large corporations such as Unilever, Ikea, Marks & Spencer and GlaxoSmithKline to tackle poverty, hunger, health and education needs. Yet many in governments and NGOs worry that they will be seen as selling out to commercial interests if they team up with big business.

There is less resistance to involving local companies in peace processes. In Sri Lanka, South Africa and Ukraine they have been part of attempts to use economics to drive peace.[30] US politician Richard Haas, speaking to business leaders in Belfast in 2002, told them they were 'central to the quest for peace and stability. In fact, we have seen time and again that business leaders constitute some of the strongest voices urging Northern Ireland's politicians to do the right thing.' Another notable exception is Colombia, where the world's longest-lasting civil war was declared at an end in 2016 when the government signed a peace agreement with the main guerrilla movement, the Fuerzas Armadas Revolucionarias de Colombia (FARC). The agreement included an explicit invitation to Colombia's companies to become part of the process of implementing the peace agreement, calling on them to invest in areas where the FARC had ruled rural communities for five decades, as well as to take responsibility for abuses that they themselves had committed during the conflict.

But global corporations pose ethical and practical challenges for peacebuilders. Transnational companies are the elephant in the room: large and potentially destructive, but at the same time so big that not everyone wants to acknowledge their presence, let alone harness them to a collective effort of building peace. Despite possessing many of the logistical, information-technical and political resources needed to achieve the goals of international interventions, the big beasts of commerce are not seen as a positive force. So business and security, peace and profitability remain largely disconnected, stranded in separate policy domains.

CONFLICT AND THE CORPORATION

Unbundling the private sector

The failure to understand how companies can be important in creating a peace that lasts, and development that endures, involves looking at complex sets of processes that cannot be reduced to economics or commercial behaviour, which are the classic lenses for looking at the private sector. The corporate conundrum in international politics is how to deal with the fact that companies have multi-faceted and often ambiguous impacts on peace and development. Having an either–or approach, which is ambivalent as to whether to co-opt or constrain companies in conflict zones, risks treating them simplistically. It ignores the fact that their presence in situations where insecurity has many guises is part of a complex pattern of daily life in fragile societies, including unglimpsed possibilities for companies in preventing and mitigating violence.

As I began to delve into the realities on the ground where foreign companies operated, and their puzzling absence from international peacebuilding, I could see that the mix of foreign money, vulnerable communities and aggravated insecurity could produce unexpected results. Companies themselves could not be labelled systematically as either benevolent or abusive, designated as 'good citizens' or cruel machines. Above all, I felt that where daily life is a struggle against small types of insecurity, as well as grave danger, and where coping strategies to survive may look ugly—even corrupt and nefarious to the outside eye—business impacts are personal to each individual, family and situation. In understanding how global capital fits into the dystopian picture of conflict and insecurity, the variegated, nuanced effects of companies could best be seen in terms of specific experiences. This side of the picture where companies influence even the most intimate aspects of life is not reflected in most academic studies of conflict and development, or in policies to build and sustain peace. The paradigm that sees foreign investment as a financial phenomenon, including the tendency to view it as simply positive or negative, could not fully uncover the opportunities and pitfalls of foreign businesses in contexts of conflict.

Our typical vocabulary for companies includes terms such as 'business confidence' and 'business interests', as if all companies are the same and shape our social and economic landscape in the same way. We often talk about the private sector as if it is a single entity, which has to be engaged, rather like a car's gearbox, in order to drive the economy forward. But business is not monolithic. Each company is different, and to understand how companies affect our security and to see their potential we need first to lift the lid off the one-size-fits-all box we put them in.

The narrative of foreign corporations in conflict zones is not the standard tale of investment plans and management strategies. As we will see, in the Middle East and at the time of a deadly health epidemic in Africa, operating in the middle of conflict and crisis challenges emotions and the moral standards of business leaders. The story of this book is personal—about how people with financial and commercial power come together with people facing an existential kind of risk, and what that interaction tells us about the nature of security and insecurity in today's world.

Human security is a term that policy-makers and academics use to describe what ordinary people need in order to live tolerable lives, at moments when they are overwhelmed by conflict and disaster, when normality is disrupted and the very core of their existence is threatened. It means focusing on basic needs such as clean water, a roof over your head and an income, protection from physical threats such as death, injury or torture, and psychological welfare such as dignity and a chance to determine your own future, rather than have it imposed on you by strangers or foes. A tolerable life also requires being treated with dignity. The challenge here is more than getting companies not to commit human rights abuses. It is about tackling deep-seated threats and risks that people face, seizing opportunities and making the most of their capacities to improve their lives.

Ensuring personal well-being and safety is about 'the security of small things'. It does not rely on armies and weapons, the control of territory and defence of state borders, which are the classic concerns of those in defence ministries and government departments, or many international organisations. It means supporting people on the ground to make and sustain their own versions of peace.

This kind of security is often controversial because it means taking control away from the exclusive grip of an elite who work inside policy establishments, and making security a concern for all of us.[31] Critics claim that human security is too vague as a prescription for how to navigate the political challenges we face. The counter-argument is that individual experiences matter, and how people and communities react to existential predicaments has a fundamental bearing on the prospects for peace, not just locally but also globally. Wars do not end solely as a result of diplomatic treaties or sending troops, by the taking of territory or bombing insurgent militias. Lasting peace requires that there are incentives for people not to fight or take part in organised criminal ways of making a living.[32]

This book proposes that re-imagining security as something that deals with individual, family and community safety and welfare, offers a new lens for looking at the role of business. Rather than concentrating on the visible abuses that attract public attention, I set out to examine the multiple, often contradictory, effects that companies create at moments and places of heightened risk amongst ordinary people. I wanted to see how they influence the things that matter most to families and communities, creating impacts that shape the security of the world beyond fragile states and conflict zones. Economic statistics don't always capture this type of picture. They miss much of what is going on in small villages and between different kinds of people. Perhaps stories could shed more light on what is happening.

Foreign corporations are an essential part of delivering physical, material and emotional security, because of their daily contact with individuals, and how lives depend on so much of what business does in a community, through investment, environmental effects, new cultural norms and in changing the local social fabric. Such impacts are often unwitting, and companies miss opportunities to improve well-being that can help build peace. At present we do not know enough about how this happens, and the conditions under which corporate power can contribute to the public good, rather than act as a peace spoiler or conflict driver. This book is about throwing some light on that puzzle, starting at ground level where companies' influence is most acute, and least observed.

The story of Fiat in Serbia, told in Chapter 4, is an example of how businesses can be myopic, even naïve, when it comes to understanding what they can do. The first time I approached Fiat about its investment,

17

I was told that I would probably not find it very interesting. Nothing to see here. Everyone had welcomed the company for handing the country an economic lifeline. This was true, but not the whole story. Fiat's arrival had ripple effects, which were not immediately obvious, including changing ordinary lives and affecting party politics. Its story is not about corporate abuse or classic economic development, but of a social phenomenon, planted in the midst of a fragile society.

This book is not just about the 'bad' company, which is the chief character in the business and human rights narrative. Nor do I want to suggest that companies mostly do good things, and are simply misunderstood. The stories in the next few chapters show some of the ways in which company actions have repercussions for peace and the quality of development, and therefore the life chances of ordinary people. Corporate strategy becomes entangled in complicated logics and relationships, and sometimes goes awry. It comes up against messy and chaotic environments, and it also reshapes them. What does this mean in an increasingly hostile world, where so much effort by governments and organisations is directed at trying to stem insecurity, chaos and conflict?

The practice of keeping business at arm's length from efforts to build peace has started to change. Business in conflict zones is no longer the 'blind spot' in the eye of key international organisations such as the UN, the World Bank and some governments.[33] 'In the face of diminishing resources and increasing disasters and crises ... it is imperative to bring in innovative resources,' said Mamissa Mboob of the Private Sector Section at the UN Office for Coordination of Humanitarian Affairs (OCHA). 'It's almost as if we have no choice. ... The humanitarian system is stretched to its capacity. ... It's becoming more clear that no single entity can solve a lot of these world problems.'[34]

The example of private companies responding to the Ebola epidemic in West Africa, told in Chapter 7, is notable for the fact that, with little cash changing hands, the companies surprised aid agencies and governments by being able to fill a vacuum in the international humanitarian response to the disease.[35] That story represents one small turning-point in changing public perceptions of what companies can do. In the next chapter we will look at other shifts in public views of business, and our understandings about making the world safe.

CONFLICT AND THE CORPORATION

Many companies have long believed that no one saw or bothered about what they did in faraway countries, when they operated in contexts where ethnic cleansing, government corruption and social disintegration were happening, or where there was chronic and persistent failure of livelihoods. That is changing. People are watching, and the chapters that follow are intended to help us understand what we see, and reveal some of the reasons why future peace depends on good business behaviour.

The story of change begins not today, but much further back, in seventeenth-century Europe, with ideas of state protection and responsibility, and how they have evolved over time to end up today in the hands of global corporations. The tale continues in 'faraway' places across four continents. In the world of drug conflicts in Latin America, or in the frozen conflicts in the Caucasus, we start to see ways in which big companies navigate uncertain and dangerous terrains, and can play a positive role in keeping people safe. In the Balkans, proximity to a market of 500 million European consumers and cheap production costs attracted Fiat to a country still struggling to emerge from authoritarian rule and a bloody civil war, but it had to understand the particular challenges this posed for its vision of low-cost global manufacturing. In the Middle East, French conglomerate Veolia misunderstood what was at stake when it decided to take on a transport contract in the Occupied Territories, with more dramatic consequences. These are cautionary tales about the sometimes unimagined impacts of commercial decisions. In Africa insecurity comes not only from conflict but also from natural disasters such as the Ebola epidemic. How did a leading steelmaker from its offices in London's Mayfair confront a catastrophe that threatened to wipe out thousands of the inhabitants of West Africa?

In turning the spotlight onto these corporations, I have tried to avoid a blame game or sweeping judgements in favour of simply telling what happens as a result of them being present in these environments, in order to reveal a bigger picture about peace, conflict and development, and how they connect to companies.

Activists call this the era of the 'regenerative' business, where companies cannot be content with merely reducing the bad impact or so-called negative externalities of their operations, but must seek opportunities to create value for society—through locally attuned policies, replacing exploitation with empowerment, and through 'distributed decision-making' rather than remote management.[36] This book attempts to alter our line of vision about global business and explain how it can contribute to those new opportunities, and in doing so, break the perpetual cycle of crisis and conflict that grips so much of the world.

2

A DOUBLE CRISIS AND A TURNING-POINT

Two developments have helped catalyse a change in the place of business in our world, breaking down barriers between companies and peacebuilding, and paving the way for a closer alignment between global security efforts and global corporations. The first significant development is in the way we try to manage problems that cross geographical and cultural borders, and deal with emergencies from wars to natural disasters. The second sign of change is the emergence of tougher attitudes towards what companies should do, and greater expectations of their contributions to society at large.

The changes that are taking place reflect a double crisis—of liberal peace and security on the one hand, and of neoliberal capitalism on the other. These crises could trigger changes in the relationships between business and traditional sources of action to ensure peace and stability within governments and aid agencies. The shift they represent could potentially carve out a new role for corporations as part of efforts to create a safer world.

The crisis of liberal security

On 4 February 2012 the UN Security Council (UNSC) met to discuss international action in the face of mounting violence in Syria between rebels and government forces. The regime of President Bashar al-Assad and its policy of suppressing uprisings had already caused more than 7,500 deaths. An estimated 100,000–200,000 Syrians had fled their homes. The USA, under President Obama, stung by the aftermath of its invasion of Iraq in 2003, was reluctant to commit to another foreign military campaign. The British Parliament subsequently also vetoed military action over a chemical weapons attack on the outskirts of Damascus. After more than a decade of stepping in to stop other people's wars, the international community was growing tired of pacification interventions that were costly and lengthy.

The term peacebuilding, like much else in the lexicon of conflict, originated with the UN in 1992, to describe actions taken to strengthen societies after war, in order to prevent a relapse into conflict. Peacebuilding means more than calming hostilities, or an absence of violence. It is meant to create positive measures to ensure peaceful futures. UN secretary general Boutros Boutros-Ghali coined the term, to set out a civilian vision of intervention: 'to build peace, stability and security must encompass matters beyond military threats in order to break the fetters of strife and warfare that have characterized the past'.[1]

The opening ceremony of the era of liberal peacebuilding through foreign intervention was a speech by British prime minister Tony Blair in Chicago in April 1999. Blair outlined a doctrine of 'international community', which required states to collaborate, and intervene if necessary in the internal affairs of other states on humanitarian grounds, and as a matter of domestic self-interest. The doctrine marked a departure from the idea of non-intervention enshrined in the UN charter, and in the paradigm of the sovereign nation-state, which had prevailed in international relations since the seventeenth century.[2]

As Blair was speaking in Chicago, NATO planes were bombing Serbia in a bid to halt Slobodan Milosevic's ethnic cleansing of the majority Albanian population in the Serb province of Kosovo. It was the start of a spate of local wars, which commanded global attention and resources as the international community attempted to counter local violence with a mixture of humanitarian intentions and the aim of ensuring global peace.

Whereas so-called early interventions focused on narrow goals of keeping the peace and assisting transition through democratic 'fixes' such as organising elections, by the mid-1990s a second phase triggered by social and development problems in countries such as Angola and Cambodia shifted the focus to reforms and institution building. In the early 2000s crisis management extended further to connect security with economic and governance issues, creating an arc of social control by foreign 'experts' across a range of policy areas.[3] The United Nations defined peacebuilding as including but 'not limited to reintegrating former combatants ... strengthening the rules of law ... improving respect for human rights ... providing technical assistance for democratic development ... and promoting conflict resolution an reconciliation techniques'. It was about 'everything from the legal and political system to education and health and welfare'.

As a result, interventions turned into lengthy affairs, in many cases with no end in sight. Martti Ahtisaari, the former Finnish prime minister and an expert in external peacekeeping who had brokered a peace agreement in Aceh in Indonesia in 2005, and was the architect of a plan for Kosovo independence in 2007, was asked how long Kosovo would require international supervision. He shrugged, and said it could be years.[4] He proved right: the international community has been in Kosovo since 1999, in Bosnia since 1995, and in the DRC since 1999. Although these missions have scaled down, only a minority has ever been officially concluded.

Governments and international organisations began to talk about 'exit strategies' amid concern at the mounting costs of dealing with other people's conflicts.[5] The UN budget for military peacekeeping in 2012 was around $7.3 billion. The UK's Overseas Development Assistance budget in 2016 to promote sustainable development and address global crises was £12.2 billion. In the USA, Nobel economist Joseph Stiglitz published a book in 2008 entitled *The Three Trillion Dollar War* setting out the hidden and published costs of the invasion of Iraq.[6]

Peacebuilding morphed into *state* building, and one solution to its spiralling cost was to outsource some of the tasks that went with such a large-scale enterprise. As a result, the Iraq war became the most commercial conflict in history, with private contracts worth £138 billion awarded to over 48,000 different companies, including Halliburton, Kellogg, Brown & Root and DynCorp.[7]

Many of these contractors took on tasks previously carried out by the armed forces. Security itself became a marketable commodity, and

23

the demand for protection and guarding—of buildings and people—spawned an industry of its own, which has spread globally, blurring traditional distinctions between those working for public services and private forms of authority.[8]

Yet, as fast as the commercial enterprise of peacebuilding expanded, the results looked increasingly mixed. NATO's senior civilian representative, Mark Sedwill, assessing its security mission to Afghanistan in 2010, stated that the country would remain poor and undeveloped for many years to come, and that progress in creating a governed state with laws and a functioning administration was scant.[9] The UK's Royal United Services Institute, commenting on the effects of a decade of British presence in Afghanistan, wrote: 'However we eventually interpret the outcome of Britain's fourth Afghan war ... the process of engagement in it ... was less than satisfactory from almost every point of view.'[10]

In the Balkans, nearly twenty years after the first peacekeeping missions and reconstruction aid, the record of achievement is mixed. An assessment of Kosovo found that between 2006 and 2010 there had been little or no progress recorded in around half of the policy areas covered by European Union assistance. The worst performance related to economic and market reform, where headings such as 'functioning market economy' and 'sectoral and enterprise structure' looked hopeful but in fact recorded no progress at all.[11]

These findings were borne out on a visit I made to Kosovo in 2009, a year after its independence. I was struck by the unreal nature of a society still in the grip of a civilian army of foreign experts: lawyers, policemen, government advisers and economists. Despite independence, the country was still reliant on a raft of international organisations and development agencies. The European Union alone had six different agency headquarters in the tiny capital city, Pristina. The number of local NGOs had grown from 65 to 2,300 between 1999 and 2004, responding to an influx of donor money and all promoting an agenda of democracy, human rights and governance reform. In contrast, the private sector consisted of one or two European banks, a mobile telephone operator, a few medium-sized construction businesses and some local enterprises. There was almost nothing to stop Kosovo from being run by international civil servants and overrun by international NGOs. No other organisations existed to provide jobs and the beginnings of a 'normal' economy. Kosovo was a paragon of 'Peaceland'.

Peacebuilding by outsiders is riddled with contradictions such as dispensing aid with conditions attached, invoking universal values to resolve local problems and the imposition of democracy by undemocratic means such as executive administration. Critics question whether these contradictions simply amount to operating challenges, which could be fixed by better policies or more adept implementation, or whether they are evidence of more fundamental faults in the whole premise of external intervention.[12] The UN's review of its own peacebuilding architecture in 2015 acknowledged the perception that it was overly technocratic, focused on capitals and elites, and failed to take account of local needs. Its report summed up what many critics had been saying: that outsiders were ill-equipped to resolve conflicts that were complex, fragmented and intractable.[13] State building in particular had become associated with isolated pockets of interventionist activity, which failed to penetrate the deep-seated causes of conflict and fragility, and was increasingly seen as an illegitimate abuse of Western influence. In the face of growing opposition to large-scale external interventions, peacebuilders turned to different approaches, going local, becoming 'pragmatic'.[14] The answer was to find durable solutions through engaging with everyday life and build the self-reliance, resilience and empowerment of conflict-affected societies.

A crisis of capitalism

At the time that the liberal peace project was taking on water, the global corporation also found itself in the middle of a public storm. The backlash against hyperglobalisation that began in the 1990s was given new momentum by a succession of environmental, governance, financial and human rights disasters caused by global companies. The 2008 financial crisis crippled trust in banks, while examples of corporate greed and mismanagement, de-industrialisation, cost cuts and job losses combined to create a chasm between the private sector and the rest of society.

Corporate social responsibility (CSR), a management strategy that had grown out of philanthropy, was no answer to this crisis of legitimacy. CSR was exposed as unfit for purpose: vague—since it depended on the voluntary acts of corporate executives—or worse, a ruse by executives to divert attention from the negative impacts of corporate behaviour in order to protect their licence to operate.[15]

Business behaviour in conflict areas had begun to attract adverse attention, and consumer and investor opposition could damage revenues and risk reputational damage. Among a digitally connected generation of young people, corporate abuse might lead to court actions, and sanctions and boycotts by international organisations, but it could also make it more difficult for companies to recruit the best staff, a threat to competitiveness that many took seriously.

As a result, some companies, often led by the very extractive companies that had been the foremost targets of civil society and public outrage, began to re-examine ideas about corporate care and responsibility. They started to look at risk in a new light, seeing their relations with communities as central, not merely incidental, to their success.

The CEO of Barclays Bank, in making a plea for a new culture of responsibility and citizenship at the end of 2011, admitted that five years earlier he could not have imagined such a change in corporate priorities: 'I came to the firm conclusion that banks—and the private sector—would have to adopt a broader set of objectives and responsibilities in order to truly restore trust. They would have to become better citizens.'[16]

While many of the reforms that companies began to initiate have been token, they are also a sign that a new truth is taking hold in the boardroom and among lawyers, investor relations and brand consultants: companies must not only bear the consequences of doing business, they must also play a more active role in shaping wider society. The so-called 'triple bottom line' of social, environmental and economic goals and achievements became a new reference point for the private sector.

For the growing number of companies that cannot avoid having some involvement in conflict-affected areas of the world—because they are connected through long global supply and value chains—this means engaging with, even joining, the peacebuilding industry, and thinking about how to achieve human well-being.

Unilever chairman Paul Polman, accepting a prize from a committee of Business for Peace, called for companies to develop new ways of doing business that will increase the social benefits from their activities. Referring to the unprecedented number of interrelated crises on food, health and environmental security, he said that business needs to be part of the solution, 'not simply a bystander waiting for governments to act'.[17]

Operating on the edge

Fragile states are defined as places where social and economic problems, coupled with weak public institutions, create cycles of violence and underdevelopment. The impacts of foreign corporations in such places are magnified compared to those in peaceful and stable societies, because of the level of vulnerability of local people, coupled with a reliance on the corporate presence. Foreign investment holds out the promise of breaking with a turbulent past, survival in the present, and prosperity in the future. In many isolated societies there is total dependence on the local presence of a foreign corporation because it provides not just the only employment in the area, but public goods such as district heat and lighting, roads, and services such as education and healthcare. However, in conflict-affected societies with fewer safety nets such as social security systems, workable laws, effective media or civil society, this relationship of reliance can go wrong. Foreign money is powerful and difficult to gainsay, when there are disputes between the company and the community. It represents a chronic imbalance between the influence of business and the weak voices of local people; but foreign money also generates exaggerated expectations of what it can achieve. It courts resentment at undelivered promises, as well as fear of business intentions. People feel they have little control over foreign companies and how the benefits from investment are distributed. This mixture of hope and expectation, nervousness, uncertainty and disillusion is felt most deeply at the grass roots, among individuals who work for international corporations and in the communities that surround them. And it can be toxic. As we shall see in later chapters, the emotional connection between a company's presence and the local community is often lost in translation somewhere between the ground level and corporate headquarters in Western capitals. In Africa, the Balkans, Mexico and on the West

Bank in Jerusalem, disagreements and festering resentments between locals and foreign companies that operate in their neighbourhoods can combust like a bush fire, spreading unrest, and licking at the heels of disenfranchised and disaffected individuals in particular. Young men who are out of work are most prone to be caught up in this dangerous disillusionment around big business.

Attempts to understand and resolve conflicts drew attention to their economic drivers, and the phenomenon of war economies, which thrived on the violence, chaos and absence of stable order. This economic focus led to efforts to rein in corporate behaviour and cut links between business and armed groups. Companies mining diamonds and other precious resources found themselves subject to new rules on transparency, as conflict-resolution policies aimed to expose nefarious networks that connected conflict, commerce and Western consumers. 'Blood diamonds', identified as coming from conflict areas and being sold to finance violence, were ostensibly outlawed and driven out of the market by an international system of certification, the Kimberley Process. Mining companies had to prove that they were not selling conflict minerals sourced from rebel areas of the DRC. Other codes of conduct and transparency standards sought to lift the lid on what companies did in fragile countries, and tie them into public accountability for their activities. The effectiveness of such measures has been disputed. Critics claim that these efforts are often piecemeal and flawed. They can also give rise to a boomerang effect whereby restricting sales of minerals to foreign companies simply encourages informal resource extraction, drives down legal revenues and leaves unregulated miners more vulnerable. Preliminary evidence from gold mines in the DRC suggested that it had led to more, not less, violence.[18]

In the DRC in 2008 the crisis of security collided with the crisis of capitalism. The US Congress passed legislation which attempted to control the behaviour of investment banks that had brought the financial system to the brink of disaster. The Wall Street Reform and Consumer Protection Act was the most significant revision of US financial regulations since the Great Depression. Among the most innovative and controversial features of the new Act were provisions requiring corporations to disclose whether 'conflict minerals' originating in or around the DRC were used in the manufacture of their products.

Section 1504 of the Act required companies to disclose payments related to extraction of oil, natural gas or minerals. It was an extraordinary and unprecedented fusion between peace and security policy on the one hand, and corporate regulation on the other. A crisis at the very heart of the capitalist system on Wall Street had spilled over into how global companies did business in a conflict zone. A law that set out to protect the interests of small investors caught up in the worst financial meltdown in eighty years was being used as a way of protecting Congolese miners who were the victims of a vicious civil war.

3

NEW LEVIATHANS

Any hope of subduing him is false
The mere sight of him is overpowering
(Job 41:9)

In 1651 the political philosopher Thomas Hobbes drew on the biblical image of a fierce sea creature to set out a proposition about power, purpose and responsibility in the modern state. Hobbes made the Leviathan a metaphor for strong government, and used it to argue the case for popular support of a unitary state and its absolute, sovereign power.

Hobbes proposed that there should be a political contract between the government and the governed, in which there was a mutual dependence between them. In exchange for protection by the Leviathan, its subjects agreed that the state could maintain order and control within its borders. The Leviathan's powers and legitimacy came from that consent of citizens to support it with obedience and allegiance, and to delegate their right to be protected. In turn, the state's duty was to act on behalf of all the people and in the people's name to promote their collective interest.[1] Hobbes's declared purpose behind his strange—and at the time shocking—metaphor was to set out the 'mutual relations between protection and obedience', the one conditional on the other.[2]

So resonant and enduring was Hobbes's prescription for social and political order that his metaphor of a protective force, able to repel all threats and also to command the allegiance of the people, served as a shorthand description of state power for 300 years. A century after Hobbes, Jean-Jacques Rousseau articulated a 'social contract' between people and rulers in a pamphlet which influenced the French revolutionaries, and drew directly on Hobbesian ideas of an agreement between rulers and those they ruled, a swap of sovereignty for protection. The German political scientist Carl Schmitt, interpreting *Leviathan* through the prism of the desire for a strong German state after the collapse of the Weimar Republic and during the rise of Nazism in 1932, declared that Hobbes's message of *protego ergo obligo* (I protect therefore I oblige) was the state's equivalent of Descartes's definition of man: *cogito ergo sum* (I think therefore I am).[3]

Globalisation, communications technology and a history of state failures since the end of the Cold War have redrawn the contours and relevance of a contract based on a sovereign state controlling a defined territory and a submissive citizenry. In a world where state borders no longer always determine allegiance or mark out the boundaries of protection, the relation between people and power has shifted. It no longer seems realistic that single states can defend their citizens against the kinds of threats that now include global pandemics, climate change, international terrorism and mass migrations.

The next two chapters look at the purposes and power of corporations and their relationship to the rest of society, in terms of two ideas that go back to Hobbes's *Leviathan*: protection and responsibility. This chapter begins by looking at the historical precedents of commercial companies assuming an obligation for security and welfare, and providing the most basic of public goods, and then examines how the notion of corporate protection fits with the kind of contemporary threats in a hostile world. In Chapter 4 the currency of responsibility for protecting against human suffering and underdevelopment offers a way of seeing how modern business might reach beyond a narrow concern for profitability to take on roles that involve not only protecting its interests and its own workforce, but a wider obligation towards community and society at large.

This is the prelude to exploring, in the chapters that follow, examples of how global companies have reacted to contexts of vulnerability and danger, and what kind of thinking drives corporate behaviour, and might govern their impulses to protect. What are the influences determining the roles that companies adopt as protectors? And what could lead us to imagine that corporations could be modern-day Leviathans, endowed with sovereign-type rights, but also capable of building a 'common wealth' of protection against external harm? In circumstances where state power is in rapid and chaotic retreat, are companies able to replace, augment or authenticate state authority and power, and are they willing to do so?

Any proposition that companies should accumulate additional layers of influence is deeply unpopular. Most public discourse is about curbing business power, and establishing, through law, regulation and public scrutiny, systems for identifying and restricting enterprises that overreach and abuse their position. Asking business to assume a mantle of authority, expecting companies to take on tasks that we regard as properly belonging to elected institutions, carries ethical risks and makes many people feel uneasy. Whatever form this extension of responsibility takes—either as acts of corporate philanthropy or pragmatic responses filling gaps in public services—this 'mission creep', which sees companies taking on functions of providing security and well-being, has implications for democratic governance.[4] If we don't trust companies to hold our money safely, deliver utilities at an appropriate cost, organise social media platforms in ways that prevent harm to vulnerable people, or even pay their share of national taxes—all issues which currently preoccupy us about the way global business operates—then delegating responsibility for global security constitutes a quantum leap of faith.

Moreover, most companies are reticent about taking on that kind of responsibility. Very few want to be seen as agents of development or guarantors of public safety. If global corporations are the new Leviathans, with protective powers that once only states had, then they are largely silent beasts.

The precedents of protective power

The historical experience of private enterprises acting in place of the state has been to show that corporate protection comes at a high price for ordinary people. In Congo, as with other countries across Africa and Asia, the reliance on foreign trading companies to create transformations that combined economic benefits and social improvements proved all too deadly. In the nineteenth century, investment and trade arrived with foreign rubber planters, who built schools and hospitals while they subjugated, brutalised and killed local people in order to fulfil export quotas. The pattern was repeated elsewhere from the Dutch East Indies to sugar and fruit plantations in the Americas. Andrew Philips describes trading behemoths such as the Dutch and British East India Companies as 'imperialism's violent vanguards', playing a key role in Western colonial expansion, from the seventeenth to the twentieth centuries, not only extracting tradeable commodities, from minerals to slaves, but levying taxes and imposing order on behalf of their sponsoring governments.[5] The British East India Company, sometimes called the first transnational corporation, was granted a royal licence on 31 December 1600 to monopolise Asian trade and fight for the 'Honour of the nation and the Wealth of our People'. Nearly 200 years later, maintaining an army of 60,000 men and holding sway over 30 million subjects in India, the East India Company had become 'a Commonwealth without a People'. It had strayed from its original founding purpose and was largely unaccountable. Its critic Edmund Burke provided Parliament with a lengthy philosophical argument that such extensive political power and privilege should be exercised for the benefit of the people, not for the company's narrower interests.[6] The company's overreach had made it a Leviathan without popular licence.

In the Congo the marriage between the trading ambitions of Western companies, following a path originally beaten by ivory merchants and slavers from Egypt and Zanzibar, and the mobilising force of nationalism in the nineteenth century, created a colony rooted in administrative force and commercial greed.[7]

In a hierarchy of protection, it was commercial interests and the welfare of colonists that prevailed over care for indigenous populations in such proto-states where governance was arbitrary and piecemeal. Only occasionally did these interests align in Asia, North America and the African colonies, leading to glimpses of how commercial and political power could work together in delivering stability and well-being.

Debates about the relative powers of states and corporations punctuate the history of empire, and before Hobbes wrote about a new understanding between people and their government, international trading companies fused politics and commerce. These companies were originally the creation of the state, and it was a political decision to grant joint stock companies the advantage of limited liability to enable them to expand their capital and thus their trading potential. The fact that these 'little republics' became a form of law unto themselves raised questions from the outset about whether companies were private associations or public institutions. The corporation was the first autonomous entity to be created in hundreds of years, and the first to represent a centre of power that was within society yet independent of the central government of the national state.[8]

In 1600 the East India Company was a collection of merchants, chartered by the Crown and granted 'semi-sovereign' rights to run its trading interests in the colonies. The English East India Company and its Dutch equivalent not only held monopolies in their domestic markets, but, with the collusion of governments in England and Holland, they shaped how world trade developed, using armed force to secure trading territories and spearhead imperial expansion. The company was licensed to wage war on behalf of the Crown, and prospered through a combination of close ties to government, a swaggering entrepreneurial ambition, a fortified presence abroad and a far-reaching administrative system. It demonstrates how a corporation is, among other things, a mechanism for blending business and politics, conquest and commerce.[9] 'In its business outlook, capacity for bureaucratic management, or the sheer breadth of political ambition there was nothing diminutive about the East India Company's operations.'[10] By the eighteenth century the company controlled the internal trade and tax revenues of Bengal, supplanting the authority of the ruling nawab and becoming the spearhead for British imperial rule in India.[11] In 1773 the company's Warren Hastings became the first governor-general of India. Later accused of extortion, bribery and corruption, Hastings became infamous for his ruthless exploitation of Bengal's natural resources, including smuggling opium into China in defiance of a ban. However, he is also remembered for his cultural philanthropy, leaving a mark on India and Anglo-Indian relations that went far beyond mere business. The spread and influence of the East India Company was such that in the eighteenth and nineteenth centuries it touched vast swathes of both the

British and Indian populations. Not unlike today's global corporations, people were connected to the company through employment, family links or as customers.[12] Foreshadowing today's complex relationships between foreign business and local people, histories of the British conquest of North America reveal how the Hudson Bay Company in northern Canada simultaneously exploited and protected indigenous fur trappers, with systems of employment, credit and accommodation in an era of ambiguous and frequently disputed sovereign statehood as Britain and France vied for commercial and political control of the territory. Archaeological data have shown that the impact of commercial expansion across the northern seaboard by French and British traders cannot be viewed as entirely negative, despite the violence it entailed. The Inuit in today's eastern Canada became resilient and organised as a result of interactions with the trader colonists. Accounts of colonial relationships show how protection was institutionalised by the Hudson Bay Company, which contrasts with how locals fared at the hands of unorganised bands of whalers and fishers. In any case, these encounters suggest a long-standing reality that where protection was afforded to locals it was uneven and conditional, giving privileged status and rights for a few who co-operated.[13]

In Africa, as part of colonial rule, foreign trading companies' intervention was more explicit in mixing commerce with cultural conquest. Today's corporate giant Unilever began life in Liverpool as a soap producer, Lever Brothers. In the 1890s the company set up operations in the Congo to source palm oil from the country's rich plantations. It controlled an area covering 1,000 miles, and employed 17,000 local workers. By 1926 it was running 15 hospitals, 5 schools and 1,200 houses. All this was underpinned by an evangelical determination to 'bring ... progress to grateful natives'. Describing the move into the Congo, a hagiography of the company's founder, Lord Leverhulme, by one of his managers, Jervis Babb, extolled the virtues of the mix of commerce and social engineering: 'Sunlight was brought to the darkest forests. Steaming swamps were drained; malaria and other diseases stamped out; roads, schools and hospitals were built; villages were constructed and new meaning and purpose brought into the lives of primitive and aimless savages.'[14]

Lever Brothers also perfectly represented British government attitudes to development in West Africa, where the colonialists ascribed to themselves a dual mandate to exploit local resources in order to promote 'civilisation' and a responsibility to natives to improve their welfare. Writing to one of his managers in 1908, Lord Leverhulme explained that 'in developing and improving [the Congo], we do so in a way that will equally benefit the consumer in Great Britain'.[15]

Companies and colonial administrators shared a language of trusteeship and guardianship towards local populations, which was a thin veneer for racist views that infantilised indigenous people as incapable of their own development.[16] Corporate and state interests aligned perfectly. The colonial tax policy was changed to increase the amounts individuals had to pay while collection was spread throughout the year to ensure that plantation workers would continue to work in order to pay their tax dues, guaranteeing Lever Brothers a steady supply of labour. While slavery was officially abolished in Leverville, the company town in south-west Congo, a pattern of forced labour was part of the colonial administrative and corporate system.

Seen from the viewpoint of this history, contemporary globalisation is another turn in a long story of subordination of indigenous interests that goes back to colonialism and beyond. Today, expanding world markets may deconstruct the boundaries of the nation-state, and render other national entities—markets, industries, corporations—less salient, but this growth continues to entrench social, economic and political divisions between those inside networks of power and local populations excluded from them.[17]

Fragmented security

In Latin America 'the incomplete state'[18] meant that domestic businesses were given a privileged social position. The logic of statehood here was complicity between domestic companies, officials and even criminal organisations, with each group protecting its own interests in an environment of government weakness and dysfunction. When governments can only offer selective security to an elite clientele, who are part of powerful networks, the result is a 'fragmented security state', which breeds rather than prevents or counters violence as citizens compete to make themselves materially and physically safe. Fragmented security is visible today in current conflicts in Mexico, Colombia and

Central America. It is no accident that some of these countries have strong business sectors, and, as in the case of Colombia and Mexico, vibrant economies, as issues such as land rights, taxation and other privileges are part of the symbiosis between business and state. This type of state does not guarantee security protection and welfare for the mass of the population. Violence is perpetuated, and the growing wealth of those in business circles is not linked to any progress in upholding and improving the rule of law. Indeed, historically there are no incentives for these entrepreneurial elites to support governance reform or build public institutions, which might ensure development with security.[19]

Examples of 'societal corporatism' in the shape of private Colombian business foundations and influential business associations such as the coffee growers' federation, described as a 'state within a state', demonstrate that welfare provision and philanthropy delivering benefits not available from the state, characterise a history of national business substituting for government as a protector of citizens, although the forms and conditions of this protection are many and variegated.[20]

Corporate social evangelism by transnational business had roots in nineteenth-century industrial Britain, but was a feature of the growth of a European-based enterprise empire. William H. Lever, who was described as 'a commercial genius ... probably of good heart, but also hard, who sees humanity as a vast engine of production without soul or desires or ambitions',[21] was among a group of industrialists who expanded their commercial empires based on paternalism and authoritarianism. Model villages such as Lever's Port Sunlight, Sir Titus Salt's Saltaire and Bourneville, created by the Cadbury chocolate family, were among around thirty similar institutions which housed workers and provided education, healthcare and civic amenities. In Germany, the Krupp engineering and armament works in Essen, and Pullman, which made railway carriages in Chicago, followed similar lines.

The motives for this corporate philanthropy were mixed. Worker towns were usually the creation of individual business owners, some with a nostalgic sense of a feudal past. Creating employee housing in easy reach of the mill or the factory helped recruit and keep a workforce, providing facilities that employees would not find if they left to work for rival firms. It was also about establishing order and Christian religious values. In each town the provision of schools, churches, a theatre, library and museum was part of a regime of surveillance and discipline that aimed to influence workers' social behaviour. A biography of George Cadbury described his Bourneville village as a social experiment 'whose underlying purpose was to show that business success was not only consistent with a high regard for the welfare of the workpeople, but the corollary of it'.[22] The common view of many business owners from the beginning of the Industrial Revolution was to regard employees as human forms of the new machinery that was powering the growth of the British economy. While some observers praised the 'good will and thoughtful attention of employers towards the interests and welfare of their subordinates', critics observed that the paternalism of the new social cities and mill towns amounted to a form of white slavery which created an excessive dependence by the workforce on the goodwill of the business owner.[23]

The record of more than three centuries of business engagement with communities in developing countries suggests that corporate contributions to improving the security and safety of local people come freighted with conditions, are motivated by diverse factors and are ultimately unreliable, depending often on personal whim.

In modern polities the convention is that the state offers the most reliable and resourceful single source of security provision for millions of people worldwide, even in the absence of a formal monopoly on protection. However, absolute, indivisible and inalienable sovereign power began to ebb away, and on the evidence of twentieth-century atrocities, from the Holocaust to post-Cold War genocides, it came to be recognised that states cannot always be counted on to shield their citizens from harm—and may themselves be the perpetrators of harm against individuals. In that case, who or what should step into the gap opened up by uncertainty over the will and capacities of the caring state?

Private or public?

As state provision of public goods has diminished, it is private actors' transactions that have filled the gap in meeting basic needs through supplying vital services and commodities. Alternatives to state actors became visible in the aftermath of the Cold War. Even the conduct of foreign policy and diplomacy, the quintessence of statecraft, looked different. Commentators remarked on the shift away from 'pin-striped diplomats [to] NGO activists in jeans and saris, baseball caps and turbans who spoke a more direct, aggressive and jargon free language'.[24] Political scientist Susan Strange, analysing the changes to the state's role, observed that modern statehood was about economics as much as security politics. States no longer competed for territory but for market share in a world economy, and for credibility in addressing urgent contemporary problems. Their authority was leaking away—upwards to global institutions (although most of these are composed of state representatives), sideways to non-state organisations, and downwards to popular movements. Sometimes state authority had not gone anywhere that could be located, it had 'just evaporated'.[25] A multipolar world where geo-political power had fragmented could allow governance theorists to safely say 'there is no global Leviathan'.[26] Meanwhile international organisations, NGOs and social movements jostle to display their rival capacities and offer individuals protection against a variety of harms, from poverty to conflict and climate change, challenging the failures of governments on these issues.

Every year in mid-winter this new global protectorate meets in luxurious settings to discuss the most urgent topics in politics, security and economics. The settings are cosmopolitan, the kind of places inhabited by international travellers and tourists rather than everyday citizens. Over 2,000 participants gather in the ski resort of Davos in Switzerland for the annual meeting of the World Economic Forum, where the agenda ranges from technology to terrorism, climate change to conflict prevention. More rock festival than political summit, this 'meeting place of the masters of the world',[27] whose stated aim is 'improving the state of the world', stages headline acts such as Bill Gates, the founder of Microsoft, speaking on ending poverty or infectious disease, or Pope Francis on the 'fourth industrial revolution'. Davos sets the global agenda and terms of debate, and never fails to capture headlines. In four decades it has expanded from a swanky conference to a system of knowledge, information and politics, in which governments are only one type of participant.

The Munich security conference in the opulent surroundings of the Bayerische Hof Hotel is another example of an event which has become a pilgrimage of power, where elected politicians are frequently outclassed by voices from business and civil society; where policy and positions are crafted that chip away at states' grip on foreign and security policy, to create new sources of influence. The Munich conference, which began as a closed gathering of names such as Henry Kissinger and former German chancellor Helmut Schmidt, is now an annual outing for 350 members of governments, military leaders, business executives, NGOs, scientists and other academics, who go to listen but mostly to be heard and seen.

One reason why nation-states have had difficulty maintaining a stranglehold on global politics, and their 'monopoly of the legitimate use of force', which had been the classic definition of the modern state since 1688, is an awareness of new threats, against which military force, borders and weapons appear to be inadequate solutions. In the late 1990s urgent policy challenges were grouped under headings such as 'global capitalism, environmental danger, identity politics and post-nuclear geopolitics', but part of the problem was that often abstract threats of this kind, unlike state borders, were topical and highly fluid.[28] The UN listed seven types of insecurity to be addressed: economic, food, health, environmental, personal, community and political security. The point about these 'new' but not-so-new threats was that they threatened individuals rather than states, and they could arise in varying degrees of severity at any time or place. Solutions had to be found by assembling new coalitions of actors as well as through new ways of thinking about public policy.[29]

Faced with a kaleidoscope of unpredictable and never-ending threats, effectiveness was one requirement of security policies, but so was cost efficiency. The reformulation of the state, confronting problems it could not control and requiring resources beyond its means, led it to outsource key functions, devolve authority and privatise assets, including those associated with protecting citizens. Since the 1980s the private sector had been seen as an alternative to unwieldy and expensive state industries and management by government. Privatisation and deregulation of transport, energy and telecommunications infrastructure had delegated management and transferred ownership to private companies in key areas of the economy.

By the end of the twentieth century this trend had spread to security, conflict and the waging of war. Private security became an emerging phenomenon in the international system. Military contractors and security consultancies not only began to take on routine service functions such as guarding buildings and staff or organising the logistics of defence ministries, but moved up the value chain to train local security forces and take strategic decisions on fighting insurgencies and undertaking governance reforms. The invasion of Iraq in 2003 by US-led coalition forces became a byword for the rise of private security. Estimates vary (and indeed, one troubling aspect of this development is that neither the US Congress nor the Pentagon knows or will say exactly how many private contractors were on the government's payroll) but between 48,000 and 180,000 private contractors had been hired by 2007, outnumbering US army troops.[30] Many private military and security companies (PMSCs) came out of the Iraq war with revenues and reputations that laid the foundations for rapid growth and a wave of takeovers to create new types of corporate empires. In some cases their reputations were highly dubious: five employees of Blackwater, one of the biggest US contractors, were eventually prosecuted for opening fire on Iraqi civilians in Nisour Square in Baghdad, killing seventeen and wounding twenty more while escorting a US embassy convoy. Seven years later a US court found one employee guilty of first-degree (premeditated) murder and three more of voluntary manslaughter. They were sentenced to between thirty years and life in prison. Blackwater has since changed its name twice and has been taken over by a group of private investors. Private security firms grew rich on wars in Iraq, Afghanistan and African countries which states and public actors could not afford to fight.

The value of private contracts to support the US global War on Terror between 2002 and 2011 was over $139 billion. Names such as G4S, DynCorp and Executive Outcomes are not simply modern forms of mercenary soldiers. They are the centre of an expanding 'market for force', estimated to grow from approximately $180 billion in 2017 to $240 billion in 2020,[31] with global reach and a range of services that only in some cases includes fighting in wars. These services have far-reaching political and ethical implications.[32] Where once it was rogue regimes in the Third World that hired 'Dogs of War', bands of former soldiers, to boost their fighting forces and to hold onto or seize power, now the consumers of private security range from commercial companies who don't want to rely on state police forces to keep their employees and plants safe, to democratic governments trying to make shrinking defence budgets stretch further, and even humanitarian organisations and the UN, who use private companies to deliver emergency assistance and protect aid workers.

Private security contractors are assigned tasks as diverse as training foreign armies, analysing conflict risk, intelligence, running prisons and keeping shoppers safe in shopping malls. As P. W. Singer points out in his seminal study of the privatised military industry, *Corporate Warriors*, the industry both represents the changed security and business environments at the beginning of the twenty-first century and is an ironic reversal of the processes by which the modern state began: to gain power, new and fragile states no longer develop economies and raise taxes to pay their armies, they obtain revenue by granting a resource concession, and bring in a private security contractor.[33]

The global private security economy is about more than just the exponential growth of a new breed of for-profit security providers. It is the marketisation of protection and the rise of new centres of private authority and governance. It is a phenomenon which reflects another form of complicity between states and non-state actors, this time with the consent of citizens, persuaded to have their daily lives monitored by CCTV cameras, their personal data stored by commercial companies and a wide array of unofficial police, military and other security forces licensed to use multiple forms of coercion as the price of protection against perceived dangers.

The private security economy is a breeding-ground for new Leviathans, who are outside the state, but deeply integrated in financial and consumer markets, and part of global trade flows as purveyors of must-have goods and services. This burgeoning industry is where the shift in state power and the state's role as protector is particularly visible; but it is not the only or most significant source of authority in a novel political landscape where *government* is public, but *governance*— the setting and enforcement of rules and norms and the capacity for collective problem solving—is increasingly private.

I was struck by the influence of private security contractors at a meeting held at the headquarters of a UN peacekeeping mission to brief the local representatives of foreign companies in a recently stabi-lised war zone in Africa. As the corporate guests filed into the meeting wearing buttoned-down shirts and pressed trousers, they were accom-panied by other individuals wearing jeans and T-shirts, sporting well-honed biceps, the odd tattoo, and good-luck charms. One had just flown in from the Balkans, another had seen service in Iraq and Afghanistan. Where corporate managers in London or New York might bring their lawyers or accountants to a meeting, in this context it was private security guards who were whispering in managerial ears. Corporate 'armies'[34] are part of contemporary war and post-conflict zones, not just because governments hire them to fight wars and clean up the aftermath, but because they are an integral part of how corpora-tions manage their own operations in these environments. As a result, the presence of private contractors will increasingly shape conflict and post-conflict environments.

This is not a tale of private security contractors, but of their paymas-ters. The story of this book is the face-off between mainstream com-mercial companies and states, as to who should be responsible for security in fragile neighbourhoods where authority and legitimacy are unclear and fought over. Private security contractors are the means that governments, companies and society turn to in order to provide stabil-ity and safety. They illustrate how the balance of power has swung away from the state towards non-state actors in civil society and the private sector. The increase in the number and the geographical spread of global corporations means that they rival state power as sources of authority across the globe in all aspects of security, from physical pro-tection to thought leadership and knowledge.

Transnational corporations (TNCs) account for 80 per cent of exports and foreign direct investment.[35] In the world's biggest econo-mies, the United States and China, TNCs account for around three-quarters of GDP.[36] A common measure of how global companies dwarf the financial firepower of states is the contrast between the annual sales of TNCs and the GDP of states. The world's largest company according to the Fortune 500 rankings between 2013 and 2016 is the retailer Walmart, which owns Asda in the UK, and which is wealthier than either Australia, Spain or the Netherlands. At half the size of Walmart, Shell is bigger than Greece; Apple is bigger than Ireland. The 100 wealthiest economic entities in the world include 69 corporations and only 31 countries. According to the economic and social justice advocacy group Global Justice Now: 'At this rate, within a generation we will be living in a world entirely dominated by giant corporations.'[37]

The emergence of transnational corporations as influential actors in international politics exists in a new political space. It is 'not embedded in either a realistic political sociology of the state or an appropriate normative framework'.[38] It is not clear how they should be categorised in relation to NGOs, social movements and other forms of civil society. Business may represent a new kind of political actor but companies themselves have taken an ambiguous attitude towards their role as agents of change, progress and protection.

Big numbers remind us of the scale of corporate muscle, in a world of fluid governance arrangements with no clear and uncontested global authority. But numbers are only part of the picture. Power comes in different forms, including through the use of culture and the strength of symbolism. Companies' ability to establish and maintain networks of influence across national borders reflects their social power as much as their financial resources and economic importance. Western corporations deploy this power by lobbying governments and seeking to determine political agendas, but also through trying to shape our social landscapes, creating consumer markets for the goods and services they produce and contributing their voices to how we understand public issues such as climate change, health risks, energy and technology. It is on this basis that a new kind of enterprise authority and legitimacy has arisen.[39]

Campaigning journalist Naomi Klein's book *No Logo* tells the story of how corporate marketing and a 'web of brands' became the marker of globalisation to the extent that the main point about pan-global companies is not their products, but rather instant name recognition and image: 'Nike isn't running a shoe company, *it is about the idea of transcendence through sports*, Starbucks isn't a coffee shop chain, *it's about the idea of community*.' Creating meaning, more than just goods and services, is the task of the modern corporation, according to Klein.[40] She is at the forefront of a generation of writers who have attacked the power of business to control not just economic flows but the arteries of culture and society. To these critics, companies have encroached onto public space, turning it into a commercial marketplace, to the point where we as citizens no longer even notice how deeply ingrained the consumer ethic has become. Corporations aggregate the wishes and interests of millions of citizens in order to represent a new common-wealth of consumption, while they in turn achieve legitimacy through their ability to command the allegiance of a worldwide customer base.

In places affected by conflict and violent change, where the power of state authority has been undermined by rebel force, or has withered through incompetence, corruption or dysfunction, corporate power has a different hue. Foreign investors step into the vacuum left by failed governments, absent laws and a lack of social safety nets. The influence of foreign companies over local communities is magnified because they represent a form of stability, a locus of apparent physical safety and a lifeline in terms of jobs and income. Organised production provides a form of social order and the potential for a regulated 'commonwealth' within the territory of its operation. Companies are often at the hub of a web of local relationships and alliances, between government offi-cials, local suppliers and external peacebuilders, such as the UN and international aid agencies. Investment cycles are longer than crisis interventions by the international community, so companies are often physically present over longer time periods than many other types of outsider. When they enter crisis and conflict environments where every aspect of political, economic and social life may be in chaos, their pres-ence may contain the promise of stability and normality. This promise represents leverage for companies to exert their influence over local populations and their rulers. At the same time, in many fragile societies there is a monolithic economic culture based overwhelmingly around one type of resource or commodity such as oil or minerals. The con-centration of corporate power in terms of economic and social influ-ence associated with this creates conditions of excessive dependence by local populations on a few companies.

An example of this occurred in eastern Ukraine in 2016: a year earlier, as separatist groups backed by the Russian military gained con-trol of the industrial heartland of the country, government troops were forced to retreat. The area became a no-go zone, cut off from the rest of the country with no public administration, services or indeed func-tioning economy. Ukraine cut most transport links to the region in an attempt to starve out the rebels, so industrial production stopped. Many businesses fled, but for the giant industrial plants—processing coal or making steel—this was not an option. Their assets and work-force were locked in the middle of a battleground between Russian-backed separatists and the Ukrainian state. Land between the two opposing sides is littered with mines. Oligarch Rinat Akhmetov, who, with an estimated net worth of $31 billion, owns around half the steel mills, iron-ore and coal mines and power plants in the Donbas region as part of an empire of more than a hundred companies, which employed 320,000 people at its peak, was Ukraine's richest business-man. A critical question as conflict intensified in eastern Ukraine was whether Akhmetov was funding the Russian separatists or whether he was loyal to the Ukrainian cause. By 2016 Akhmetov had fled the besieged city of Donetsk and the value of his empire had more than halved. Some of his industrial assets have become fortifications for the separatist militias. His Azovstal iron and steel works is producing at just one-third of its capacity. He even withdrew his football club Shakhtar, whose players, coaches and administrators lived in Kiev's Opera Hotel, and played their home games in Lviv, 40 miles from the Polish bor-der.[41] Despite the disruptions to production—railway links to the west are supervised and restricted by the Ukrainian government in an attempt to starve out the rebels—Akhmetov continued to pay his fac-tory workers even though they could not work, because they had no other form of support in a land without government.

In place of the state the company stepped in to keep families alive by keeping factories open, and continuing to pay wages. Protection in return for allegiance. In places of extreme vulnerability such as eastern Ukraine in 2016, it is not fanciful to imagine corporations as alterna-tive authorities. Is this the shape of modern Leviathan? Powerful, pro-tective, but also potentially dangerous.

While the critics of hyperglobalisation such as Naomi Klein indeed view corporations as sources of 'monstrous' power, few use their power to assume a protective role. In practice, power and protection are antithetical, not consequential, as Hobbes had envisaged, and cor-porate clout is often deployed in ways that do not focus on human well-being or taking care of the vulnerable. Forays into emergency humanitarian aid and crisis response, public–private partnerships to provide infrastructure, medicine or education, and self-regulation initiatives to demonstrate good behaviour suggest that some companies may take an enlightened view of their social obligations, but this rarely extends to deciding to act as a positive force for global security. Little attention is paid either by managements or policy-makers to precisely how business can be connected to the challenges of either local or global stability and well-being. The corporate voice on mass migration flows, violent extremism or issues of inequality is rarely heard.

4

THE RESPONSIBILITY GAP

Havana, Cuba, November 2016: the Colombian government signed a ground-breaking peace deal with members of the FARC guerrilla group, to end the world's longest-running civil war, which had gone on for half a century. On page 210 of the 300-page document that set out the terms of the agreement, something novel appeared. Private companies were invited to help ensure the success of the peace settlement with FARC. Business support was required to guarantee the peace agreement, and the transition to peace, particularly in rural areas, would be accompanied by new investments to deliver public goods and legal jobs in a country where the conflict was deeply entangled in drug trafficking, a lack of legal livelihoods and economic inequality.

Corporate involvement was critical to the government's proposals for a programme of comprehensive rural reform with the goal of eradicating poverty, improving land use and increased opportunities for nearly one-quarter of the population living in the countryside. Peace in Colombia was defined in the agreement as 'territorial peace'. Large swathes of the country had been ungoverned for fifty years as armed groups assumed control of villages, towns and jungle. In many areas that had not seen a government official for all that time, the only outside groups apart from military forces were mining, agricultural or natural-resource companies. Now the government needed these companies, and others from the private sector, to help establish state presence, the rule of law, sustainable employment and peaceful coexistence. Victims of the violence and former combatants alike had to be made part of a new post-conflict economy.

There were several problems with this unusual invitation. The response of companies was lukewarm. Although many undertook projects that would contribute to developing areas previously controlled by armed groups, or hired former combatants to reintegrate them into society, almost no companies I spoke to admitted to wanting to help the peace process itself because they saw it as too politically charged.[1]

Secondly, government arrangements for managing business contributions proved to be chaotic. The overwhelming majority of companies, when asked, said that they were unaware of government plans to mobilise business in building peace.[2] A scheme of allowing companies to offset their tax bills if they invested in infrastructure projects, Works for Taxes (Obras por Impuestos), quickly became bogged down in difficulties of translating public policy into projects that companies could implement. Finally, what was meant by 'peace' in Colombia became a deeply contested and divisive issue. Half the country rejected the peace agreement with FARC, and even Colombia's next government played down suggestions that it was involved in peacebuilding in order to get elected.

Two-and-a-half years after the Havana accords, and despite the peace process falling out of fashion in public debate, most companies continued to believe that peacebuilding was a moral obligation. Around a quarter thought that engagement would provide new business openings and would result in new commercial markets. Others when questioned said they would make social investments in peace because of a combination of duty and business sense.[3]

These replies suggested that, although Colombian companies faced practical and political challenges in contributing to the peace, and indeed were largely pessimistic about the prospects of the peace agreement ending the conflict, they felt a strong sense of duty towards helping to implement it. This was a response rooted in an abstract idea of responsibility, rather than experiences of protection and stewardship.

Responsibility to protect

A recurring theme in international politics as part of the post-Second World War discourse of human rights has been to combine responsibility and protection, and to mobilise responses to conflict and crisis, through appealing to the capacity of outsiders to help, whether through humanitarian assistance or as a guiding principle of peace interventions. The two concepts were explicitly linked in 2000, when a Canadian-led international commission put forward proposals to increase the protection of citizens of states that were either unwilling or unable to guarantee their most basic rights to life, livelihood and dignity, and suggested that this was an issue of responsibility for those with the means to help. The International Commission on Intervention and State Sovereignty (ICISS) formulated the idea of Responsibility to Protect (R2P), to help populations at risk from grave dangers such as mass murder or starvation, in cases where the state itself was either the perpetrator or unwilling or unable to defend its own citizens. R2P was the response to atrocities such as the Rwandan genocide and ethnic cleansing in former Yugoslavia. It set out an idea of limited or contingent sovereignty—that states could not invoke automatic and unlimited rights over their own territory if they could or would not defend their own people from harm.[4] By qualifying the idea of state power, R2P proposed limiting the unfettered authority of states, reversing a tradition of deference and obedience to the state, raising the ideal of protecting the vulnerable to a condition of statehood, and recognising alternative forms and levels of protective authority in the modern world. This was more than just an idea: under its acronym R2P, Responsibility to Protect was a political commitment by UN member states to assume an obligation to act on fragility. Governments that failed to shield their own people could no longer hide behind the established convention that they could do what they liked—in other words were sovereign—within their own territorial borders. Other governments were mandated to take on the duty of protecting another state's citizens, including by force.[5] Because this duty to intervene in countries against their will was seen as giving licence to dominant powers such as the USA, R2P became one of the most contested and controversial concepts in international politics.[6] But it meant that responsibility for others, and the idea of protection, had gone global, superseding the historical power of the state.

Despite an increasing international concern to defend individuals against abuses of power and derelictions of their rights, the question of parallel forms of non-state protection, including apportioning respon-sibility to private-sector actors, is fraught with moral uncertainties and practical difficulties. There is a legal issue: whether companies have personalities independent of the individuals who manage them, which enable them to assume obligations beyond their duties to their owners and stockholders. This legal/philosophical hurdle has a bearing on whether companies can be forced to act in the public interest. The Archbishop of Canterbury, Justin Welby, who later led a campaign to stop financial companies offering pay-day loans to poor people at exor-bitant rates of interest, argued that companies had features of social existence and personality that consisted of moral agency and a capabil-ity for sin.[7] Welby proposed that fines should be deducted from divi-dend payments, or *in extremis* that companies should be forcibly sold, with the proceeds going to the victims of its misdeeds.

Other efforts to encourage corporate responsibility have been less draconian. Initiatives such as the UN Guiding Principles on Business and Human Rights (UNGPs) use a mixture of voluntary and self-regu-lation measures, with the goal of limiting the adverse impacts of com-panies and invoking a principle of 'do no harm'. The language of the UNGPs was a conscious echo of the R2P formula of a responsibility to protect, but it distinguished between what was seen as a duty on the part of states and a (lesser) responsibility of companies to respect human rights. Critics of the UN principles say this has resulted in low-ering the ethical pressure on companies. What are required are legally enforceable obligations with regard to human rights in the form of a binding treaty on states and companies. Moreover, while human rights standards for business have begun a process of curbing corporate power, they fall short of bending that power to improve human well-being. The UNGPs have succeeded in linking responsibility to protec-tion, but the connection between corporate influence and action to prevent conflict and address long-term vulnerability remains weak.

Here is the conundrum about corporate power and purpose: unlike the state, which justifies itself by claiming to protect its citizens from violence[8] and exercises considerable power over them in the form of laws and surveillance as part of a political bargain, the corporation has to be cajoled or coerced into exercising its protective capacities, through imposed standards about human rights, transparent reporting, environmental protection and rooting out corruption. There is little that pushes companies to assume responsibility for general public order or social welfare. The status quo is that, rather than grabbing additional powers for itself, business waits upon government, international institutions, and even civil society, to take the lead and organise such efforts.

A study of Danish food and infrastructure companies in 2008 illustrates the problem. The research found companies unwilling to contribute to the government's counter-terrorism efforts, because they were reluctant to take on what they saw as an overtly political role, which they felt held no economic logic.[9] What explains such reticence, which seems at odds with public perceptions of overweening corporate influence and capacity? Why is this one area where corporations are reluctant to tread?

One answer is the persistent image of a protective and welfare state as the primary entity responsible for individual security—both physical and material—that was written into politics in the seventeenth century. This has been overwritten by a neoliberal discourse, which insists on a distance between government and the private sector, and assigns separate roles and tasks to each.

Where the era of the protective state had a fixed quality, centred on a distinct geography and including an emphasis on citizenship and strong institutions, the neoliberal world order is populated by highly mobile transnational corporations and country-hopping cosmopolitan citizens. Global business cannot be tied down by requirements to look after the vulnerable. The profit imperative absolves it from obligations to assume social duties, while at the same time questioning its legitimacy to become a guardian or active provider of citizen welfare.

This neoliberal world of untrammelled corporations also assumes that states will limit their protective duties through adopting light touch regulation, as well as delegating their obligations through the privatisation of key goods and services. If things go wrong, citizens will not look to the state for protection, but will 'simply up sticks and go elsewhere'.[10]

Neoliberalism discounts the idea that there can be a self-interested version of corporate social responsibility. Although companies benefit from secure and stable societies, where production is not threatened by crime and violence, communities are able to buy the goods they produce, and there are level playing fields thanks to rules and guarantees against corruption, few regard it as part of their remit to help deliver such conditions.

The Nobel economist and neoliberal philosopher guru Milton Friedman famously declared at the start of the modern era of multinational business that social responsibility by companies was 'a fundamentally subversive doctrine. There is one and only one social responsibility of business—to increase its profits.'[11] Others oppose the idea of allowing companies to take over protection and security functions for different reasons, seeing an encroachment by private companies into the protection business as a threat to democracy. A senior official from the European Commission's Enterprise Directorate delivered a speech in 2012 outlining how important it was that companies should recognise and be accountable for their impacts in conflict zones, yet concluded by saying: 'Companies don't have a responsibility to protect, or actively build peace. It is important to keep this distinction otherwise we risk confusion.'[12] There is even an argument that an 'oversizing of the moral responsibility' of companies could undermine personal freedoms and individuals' autonomy. If corporations are allowed to distribute to citizens rights to public goods such as security and essential commodities such as water, electricity and infrastructure (as distinct from selling them at market prices), then this will aggrandise corporate power and weaken the ability of government to regulate corporate behaviour. Such a tendency would, the argument goes, sweep away citizens' protection by effacing the difference between the public and private spheres.[13] Companies usually raise the legal argument against providing public goods and services that it will involve them in contractual liabilities, which conflicts with overriding responsibilities to their investors.

Thus there are contradictory arguments about what the respective roles and duties of key social actors around the question of citizen protection should be. All point to the existence of a responsibility gap in the provision of security and a hole in governing and legal arrangements when it comes to factoring in the presence of companies. The distinction between business and society, which is a central tenet of the neoliberal argument, and the idea that the world of the corporation exists apart from the worlds of government and politics, represents an artificial construct, as well as a historical anomaly. For most of the modern period, which has seen the growth of cross-border commercial interests, such limitations have not prevailed. The links between corporate, economic and political power run deep in all societies even if governments and business sometimes go to great lengths not to reveal them.

The most notorious case of corporate interference in the politics of a conflict region is Shell in the Ogoni Delta in Nigeria, where years of protests by local populations against pollution, land grabs and human rights abuses by the company culminated in violence, and the deaths of activists.[14] Revelations by Wikileaks showed close links between the company and Nigerian politicians. Shell had boasted behind closed doors that it had seconded people to all the relevant ministries so that it had access to all ministerial decisions and initiatives.[15] A report by the oil watchdog Platform noted that, although the company claimed to have nothing to do with Nigerian politics, 'In reality, Shell works deep inside the system, and has long exploited political channels in Nigeria to its own advantage.'[16]

As late as 2004 Shell was asked in a press conference what its 'foreign policy' in Nigeria was, a question its spokesman dismissed as irrelevant for a businessman to answer. Yet if Shell were a state, its overseas operations and relations with foreign governments would be described in exactly these terms. Shell exercised all the powers of a state in its dealings with the Nigerian government. Its concessions in the Ogoni Delta effectively gave it sovereign powers over the local population, yet the government and the company persisted with the fiction that there was a separation between business and politics.

A sense of purpose

From seventeenth-century buccaneering merchants to nineteenth-century industrialists and imperialists to modern-day creators of global production networks in search of resources, markets and cheap labour, companies have criss-crossed the boundaries between business and society, between corporate profits and culture, so that the demarcation lines between them have always been blurred.

The annual statements of Lever Brothers at the turn of the twentieth century would not be out of place in the later political discourse of social progress and the welfare state, in their references to 'the human element in industry' and affirmation of a duty to use modern science to enhance the welfare of 'the greatest number of people in any country'.

Corporate protection and paternalism represented two sides of a coin, minted out of a quest for profits, and the belief that looking after people's welfare made good business sense. Companies not only provided basic needs and material for a good life to workers and their families, they assumed other functions, which went beyond straightforward financial and business competences.

Singer Sewing Machines of New Jersey saw its expansion into foreign markets as a civilising mission that went beyond commercial gain. McCormick, inventors of the mechanical reaping machine, similarly referred to its new model as part of the 'grandest army of all ages and bound on the greatest mission, peace' as it opened up foreign markets.[17] Western companies that sought to exploit natural resources overseas emphasised the benefits of exporting technology to poorer countries as part of a civilising force. Lord Leverhulme asserted that the profit motive and the free enterprise system ensured that his company could 'listen for the faintest signal of a shift in society's priorities'.[18]

By the mid-twentieth century David Packard, the founder of Hewlett-Packard, addressed head-on the question about what a company was for in a speech to employees:

> I want to discuss why a company exists in the first place. In other words why are we here? I think many people assume, wrongly, that a company exists simply to make money. While this is an important result of a company's existence, we have to go deeper and find the real reasons for our being. As we investigate this, we inevitably come to the conclusion that a group of people get together and exist as an institution that we call a company so they are able to accomplish something collectively that they could not accomplish separately—they make a contribution to society, a phrase which sounds trite, but is fundamental.[19]

Companies began to speak about corporate citizenship and good behaviour towards society 'for business as well as moral reasons'. The concept of corporate social responsibility (CSR) had emerged in the United States as a business function, and it began to percolate into management debates. Howard Bowen's book *Social Responsibilities of the*

Businessman, published in 1953, argued that as vital centres of power and decision making, which touched the lives of citizens at many points, large companies had a duty to pursue goals and make decisions which were in the interest 'of the objectives and values of our society'.[20]

In 1971 the US Committee for Economic Development noted that businesses were being asked to assume broader responsibilities to society, and serve a wider range of human values. It defined CSR in terms of three circles: an inner circle, where the company was responsible for products, jobs and economic growth; an intermediate circle, where it had to be sensitive to social concerns about the environment, labour relations, the right to information and worker protections; and an outer circle, where business should be engaged in actively improving living conditions, influencing issues such as poverty and urban blight.[21] Although proclaiming its 'fundamental principle' to be a good citizen in the 1970s, Unilever's management also played down its influence, saying the only real power of a multinational company was the power not to invest, start new ventures or run down old ones.

Where neoliberalism, privatisation and globalisation had reinforced a view that the corporation's social character was limited, and its responsibilities circumscribed by financial interests, geared primarily to its shareholders, by the beginning of the twenty-first century global corporations were being increasingly pressured to demonstrate that they were ethical. In a significant expansion of what was seen as the 'outer circle' of corporate targets, which are non-financial, and include social and environmental goals, companies began to compete to be seen as sustainable and, most recently, 'purposeful'. This is the text of a 2016 report by a corporate think tank:

> The purpose of a great company is its reason for being. It defines its existence and contribution to society. It determines its goals and strategy. Underlying it is a set of values and beliefs that establish the way in which the company operates. Purpose is as fundamental to a corporation as our purposes, values and beliefs are to us as individuals. Purpose operates on four major planes—a covenant with customers, a reciprocal human contract with employees, mutuality of interest between society and firm and the desire to contribute to human betterment.[22]

CSR is now a growth industry in its own right, with consultancies, information centres, conferences and guidelines[23] although ideas such as the 'triple bottom line', which seeks to rate social goals for business as on a par with profits, 'bottom-of-the-pyramid capitalism' and the mantra that companies should emphasise ESG—environmental, social and governance standards—are still mainly part of a discourse that circulates among Western companies. Chinese, Indian and other non-Western businesses, which are increasingly powerful not only in global trade but also in areas of underdevelopment and social tension in Africa and Latin America, have different traditions for dealing with what are termed 'negative externalities'—in other words, the adverse effects of business operations.[24] Even in Western society the meaning of CSR remains highly elastic, ranging from simple acts of random business philanthropy to more fundamental concepts of duty and obligation.

As the early pioneers of CSR thinking recognised, the ways in which business and society connect and shape each other change constantly, as public expectations of states, companies and civil society ebb and flow. Particularly where corporations come into contact with fragile societies, CSR is seen as no longer fit for purpose, because it tends to create token attitudes of compliance which do not address the complex vulnerabilities that businesses increasingly encounter.[25] As we shall see in subsequent chapters of this book, classical CSR also suffers from a disconnect between the goals and declarations of principle made at company headquarters level, which can be found written in countless corporate brochures and websites, and the often more limited exercise of responsibility by companies on the ground.

This points to a deeper flaw. CSR is not only disconnected from mainstream management functions in most companies, regarded as an additional operating cost rather than a revenue centre, but it also represents a unilateral effort by business rather than a meaningful two-way engagement with people on the ground. Many companies address social and environmental issues as the cost of expansion into new markets, and a social licence to operate.[26] As a result corporate responsibility initiatives often fluctuate, depending on profit cycles and global commodity prices. Often they are simply misguided. Underdeveloped countries abound with examples of schools built with no money for teachers, football pitches in places that locals cannot readily access, or health centres in unsafe locations. Michael Porter and Mark Kramer of Harvard Business School suggested that companies were being trapped in a vicious circle of corporate responsibility: the more they embraced it, the more they risked being blamed for society's failures. Porter and Kramer proposed that the way out of this dilemma was for business to 'take the lead in bringing business and society back together', make societal issues at the core not the periphery of corporate management and pursue an idea of shared value.[27]

Other scholars argue that the next step should be corporate *security* responsibility, which recognises that companies are political and social actors, and should not just be occasional philanthropists. The idea of a corporate security responsibility is intended to encourage companies to take more positive action towards ensuring security as part of their operations in environments where there are physical and material safety concerns.[28] Claiming that 'the most important corporate social responsibility issue of our time is that of contributing to sustainable peace',[29] advocates for an explicit security dimension to company obligations are arguing for a significant step change in what we have a right to expect of global business.

Such attempts to politicise the global corporation change its image, seeing it as an essential provider of the most basic rights and fundamental public goods. Understanding corporate responsibility in this way is about changing a fundamental basis of society, and advocating a new form of capitalism, which integrates ethical, social and political behaviour into business rationale, ending the barriers between corporate responsibility functions and commercial divisions, and establishing new driving forces for the business sector.[30]

Compare this quotation, by the head of the world's largest investment fund, which manages assets of $6 trillion, with earlier beliefs that the only responsibility of business was to make money:

> The public expectations of your company have never been greater. Society is demanding that companies, both public and private, serve a social purpose. To prosper over time, every company must not only deliver financial performance, but also show how it makes a positive contribution to society. Companies must benefit all of their stakeholders, including shareholders, employees, customers, and the communities in which they operate.[31]

Yet examples of progressive attitudes like this are still the exception, not the norm, even if they grab attention in media, academic and expert circles. A more minimalist approach, called 'business case CSR', where companies engage with communities in order to pre-serve their licence to operate or simply as a method of reducing oper-ating risks, is more common. Companies address social and environ-mental issues as a cost of expansion into new markets, or in order to secure their acceptance locally.[32] Responsibility, alongside account-ability for their actions, are concepts that exist at the top of the man-agement chain, in headquarters offices, which regard them as neces-sary to meet the demands of a new ethical generation of financial investors, consumers and labour organisations. As we shall see, it takes a fundamental change in attitudes and corporate organisation to ensure that they percolate down throughout the entire firm. Corporate responsibility in the sense of offering a backstop to pov-erty, underdevelopment and insecurity remains on the radical fringes of management debates about the role and purpose of the corpora-tion. In practice, few global companies embrace the kind of protective strategy that ethical capitalism argues for.

In contexts where people are most in need of protection, they face a complex mixture of different types of threat: hunger and work, pol-lution and health risks, for example. Companies react mostly by focus-ing on single-issue problems and one specific type of need rather than confronting a reality in which deprivation and instability can rarely be reduced to just one root cause or grievance. To take a couple of exam-ples, Shell in Nigeria is committed to reducing the negative impacts of their operations on the environment, which means that what they focus on is biodiversity in the Niger Delta. Coca-Cola translates its social and sustainability commitment into three types of programme—helping women to participate in the market place, water conservation and promoting healthy lifestyles.[33] Corporate responses struggle to provide integrated responses or consider how a spectrum of insecurity and combination of risks might undermine efforts that concentrate on just one area.

Compartmentalising responsibility and parcelling it into small pieces means that company engagements with communities end up being partial, and often unsatisfying for both sides. Local people do not always want to be protected on a company's terms, and their views of what threatens them or poses an existential risk are often at odds with how companies direct their social programmes. As the Harvard economists Porter and Kramer suggested, the responsibility 'trap' is that businesses create expectations that cannot be met and end up fuelling resentments and increasing dependencies.[34]

Facing new pressures of accountability and governance which attempt to identify their responsibility for harms such as human rights abuses, environmental degradation and poor labour conditions, companies interpret their duties flexibly, creating multiple different identities so that they become the 'environmental corporation', 'the risk-managing and responsible corporation' or the 'largesse-distributing patron corporation'. What critics dub the pick-and-mix attitude to issues of welfare and security helps preserve companies' traditional freedom of action to behave in a way that maximises profitability.[35]

Corporate responsibility projects often reflect a reality that global companies operate in a parallel universe, removed from those who are most exposed to their impacts. The regulations and laws of their home states, combined with a still weak set of universal norms that cover only a minority of companies, provide some restraints on corporate behaviour and help determine attitudes to responsibility. However, there are large areas of the globe that offer 'zones of exception', where transnational corporations can make their own rules and assert claims to special treatment. Limited legal liability, monopoly trading rights and preferential deals on tax and justice which originated in an imperial and mercantilist age have their equivalent today in companies that take advantage of exclusive tax arrangements in export-processing zones and offshore havens, access to politicians, and clandestine contracts for investment in countries with weak governance and deficits of development.[36]

The legal jurisdictions of global companies are diffused across borders, making their accountability to national laws unclear.[37] Meanwhile their agendas and priorities are driven by markets and demands from investors, credit agencies and customers, which override local needs. The modern corporation is 'footloose' in transnational spaces, largely unanswerable to those who are on the receiving end of its behaviour.

Thus, although a more ethical type of company is emerging from a growing acceptance that business has to include social, environmental and even political dimensions, responsibility is still a weak and unpredictable force. It is being used to mitigate companies' negative impacts, but there is less understanding about precisely how it might drive companies to catalyse positive change, and how corporate activities at local level can connect not just to an international rhetoric of commitment, engagement and sustainability, but to systems for managing conflict, crisis and development challenges, so that companies work with governments and other actors to improve stability and welfare where it is most needed. There is a lack of structures or guidance which could shape corporate behaviour in novel ways, and encourage companies to go beyond compliance or minimalist approaches, to proactively seek to change conditions in the most at-risk and needy societies.

All this might suggest limited possibilities for business to exercise either responsibility or protection and become a viable resource for addressing global insecurity. Yet the contemporary corporation, while cautious about its political and social influence, and wary of being more than a profit-maker, is being pushed inexorably to change the use of its power and purpose as its relevance in terms of the most pressing global challenges becomes clearer. In 2017 the Business and Sustainable Development Commission, established at the World Economic Forum in Davos, set out the case for companies to support radical advances in addressing underdevelopment, conflict and justice, making the case for an alignment between business interests and improvements to society:

> It is incumbent on all of us to make the case for business to be at the heart of an open global economic system ... we cannot defend a lazy return to the old model that has been so widely rejected. We must have the courage to strike out in new directions and embrace an economic model which is not only low-carbon and environmentally sustainable, but also turns poverty, inequality and lack of financial access into new market opportunities for smart, progressive, profit-oriented companies. These complex challenges need the full and combined attention of government, civil society and business. Otherwise, there is no chance of solving them.[38]

In 2019 the UN deputy secretary general stressed the need to step up the pace of change: 'Governments, the UN, and a diverse range of stakeholders from both private sector and civil society must all commit to working together in a more coordinated and integrated way. The transformation we need requires us to acknowledge that everyone is a development actor.'[39]

Over the next five chapters we will see whether companies are indeed capable of being that kind of actor; how corporations have accrued influence and power in settings where classic forms of authority, legitimacy and the provision of public goods have collapsed or are unstable; and how they have exercised that influence, either alone or alongside governments, international peacemakers, aid agencies, NGOs and even competitor businesses in ways that influence security and development at the local level. There are examples where this influence has been positive, at other times negative. Where the state is under pressure, and its ability to take care of its citizens is limited by conflict, disaster or development challenges, traditional ideas about protection and responsibility need rethinking. In these cases, can corporations step in to fill gaps in preserving well-being and safety?

5

CORPORATES, CARTELS AND A DIFFERENT KIND
OF CONFLICT

Events so incredible and at times even grotesque that ... they make the novelist's chore redundant.

Carlos Fuentes[1]

It is dawn on the outskirts of Mexico City, the most densely populated city in the western hemisphere, a sprawling conurbation held together by smog-choked freeways and *barrios* of low-rise housing, arranged on grid patterns. At 6 a.m. a couple of miles from the city centre, the residential streets are mostly quiet. This itself is eerie in a city that is perpetually, nervily restless. Daylight comes quickly at this latitude, and by the time we reach our destination the buildings are no longer black outlines, but yield up their details: iron grilles, a metal door, pitched tiles. Jorge stops the car in front of a double-gated steel entrance. It is a run-down neighbourhood with few houses. The gates part slowly, cautiously. When the opening is just less than the width of our car, the barrel of an AK47 pokes out, pointing straight at us. Recognising the number plate in the murky light, the owner of the AK47 waves it affirmatively and the gates open wider, enough for us to squeeze inside. We face a jumble of trucks, parked at all angles, and a warehouse beyond, doors open, where the business of the day is already in full swing.

CORPORATE PEACE

We have come to an independent distribution centre for soft drinks, confectionery and household goods, many of them produced by the multinational Unilever. Shelves of Lipton tea, Knorr soups, deodorants, toilet rolls and sweets reach high to the ceiling. The warehouse is a mess. Packing cases are stacked haphazardly in the aisles. The floor is a heap of cardboard and plastic. The yard is dirty. The warehouse is full of men, many in black leather jackets, smoking, drinking coffee from polystyrene cups. The atmosphere manages to be both languid and chaotic.

It seems there is a problem—which is why Jorge, a senior manager at Unilever, is here. The warehouse looks like a tip but it is also a treasure trove, its contents an easy currency of unofficial bargains and informal deals, an invitation to make a little money on the side. Stock control is lax, and goods may have gone missing—or at least there is a gap between what customers order and what is eventually delivered. This is more than an issue of 'shrinkage', the polite term businesses use for staff pinching their stock. The warehouse is potentially a site for corruption and shady dealing. It is not owned by Unilever, so any losses associated with disappearing goods will not be borne by the company, but Jorge is still concerned that the distribution centre reflects badly on Unilever. It is one link in the Anglo-Dutch corporation's supply chain in Mexico. Hundreds of small corner shops and neighbourhood supermarkets buy their goods from distribution centres like this, via small trucks which ply the roads of the *barrios*. Jorge has to decide whether to try to get the warehouse owners to smarten up their act, introduce rules and install better security, or whether Unilever should just sever its ties with the place, and find other ways to sell its products in the capital. I don't follow the conversation, which takes place in rapid Mexican Spanish in a tiny, crowded, smoke-filled office on the side of the warehouse, but as we leave, Jorge's frustration indicates that the issue is unresolved. As to security, the owner feels that his leather-jacketed heavies and the AK47 are solution enough.

The distribution centre is a cameo of business in a country where rules commonly exist more in the breach than in the observance, where informality is hard-wired into the social culture, and the desire for personal enrichment can shape encounters at every level of business and government. The possibility of criminal enterprise is present beneath the surface, and violence is often a means of asserting power.

A DIFFERENT KIND OF CONFLICT

Prelude to a conflict: invasion by investment

Mexico ranks comfortably in the top twenty wealthiest countries in the world in terms of its gross domestic product. It is classified as an upper-middle-income country by the World Bank and predicted to become the world's fifth- or seventh-largest economy by the middle of this century. Economists used to talk excitedly about its prospects in a group of countries, labelled the MINTs (Mexico, Indonesia, Nigeria and Turkey), which would be the successors to the BRICS (Brazil, Russia, India, China and South Africa) as the emerging powerhouses of the global economy in the twenty-first century. However, since the beginning of the century Mexico has been destabilised by an economic boom and bust, a political hurricane and violent conflict which traces its roots to a growth of both licit and illicit business.

Optimism about the economic potential of this huge landmass, bounded by the Pacific on the west and the Caribbean on the east, sandwiched between the United States in the north and Central and South America to the south, is based on Mexico's natural resources—oil, gas and minerals—but also its labour market, drawn from a population of 120 million—of which 45 per cent are under the age of twenty-four.[2] In 1994 Mexico and its richer neighbours, the USA and Canada, signed the North American Free Trade Agreement (NAFTA), agreeing to abolish most tariffs on products traded between the three countries by 2008, which unleashed a surge in business activity.

The new trade arrangements fundamentally reshaped North American economic relations, tripling regional trade and cross-border investment. Mexican cities along the northern border with the USA saw employment and production rise as a result of increased American investment. Foreign companies moved in to take advantage of trade incentives and cheap Mexican labour, turning sleepy border towns into international manufacturing hubs. The newcomers built export-processing plants, known as *maquiladoras*, which transformed the social, political, economic and physical landscape of the border region. The boost to American exports from this new investment was massive. For Mexico too it was a shot in the arm: products turned out in Mexican factories for the consumer economy accounted for nearly two-thirds of all Mexican exports in 2013, and a goods trade surplus with the

67

USA of $81 billion in 2018. Over three-quarters of Mexican manufacturing jobs are concentrated in the US border region.[3] Threats by US president Donald Trump to shut the border or make the crossing more difficult as part of his project to erect a permanent wall were greeted with as much dismay by some US businesses as by their Mexican counterparts. Both have benefited from the cross-border boom.

The *maquila* economy is made up of global brands such as Bosch, Honeywell, Panasonic and the Lear Corporation, which import parts and materials from the USA, assemble them in Mexico, and then export them back over the border as finished goods for car manufacturers, the clothing industry and consumer electronics, in the USA and worldwide. NAFTA turned Mexico into a workshop of the global economy. Many of its workers are drawn from peasant populations in rural Mexico and other poor Central American countries—Honduras, Guatemala and Nicaragua—and up to 90 per cent of them are women. But this border-hopping, labour-devouring corporate opportunism has also increased the fragility and transient nature of life and security in Mexico.

Instead of increasing wage rates for unskilled labour, NAFTA and the growth of the *maquila* economy had quite the opposite effect. While it benefited white-collar workers and those in the new manufacturing centres in the north, it depressed incomes for agricultural labourers and unskilled workers.[4] Agricultural tariffs had also been lifted as part of NAFTA, and the Mexican market found itself flooded by American farm goods. Wages in the countryside fell, and thousands of jobs disappeared. Meanwhile the *maquila* manufacturing economy was also gobbling up Mexican agriculture, adding to the pressures on rural communities, increasing rural poverty and driving new waves of migrants towards the borderlands. Rather than NAFTA raising Mexican living standards, it helped the country's northern neighbours to become richer, while wages in Mexico stagnated or fell. A Mexican worker can stand on the southern bank of the Rio Grande and gaze a few feet across the trickle of water dividing her from the promised land, where she could earn more in one hour than she will make in a whole day in the *maquiladora*.[5]

The narco economy

Overshadowing the upheavals in Mexican trade and the emergence of the manufacturing phenomenon was growth of a more toxic export: illegal drugs. At about the time Mexico was joining NAFTA to power up its industry to world-class levels, it began to attract a different kind of global business. The trafficking routes of Colombian cocaine production moved north during the 1980s and 1990s, to capitalise on rising US demand for the drug as both a rich man's vice and, through variants such as crack, the opiate of poor inner-cites. In terms of enforcement, Mexico provided a relatively lax area for trafficking compared to other countries in Central and South America and the Caribbean. By 1989 a third of cocaine destined for the US market was routed via Mexico. Ten years later the equivalent figure was nearly 85 per cent. The value of drug exports was estimated at $10–$30 billion, up to four times more than the country's total oil sales.[6]

Mexican cartels proved adept at professionalising cocaine transit networks, hiring accountants to keep tight books, introducing new systems of reward for traffickers, and recruiting from the vast pool of young unemployed men, organised in a hierarchy of banditry and gangs, who were prepared to take risks for the chance of work. They used the accessibility of the vast, dusty plains of central Mexico, as well as the secrecy afforded by isolated mountain ranges, to construct a network of smuggling routes into the south-western USA. They soon branched out from ferrying Colombian cocaine and marijuana to producing and trafficking other drugs, such as heroin and synthetic methamphetamine. As a US National Drug Threat Assessment Report stated in 2011, Mexican cartels 'dominate the supply, trafficking and wholesale distribution of most illicit drugs in the United States'— not just because they control key transport routes, handling small loads in private cars, SUVs and pickup trucks to avoid detection, but because of their capacity to produce vast quantities of a range of illicit narcotics. Their competitive advantage was that they could either produce or distribute nearly every major illegal drug that the US market demanded.[7]

It was no coincidence that this new export trade burgeoned as NAFTA put Mexican manufacturing on the map. Border cities such as

Tijuana, Ciudad Juárez, Reynosa and Matamoros, which had long been crossing points for immigrants and marijuana, saw an explosion of cross-border trade and people movements linked to the new manufacturing industries. The legal exploitation of the border, and the internationalisation of Mexican industry in other parts of the country, generated opportunities for the traffickers to diversify beyond drugs into all kinds of racketeering, extortion and kidnapping on an industrial scale. The breadth and depth of criminality outclassed what had happened in other narco-states such as Colombia, and meant that the cartels posed a threat across Mexico to state institutions, civic authority and communities.

The key players in this shadow economy include the Sinaloa Cartel, a full-spectrum drug supplier based around Ciudad Juárez on the Texan border; Los Zetas ('the Zs'), specialising in cocaine and marijuana, who have expanded across the north and east of the country to overtake the Gulf Cartel; and the Beltran Leyva Organisation and the Knights Templar in southern Mexico. Cartel leaders are more famous than corporate CEOs. They have personal nicknames such as El Chapo ('Shorty') for Joaquin Guzman-Loera, head of the Sinaloa Cartel, El Más Loco ('the most crazy one'), and La Tuta ('the teacher'), the primary-school-teacher-turned head of the Knights Templar. From 2009 to 2013 El Chapo had his own ranking in the Forbes magazine list of most powerful people—forty-first in the world, and second in Mexico behind mobile-telephone tycoon Carlos Slim. El Chapo's estimated (2016) net worth is more than $14 billion. The cartel leaders' exploits in evading justice further guaranteed them celebrity status. El Chapo managed to escape from prison twice—the first time smuggled out in a laundry basket, the second through a tunnel which had been built between his shower room and the outside fence, before finally being captured and extradited to the USA. La Tuta was eventually tracked down to a cave, but not before the UK's Channel 4 News managed to film an exclusive interview with him while federal police hunted him in vain. Such tales had the double effect of undermining the Mexican government's authority and raising cartel leaders to mythical status in the national narrative. The narco industry wraps itself in a thick counter-culture of symbols, such as the banners (*narcomantas*) draped at the scenes of assassinations, and songs (*narcocanciones*) which laud the exploits of members. Cartels indulge in a deliberate pornography of violence, in which images of decapitated, naked bodies hanging from bridges at rush hour, and bodies dumped in public parks or at traffic intersections, are the signatures of a vicious conflict masquerading as folklore.

By the beginning of the new century, increased demand for illegal drugs spurred an increase in supply. Cartels that had hitherto been localised and largely stable now proliferated and splintered as they competed to dominate the billion-dollar supply chain to the US market. Violent turf wars erupted between cartels and their associated teenage gangs. By 2006 narco-violence was engulfing ordinary Mexicans and destroying communities. The real-life soap opera of popular heroes breaking rules and seeking fortunes at the expense of hapless state authorities morphed into a lethal national enterprise.

On 11 December 2006 the Mexican government decided to assert its authority. President Felipe Calderón, who had been elected three months previously, declared an all-out 'war on drugs' and ordered 6,500 federal troops into his home state of Michoacán, to check the power of the local cartel La Familia Michoacana. The operation left nearly 700 dead. Far from stemming the violence, the government's action escalated confrontations between cartels, police and the army. The war spread to other states. Nationwide, the death toll from these clashes alone rocketed to 2,477 in 2007, over 6,000 in 2008, and over 15,000 in 2010.

By 2016 the war in Mexico had become one of the deadliest conflicts in the world, its casualties surpassing those in Afghanistan or Iraq in the same period. Exactly how many people died is a matter of disagreement between the government and human rights groups, but estimates range from 39,000 to over 100,000. In 2018 the government declared an official toll of over 28,000 deaths, a new record, equivalent to more than 500 a week, with areas previously regarded as 'safe' such as Mexico City and Baja California recording four-fold increases in murders. One reason the official statistics are so vague is that many of the casualties are not recorded by government officials, and it is left to civil society groups to compile and guess the numbers of victims.[8] Many bodies have not been found; people have simply vanished.

Mexico's narco-conflict also barely figures in international data. The international authority on death tolls in war is the University of

Uppsala in Sweden. Its conflict database contains records going back to 1975, and is divided into three types of conflict: state-based, non-state and one-sided. According to its calculations, the total number of deaths is only 96 if you count confrontations between the government of Mexico and civilians—while 'non-state conflict' between cartels has apparently killed just under 18,000, a figure which is less than half of most estimates.[9] According to our classic understandings of war, measured in the number of people who die on the battlefield, this is a conflict that is not happening.

In Mexico, victims are dying in the streets, at traffic lights, and sometimes in their homes. The war dead are mostly ordinary people, not cartel bosses, producers, traffickers, users or teenage gang members, because they are accidental victims, caught in crossfires, killed mistakenly and because they are unprotected. Media reports tend to focus largely on murders, but there has been a steady increase in other effects of war. Estimates of the number of people displaced from their homes vary from 700,000 to 1.6 million between 2006 and 2011. Since 2007 over 40,000 people have disappeared, their fate unknown. Kidnappings increased by nearly 200 per cent between 2007 and 2012, and by 2019 were running at an average of five per day. An estimated five times more are not reported. Most kidnappings target business people.[10] Crimes ranging from car thefts to extortion and armed muggings have all more than doubled in the same period. The conflict has spread geographically so that parts of the country that were once considered safe have become infected by the virus of organised crime, corruption and violence.[11]

Questioned in a poll in 2013, almost three-quarters of adult Mexicans said they felt insecure. In some parts of the country, 90 per cent of the population are fearful. A third of all Mexican households have been the victims of at least one crime.[12] More than three-quarters of those polled were most afraid of going to the cashpoint to withdraw money, because they risk so-called 'express kidnapping', where in a perverse inversion of reality the victim becomes a human cashpoint for the criminal.[13] At work, people worry about becoming the targets of extortion. Daily behaviour has changed. Women and men have stopped wearing jewellery; in many cities there are informal nightly curfews. The majority of families forbid their children from playing on the street. In the worst conflict spots, such as Ciudad Juárez, Reynosa and Matamoros, social life—which used to revolve around bars, street food and restaurants—dried up during peak violence. Nearly half of all crime involves weapons.

Mexico's drugs war is not just about a lethal competition between drug cartels and a fight to control lucrative trafficking routes. It is about a failure of government and a breakdown of social order, against the backdrop of massive inequalities of wealth, a corrupt and broken justice system, and a social and political culture that undermines the personal safety of citizens, unless they are rich enough to live in gated communities or employ bodyguards. Many see it as a fight for the soul of the country, that thrives on what Mexicans have termed 'fake democracy', where, despite elections, authority simply shifts between different factions of powerful interests.

An enterprise war

When Mexicans elected a new right-wing president in 2000, they broke a stranglehold by the ruling party, which had lasted for generations. During that time there had been hidden deals between government officials and the drug cartels, in a kind of *modus vivendi* that allowed organised crime to operate untrammelled. With the change of government, those relationships were disrupted. A power vacuum emerged at every level—from the federal government to local municipalities—just at the moment when competition among cartels intensified, the drug trade between Mexico and the USA expanded, and trafficking of all goods across the border had been made easier by trade liberalisation. As one author described the situation in Mexico's northern states along the US frontier: it was a perfect storm.[14]

Business is an integral part of this bad weather. Mexico's drugs war is an example of not only a 'new war', but an 'enterprise war'. Violence takes many different forms in Mexico, from drug killings to the oppression of women in society and the persecution of indigenous communities. It is linked to opportunities to make money. The growth of narco-trafficking can be seen as a perverse form of enterprise culture, which mimics legal business organisation in the way that it has professionalised and structured its operations. In transporting drugs to US con-

73

sumer markets, the cartels exploited the opportunities provided by increased cross-border traffic in people and goods, which the *maquila* economy had generated. This illicit industry recruits unemployed teenage boys known as *halcones* (hawks) to operate as runners and spotters, and report on movements within a cartel's area of operation. This juvenile intelligence service, paid in watches, trainers and the latest-model smart phone to detect any sign of competition or challenge to the trafficker's territory, offers not only an income to poor urban youth, but also a sense of belonging—to a *banda*, or *pandilla* (gang).

When cartel violence exploded after 2000, it was because organised crime was reacting to attempts by newly elected municipal and federal authorities to limit their activities, after decades when politicians and officials had turned a blind eye to criminality. Many functionaries had long been part of a web of corruption and self-enrichment, in the pay of cartel leaders. To ensure their continued complicity, the cartels employed extreme violence to murder police and government officials who turned against them, and to intimidate others who wavered in their loyalty to the narco bosses. It was a battle for authority and power, a response to threats to the culture of impunity that had allowed the cartels to flourish—a fight for supremacy, exploiting chronic state dysfunction, weak civic and federal institutions, and an absence of law enforcement. In the centres of violence, it was estimated that more than half of city officials were in the pay of cartels.[15]

The contest for control of Mexico's political, administrative, judicial and security systems does not only play out among the cartels and illicit enterprise. The Mexican conflict shows why companies cannot be sidelined from solutions to conflict because, even unwittingly, they are implicated in what drives conflict or in how it plays out. Not only do companies have to navigate a web of corrupt and deadly officialdom in order to carry on trading, in major commercial and production centres they are likely to be the targets of violent threats, from kidnappings to extortion and criminal damage. Small and medium-sized companies, particularly cash businesses, such as distribution and retailers, are particularly vulnerable to demands to pay the *cuota*—the protection bribe demanded by cartels in exchange for leaving business premises and employees unharmed. Major corporations insist that they do not pay extortion money to the drug traffickers, but it is common for middle managers and junior staff to be targeted. Sometimes the price of 'peace' and for not being harmed by the cartels is no more than a box of ice cream per week, which can be traded by the extortionists for cash.

At the same time, global businesses represent an alternative site of power and authority in a country where democratic government has such a tenuous grip, and displays of macho muscle are awarded their own kind of legitimacy. In the 1990s increased foreign investment, and the rapid industrialisation of Mexico's economy, stimulated economic growth and manufacturing to the point where financial and commercial success became the basis of political credibility. With the increasing importance of foreign capital and international companies, the free market became a new imperative, not only within the economy, but also in national political discourse. Mexicans were told to respect the commercial opportunities that came with foreign investment, and foreign investors were among the 'new viceroys' in the land: a source of legitimacy, power and protection in competition with the elected government.[16]

In the last twenty years, foreign companies have not only driven the growth of manufacturing in Mexico and the exploitation of natural resources, from oil and gas to wind energy and minerals. Their presence has also contributed to the social and political dominance of a global private sector, at a time when traditional forms of authority have faced an existential crisis. The repercussions of this corporate tide have been felt in the increasing powerlessness of the Mexican state, and its struggle to control security against the growth of the cartels. During the period of violence between 2009 and 2012 the flow of foreign capital and Mexico's global ranking as a favoured place to do business did not falter. It continued to climb. As an example, manufacturing investment in the country's most violent states, such as Chihuahua, Guerrero, Nuevo Leon and the state of Mexico, increased after the start of the war on drugs in 2006 for at least two years.[17] The global corporation is not incidental but central to the search for security, peace and law and order. Mexico's conflict shows how corporate operations are part of a picture of state weakness and chronic insecurity which threaten everyday life.

Ecatepec is a large municipality north-west of Mexico City. Like many municipalities that are not even on major narco-trafficking routes, its problem is that its inhabitants include drug dealers seeking to make money in small ways. They demand a percentage of the sales of legitimate businesses, and in the case of Ecatepec they targeted between twenty and thirty drivers of Unilever's distribution trucks. It is company policy not to agree to such *cuotas*, and drivers are under strict instructions not to pay. However, because the amounts are small—$2–3 each time—many of the vendors think it worth spending such a small sum to placate the criminals. The effect is to consolidate the cartels' control of the area and secure the loyalty of individual dealers to cartel leaders. If the company tries to deal with the problem legally, by identifying drug dealers who extort these small sums, many of the victims are afraid to go to the police. Even if the perpetrators are convicted (which is unlikely given the low prosecution rate across the country), they will walk free and be back on the streets in a short time.

Single companies, however big, find themselves unable to do much other than pull out of certain areas, change delivery routes and try to work with the government and police to catch the criminals. One distribution manager shrugged his shoulders when asked about the situation: 'These are small people, and others take advantage of them. It's about power.'

Small-scale extortion is a daily occurrence, but corruption and enrichment are not always modest. There is nothing small about Walmart. The US retail giant is the biggest company in the world, with sales approaching $500 billion, and 260 million customers. In the UK it owns supermarket group Asda. Walmart expanded rapidly in Mexico after entering the market in 1991; by 2015 it was the second-largest company on the Mexican stock exchange. It had over two thousand stores, and announced plans to increase its investment in new stores to $4 billion over five years. But in 2012 Walmart was exposed in a series of articles by the *New York Times*, systematically bribing Mexican government officials in order to gain planning permission for new stores. The newspaper found nineteen sites across Mexico where Walmart had bribed officials to allow the company to build stores without environmental permits or construction licences—and, in one case, right next to one of the country's most significant Mayan archaeological sites, at Teotihuacán.

The scandal exposed the perverse connections between business and political power, and illustrated how economic growth and state dysfunction can be symbiotic bedfellows. According to the *New York Times*, Walmart was not the reluctant victim of a corrupt local culture that insisted on bribes as the cost of doing business:

> Nor did it pay bribes merely to speed up routine approvals. Rather, Wal-Mart de Mexico was an aggressive and creative corrupter, offering large payoffs to get what the law otherwise prohibited. It used bribes to subvert democratic governance—public votes, open debates, transparent procedures. It used bribes to circumvent regulatory safeguards that protect Mexican citizens from unsafe construction. It used bribes to outflank rivals.[18]

Business watchdogs such as the NGO Transparency International say that foreign companies employ double standards, proclaiming an international image of quality but behaving as 'post-colonials' in Mexico, bribing officials and seeking to subvert the rule of law. Instead of working to promote much-needed change in areas such as human rights, the rule of law and efficiency, or to modernise public services or public institutions, the global private sector has largely directed its efforts to preserving the status quo and to lobbying for liberal market reforms.[19]

Business and insecurity are also connected in the fact that economic growth has affected the vulnerability of Mexican society, undermining its resilience and making it susceptible to external shocks. Foreign companies have devoured land—particularly agricultural land—to build factories, and have dominated the competition for public services: federal and municipal budgets have been more geared to providing facilities for business than citizens. The *maquila* economy operates in spaces that have been de facto denationalised, creating a new 'no man's land' geography which belongs to neither Mexico nor the USA.[20] Small towns have disappeared under the weight of a wave of internal emigration, while elsewhere—particularly in the north of the country, where the processing economy has burgeoned—there has been immigration and rapid urbanisation, destabilising everyday life. Mexico is the main migration (and trafficking) route for workers from other Central American countries—such as Guatemala, Honduras and Nicaragua—as they try to reach the USA, or at least jobs in Mexican factories. The *maquila* economy is rooted in the idea of transit, a perpetual to and fro of human and commercial traffic. It relies on transfers of goods and people, creating a shaky bridge between poverty, cheap wages and low land values south of the border, and an affluent, relatively safe world of jobs and consumer goods to the north.

The growth of manufacturing in frontier cities such as Ciudad Juárez and Monterrey has been a magnet for waves of population movement, as rural dwellers and agricultural workers left the land in search of jobs in the new processing plants established by foreign companies. The mass displacement of people created transient and fragile communities living in shanty-towns with few public services, no roads and limited electricity, as municipal authorities struggled to keep pace with the rapid growth in population. When President Trump threatened to strangle the tide of migration by building a wall along the US–Mexico frontier and closing the border, thousands of people from Tijuana to Panama, trying to escape poverty and violence, were corralled, unable to cross the border but unwilling to make the long journey back home.

Insecurity in border cities is not confined to unsuccessful migrants. Those who stay in Mexico even with jobs are also vulnerable. There is a high turnover of labour, low unionisation and poor working conditions inside the *maquiladoras*. Average manufacturing wages in Ciudad Juárez are $422 per month, the lowest of any manufacturing centre in Mexico—in part because there is always surplus labour. Cyclical downturns in the world economy reverberate here, directly impacting workers.[21] Competition from rival manufacturing centres led to more than 90,000 regional jobs disappearing between 2007 and 2010. The *maquiladoras* lost 52,637 jobs in 2008 alone. Workers with no income, living away from families and traditional communities in makeshift townships with no infrastructure, find themselves excluded from both civic and corporate safety nets. Against this backdrop, the lure of illicit activities or illegal passage across the border to the USA can become irresistible.

Borderline insecurity

Nowhere is the overlap between business and security more evident than at the US–Mexico frontier, where two countries, and two different destinies, are separated by the thin trickle of water that is the Rio Grande. Ciudad Juárez, Mexico's fifth-largest city, is one of those crossing points between poverty and prosperity. Between 2007 and 2012 it experienced a wave of violent killing, exceeding 10,000 deaths, accompanied by other violent crimes such as carjacking, extortion, torture and disappearances. Juárez is a prime 'onshore' location where US companies come to take advantage of a favourable tax regime, making the Mexican city the equivalent of an offshore tax haven, but conveniently placed just a bridge's width away from the safety of the USA, where senior management and those in possession of US documents live, go to school and pursue a normal social life.

'José Sanchez'[22] is from Ciudad Juárez. Now in his sixties, he worked in the state police force before becoming head of security for seven *maquiladora* plants owned by the same American manufacturer. The growth of private security is one of the features of the *maquila* economy, with companies buying the kind of protection beyond the reach of ordinary citizens. Jobs for security guards and consultants have grown as a result of the influx of foreign companies, and created a revolving door between the public and private sectors. Being a police officer in Ciudad Juárez had to rate as one of the most dangerous jobs on earth between 2008 and 2012, when police murders often topped a hundred per year, so it is not difficult to poach former officers for a relatively easier life in private security. In Ciudad Juárez's Cigar Club, José discusses the trauma that afflicted the city from 2008—when it was common to hear about half-a-dozen drug killings every day, when people stopped watching television because the news was so terrifying and there were no safe havens from the violence. It was hard to know who could be trusted. Journalists and police officers would turn up at assassination scenes to find that the victim was a friend, classmate or relative. 'At that time Ciudad Juárez lost all its humanity and its civilisation,' says José. *Maquila* workers could briefly escape the streets, bused into the foreign-owned plants in customised US school buses, via a parallel private transport system that brings the city's roads to a standstill at the end of each shift. Behind the gated and walled perimeters, watched over by closed-circuit televisions and supervised by uniformed private guards, the *maquiladoras* offered a kind of green zone in the middle of the urban battleground. Yet José tells of incidents where, following a shooting outside one of the plants, the *narcos* would force their way in and demand that guards hand over CCTV tapes to protect their anonymity. Although workers were not targeted, the *maquiladoras* were not crime-free. Thefts and crimes of passion were among the spillover effects of growing delinquency and violence in a city where the rule of law had collapsed.

For individual workers, employment in the *maquiladora* requires a tradeoff between courting the danger of the streets, on the one hand, running the risk of being caught in crossfire if you worked in a bar, restaurant or downtown office, or, on the other, opting for an environment where heat and light are freely available, but where the working day is twelve to fifteen hours long and poorly paid. Women are particularly at risk in this environment. They earn nearly a third less than the average paid to men, although their skills and their smaller hands are particularly sought after for producing clothing or micro-components. Some pay even more dearly for their employment. Young women working in the processing plants are victims of a deadly cultural prejudice: a woman's place is in the home, not in jobs that were once reserved exclusively for men.[23] Femicide became another Mexican disease.

In Mexico's drug war, the prime casualty is the everyday safety and welfare of individuals. Foreign manufacturing companies have not caused this conflict, although in many places—particularly where there are confrontations between communities and companies over indigenous land rights—many corporations are seen as part of the worsening pattern of abuse and impunity in the country. Companies are increasingly entwined with a national security crisis that targets their employees, customers and communities, and creates a spiral of violence which is indiscriminate about its victims.

Companies also contributed to a particular narrative about the drug war, which emerged during the 2006–12 period and still lingers in government rhetoric. Government and business elites sought to present the narco-violence as a clash of cartel leaders, which only affected those involved in drug trafficking. By this account, the violence was a form of extreme delinquency and an existential crisis for the Mexican state. The victims brought their plight upon themselves, because they were involved with the cartels.[24] This narrative denied what civil society organisations were saying: that the violence was rooted in poverty, deprivation, and the fact that the state was largely absent in providing services, upholding law and order, and even steering the economy.[25]

Among the *maquiladoras* there was a concerted effort to play down the severity of the violence, as business leaders feared that the stream of reports about drug killings in the international press threatened the flow of inward investment that was life blood of the *maquila* economy. They spoke alarmingly of a loss of competitiveness and global market share, and insisted that protection of the free market was the way to ensure security in cities such as Ciudad Juárez, Tijuana and Monterrey. As the bodies piled up, they touted Juárez's business attractions. A glance at the headlines on any one day painted a confusing picture: Ciudad Juárez, 'the murder capital of the world', was also the most attractive city to US investors.[26]

By 2008 even the Mexican government could not ignore the rise in violence. President Calderon's response was to send 10,000 troops onto the streets of Ciudad Juárez, to reimpose order. This military approach had a devastating effect, increasing the killing to new levels rather than curbing it. The low point came on a Saturday night in January 2010. Four civilian SUVs pulled up on a working-class residential street. Two dozen men with assault rifles entered a house where a group of teenagers were having a birthday party; the massacre left fifteen dead. The Villas de Salvácar shootings became a benchmark of insecurity in the city. Not only were innocent children killed—it turned out to be a case of mistaken identity, as some of the teenagers belonged to a football team called AA, the same initials as Artistas Asesinos (a gang affiliated with the Juárez cartel)—but the authorities were shown to be powerless to protect people, even in their own homes. Residents of Juárez describe living in a blanket of fog, from which it was impossible to imagine a way out. Ciudad Juárez was a national blackspot, but killings were happening across Mexico, engulfing not just cartel bosses and their acolytes, but people who were employed by legitimate corporations or linked to them through family and neighbourhood. Companies could no longer pretend that it was business as usual. The violence was sucking them into its vortex.

On Friday 26 May 2012 a fire started in a distribution centre owned by a Mexican subsidiary of PepsiCo in the south-western state of Michoacán. It was followed over the next seventy-two hours by identical fires at four other depots run by the same company, Sabritas (a popular brand of crisps), and gun attacks on delivery drivers by groups of hitmen. The fires were fuelled by Molotov cocktails, and destroyed dozens of the company's vans. The guns were high-calibre assault weapons. The hitmen were from the Knights Templar drug cartel, which later claimed responsibility for the attacks by draping banners on bridges and monuments. They alleged that the delivery vans were being used by undercover agents as part of the government's offensive against drug trafficking. Others speculated that Sabritas had refused to pay extortion fees (*cuotas*) to the cartel, which had launched the arson attacks in revenge. The message on the cartel's banners was clear: business should stick to business and not get involved in security and politics, otherwise other attacks would follow. The destruction of the delivery trucks and the threats against drivers and company executives formed the worst attack on a private company in Mexico's six-year conflict. Sabritas's vice-president Francisco Merino told the press that the company always operated within the law, and that it was '100% focused on its business'.[27] It was no longer enough.

Safety in ice cream

Back in the early morning in Mexico City, we leave the grocery warehouse and drive to another site half an hour away. Unlike the first distribution centre, this is owned and run directly by Unilever. In stark contrast to our previous stop, there are rows of neatly parked trucks, lined up in spotlessly clean parking bays and painted with the company's Holanda ice cream brand, purveyors of Magnum and Cornetto.

Employees wear a uniform of a red baseball cap and T-shirt. Half of them are women, many are young. They are drinking coffee in a communal lounge. On average, these employees earn just $60 per week, plus 4 per cent commission,[28] a hint of how vulnerable they are despite their sanitised surroundings and a clue to the importance of the action Unilever has taken to protect them. There are forty vehicles in the depot, and each is fitted with a black box and a panic button to protect the drivers against attack by criminals. A central monitoring station receives a signal when the panic button is activated and sends out support, sometimes in conjunction with the police:

> When we first introduced the black boxes, the drivers thought it was a
> way to check their sales. We told them no, that it was a security proj-

ect, and to reassure them we introduced a rule that the boxes could not be accessed by sales people. One of the first effects it had was that drivers started using seat belts. Within one month 100 per cent of drivers were using seat belts, compared to 30 per cent in the general population.[29]

In 2015 Mexico City ranked sixth out of thirty-two states for the number of murders, suffered the third-highest number of reported extortions, and was in the top five locations for kidnappings.[30] The drivers of Unilever's ice cream trucks face risks ranging from ambush and kidnapping to extortion and the simpler hazards of bad driving. Some of their routes are made dangerous by *narco* blockades, which may consist of just one person stopping trucks to demand 'rent' for passing through his territory, or sometimes a one-off payment. Where there are low wages and little systematic management, it is common for workers to steal boxes of goods, take free promotion samples and resell them. Petty crime is not as innocuous as it appears: it is often the tip of a much bigger pattern of organised crime, orchestrated by drug traffickers. Unilever responded to this with a strategy that focused on protection and social action: the cleanliness of the depot, the corporate clothing and a no-smoking rule are not cosmetic changes, but attempts to introduce a safety culture, and a recognition that businesses like these are part of Mexico's security crisis.

Grocery distribution is one of the largest sectors in Mexico. It used to be run by individual family firms, but increasingly these are being squeezed out by bigger companies and international conglomerates. For an owner such as Unilever, the challenge is to address insecurity in the form of many everyday threats, not least precarious road safety. To reduce accidents, Unilever awards prizes for careful driving, and congratulatory messages are dispatched to the driver's family. If an accident with an ice cream truck occurs and is found to be the result of speeding, for example, it is not the police who enforce the rules, but the company. Unilever steps into the role of regulator, enforcing driving and safety rules in place of an absentee state.

The company also teamed up with other grocery groups, such as Bimbo, a Mexican baking conglomerate with a fleet of 60,000 delivery vehicles. Collaboration between commercial rivals can provide protection to employees in an increasingly insecure climate. Other kinds of hazards require different safety measures. Shift times were changed to coincide with less traffic to diminish the risk of accidents as well as extortion and ambush. Companies shared information with the police to identify cartel members and to understand which routes might become particularly dangerous. In one factory, after a spate of night-time kidnappings, Unilever changed the working hours so that the workforce could leave at 7 p.m. rather than 10 p.m. They introduced a rule of no meetings after 6 p.m. and insisted that employees carry mobile phones. When there was an armed assault outside the gate of the depot, the company asked the employees whether they preferred to move to a better, more distant location or stay put. The employees chose to move, and commute more than an hour each way every day to work in a safer area.

Oscar has worked as an ice cream driver for ten years, and tells me he likes wearing his uniform of T-shirt and red cap. 'I am proud and my family is also proud. It's a good company—they protect us and they support us.' His colleagues laugh when I ask who they trust most to tackle the security crisis: the government, local companies or foreign companies. 'The state doesn't do anything, and Mexican companies didn't do this [install safety devices into the distribution trucks]. It takes foreign companies, where people are committed to change,' says Oscar.

The company identified first thirty, then fifty delivery routes that had become dangerous as the drug violence spread. Special delivery schedules were arranged. GPS was used to inform the company when drivers had arrived safely. New procedures were introduced for destinations once considered safe. Drivers had to arrive at their overnight hotel before dark, and not go out in the evening. Companies stepped in to provide protection to workers who do not trust police or trade unions to look out for them. Unilever sought to create a spirit of caring, which substituted for state safety institutions, and a government that insisted on denying public responsibility for the violence, and erected what amounts to a parallel system of security and authority.[31]

The company has over three thousand employees in Mexico, of whom half are merchandisers. By employing them directly, rather than as sub-contractors as many companies do, Unilever exercises an influence which extends beyond the workplace to their homes and communities, and tries to encourage a social culture that inhibits rather than enables violence. As part of a global plan for sustainability, the company has procedures in Mexico for recycling rubbish. They organise volunteer activities involving family members and neighbours. There is tree planting, and training schemes for how to park vehicles and drive carefully to promote child safety. 'We try to be part of the solution,' says Jorge. The company's ambition was to affect 100,000 people—more than three times the number of its actual workforce, and equivalent to 10 per cent of the population—to introduce islands of order in a sea of conflict and chaos: in the words of one executive, 'to make business, but not with blood'.[32]

If this sounds like the paternalism of nineteenth-century Unilever, building worker communities at Port Sunlight and in the Congo, the company sees it as a new way of exercising responsibility. Adam Mallalieu was head of global security for Unilever during an early period of the drug war. He contrasts the traditional way of ensuring security within a global company—reinforcing guards and fences—with a goal of enhancing people's lives to make them safe and insulating the business as much as possible against the dangers outside. 'Now what we need to do is understand the business context, put all kinds of risks on the table. In Mexico, the concern is the vulnerability of people on the streets. Before, different companies did not talk to each other about these things. It has been an enormous benefit that companies now come together and share best practice.'

In Ciudad Juárez, at the centre of the firestorm, international companies became part of a vocal public campaign for a change in government policy. A coalition of diverse social groups including business, NGOs, church leaders, neighbourhood associations and medical professionals pressured the federal, state and city authorities to address the underlying problems of poverty, deprivation and civic infrastructure, in a bid to retake the city from the drug cartels. The result was a federal programme called Todos Somos Juárez (TSJ: 'We Are All Juárez'), which produced hundreds of individual policy actions and programmes, and over $400 million of federal spending in 2010 and 2011. Around three-quarters of the budget was directed to investments in health, education, culture, sports and recreation. The government also emphasised that improving the business climate was a key element in improving life in the city.[33]

TSJ mobilised companies to work with civil society groups to challenge government policy and use their resources to address what they saw as the underlying causes of the violence. Companies set up security roundtables (*mesas de seguridad*) to debate solutions to the crisis. They sought to rebuild citizen trust in the city and improve civic facilities, through creating crime-reporting hotlines and web platforms.[34] Conflict had reduced the distance between business and security. Companies that had previously not only stood back from public politics and security, but had sought to deny the scope, intensity and origins of the conflict, now took up frontline positions to force government accountability and direct responses to the violence.

A thousand kilometres south-east of Ciudad Juárez, Monterrey is the industrial capital of Mexico, sometimes ranked as the best city in Latin America to do business and home to some of Mexico's largest global companies. Like Juárez it has benefited economically from its proximity to the USA, but has also suffered from a growing tide of crime and the nefarious ecosystem created by neighbourhood gangs and international drug cartels, in which violence, poverty and social exclusion have created no-go areas. As in Juárez, Monterrey's companies started to team up with NGOs, local universities and neighbourhood associations, creating hybrid organisations to respond to a growing security emergency. These new alliances focused on the roots of the violence in the urban deprivation around the wealthy sites of corporate manufacturing and production.

Cemex is a home-grown multinational, which started in one of the poorest areas in the south of Nuevo Leon, the state of which Monterrey is the capital. Lorenzo Zambrano, who built his grandfather's cement business into a leading world player, realised that the key to addressing the conflict that was enveloping Monterrey and its surrounding villages and small towns lay with the communities themselves. He commissioned a web platform, the Center for Citizen Integration, to help residents pool information about their communities and use it to make improvements to everyday life. Zambrano, who died in 2014, also laid the foundations for ensuring that his business could work to improve the conditions for peace in an increasingly violent region of the world. Cemex used its connections with Mexico's top officials and politicians to persuade them to sign agreements committing them to neighbourhood development programmes. In 2015 the company conducted its own 'Deep Impact' study to apply pressure on federal spending programmes to refocus their efforts. Maintaining that parks, basic services and infrastructure are the responsibility of the state, the company forced the government to assume responsibility and make good the chronic lack of public services ordinary Mexicans suffer from. 'Our business can only thrive in a world where people can build with our products. This is part of our sustainable business model,' explains a corporate responsibility manager. Yet Cemex has gone beyond what many corporations regard as the limits of its own responsibility. It is no longer focused on just mitigating the impacts of its own operations, but testing its capacities to galvanise change in areas where the company does not itself operate. 'We realised that the company is strong in many ways. We have a strong position with government and the capacity to make alliances. We believe we can achieve more in the fights against poverty and insecurity through strategic programmes rather than just trying to minimize our impacts.'[35] Through instigating collective action, as well as looking at the bottom of Mexican society and how to connect it to the traditional centres of power in the country, Cemex is defining new meanings of responsibility and protection amid a growing storm of organised crime, daily suffering and citizens' distrust of conventional government responses for dealing with them.

Mexico's singular conflict reveals how violence, crime and predation have escalated, not in spite of the country's business successes, but because they infiltrate legitimate enterprise, and are linked to economic growth and foreign investment. The private sector is an alternative source of power that challenges traditional authority in a state, where public officials are often corrupt and criminal. Some companies, operating in the midst of this new kind of conflict, have started to think about their roles in new ways, which include a duty of care to citizens and communities. In the face of increasingly blatant abuses by state security forces, companies have rejected government policy and official accounts of the conflict, recognising a need to intervene directly in response to a collapse of order and human welfare.

Traditional alignments that kept business, government and civil society separate have been reworked into new coalitions. Companies have not only realised that they are caught up in the war of the *narcos*, they have started to use their influence to find ways out of it. In the next chapter we move east to another seemingly intractable conflict, where corporate failure to understand its impact on the dynamics of confrontation was to prove a costly mistake.

6

GOING OFF THE RAILS IN JERUSALEM

The West Bank of the River Jordan is a barren and bleached tract of land, dotted with hills, covering 5,460 square kilometres—about the size of the US state of Delaware. It runs from north to south, in a chunk of what was once called Palestine, which now bites into the modern state of Israel. It remains one of the most contested terrains on earth, fought over since the middle of the twentieth century by Israelis, Jordanians, Palestinians and Syrians and their backers. It is also a land of lines.

The Green Line designates the border of Israel drawn after the 1948 Arab–Israeli War, which resulted in the partition of Palestine between the Israeli state, proclaimed by Jewish forces in May 1948 under prime minister David Ben-Gurion, and Jordan, which occupied most of the West Bank and East Jerusalem.[1] Under the terms of the 1949 armistice, the drawing of the Green Line was a military exercise to mark the separation of Israeli and Jordanian territory. For Palestinians living on the Israeli side and unable to return to their homes, it was an exclusion line. The 1949 settlement divided Jerusalem in half: the west of the city was Israeli, and East Jerusalem part of the West Bank. Israel's victory in the Six Day War of 1967 led to its occupation of the West Bank, breaching the Green Line and consolidating control over the majority Palestinian population. In the following decade the attitude of the Israeli government hardened, and it rejected the legitimacy of the armistice line, preventing any return of the Occupied Territories to Palestinians.[2] In 1980 Israel proclaimed its control over East Jerusalem, which includes the Old City and some of the holiest sites in Judaism, Christianity and Islam, such as the Temple Mount, the Church of the Holy Sepulchre and the Dome of the Rock.

The Green Line constitutes the formal boundary between Israel and the West Bank, and has been a reference point for constituting the boundaries of any future state of Palestine. It remains a potent symbol of what has been lost, and what remains to be fought for by both sides.[3] Like many arbitrary lines, determined by military events, the Green Line weaves through populated areas, dividing towns, villages, farms and families. It is a mapmaker's line, moved and adjusted to accommodate needs on the ground. Even in the immediate aftermath of the 1949 settlement it was endlessly transgressed—by Palestinian refugees leaving Israel, and by Israeli defence forces who launched commando raids into Arab territory.

In 2002 this fluid frontier gave way to a new line when Israel began construction of the West Bank barrier, a 620 kilometre-long, 10 metre-high wall which separates Palestinian East Jerusalem from the rest of the West Bank.[4] The wall slices through towns and communities. In places it partitions houses, cuts them off from their gardens and neighbours, with a relentless zigzag of concrete and barbed wire, forcing West Bank Palestinians and Israelis into separate zones, policed by a system of entry points and checks.

The wall has led in turn to new lines, of human and vehicle traffic trying to move between the Israeli zone and the Palestinian Occupied Territories in the West Bank. The Qalandiya checkpoint is a huge and aggressive structure that presides over the most populous crossing point for workers and families trying to get from the West Bank to jobs, neighbours, shops and amenities in Jerusalem. The checkpoint funnels a daily tide of commuters through a narrow space, controlled by guards, electronic barriers and surveillance cameras. The queue of cars, buses, lorries and people at rush hour stretches far back down the road towards Ramallah, the Palestinian capital. The wait to cross is often more than an hour as papers are scrutinised and vehicles are pulled over. Bus passengers are forced to disembark on the Palestinian side where they form another line, which moves slowly on foot through giant metal pens, where their documents are checked before they emerge on the Jerusalem side to rejoin their bus. The sick in ambulances must wait too, even if they are trying to access vital emergency services in Jerusalem or seeking treatment for serious illnesses such as diabetes or cancer.

Another line is visible on the horizon, snaking across the hilltops. Gleaming new houses with roofs that look different from nearby properties, and which stand out not just because of their newness, but also because of the towers on their roofs, meaning that the inhabitants have their own water supply. On closer inspection, many also have gardens. These are Israeli houses in an expanding series of more than 130 settlements built for Jewish families on West Bank land. Since 1993, when the number of settlers passed the 100,000 mark, the settlements have been the prime focal point of tension between Israel and the Palestinians, representing what Palestinians regard as a land grab by Israel, entrenching its occupation of the West Bank, and colonising land which would be part of any future Palestinian state. There are around 400,000 Jewish settlers spread throughout these new communities, who enjoy visibly superior infrastructure and facilities such as water, roads, electricity and rubbish clearance in comparison to neighbouring Palestinian towns. According to a 2016 United Nations Security Council resolution, these settlements constitute a flagrant violation of international law. The resolution demands that Israel immediately and completely cease all settlement activity.[5]

The latest in this historic series of lines is a tram line, the Jerusalem Light Railway, a €1 billion international transport infrastructure project, which began construction in April 2006 and opened five-and-a-half years later. The railway was designed to link the western—Israeli—part of Jerusalem with the new residential areas developing to the south, north and east of the city in occupied Palestinian territory. It provides a means of connecting Israeli settlements in the West Bank, and giving them access to Jerusalem. Line 1—the 'Red Line' of the 14 kilometre tramway—crosses the 1948 Green Line between West and East Jerusalem, skirts the Old City with its holy shrines, and, heading north, passes through densely populated Palestinian neighbourhoods of Shu'afat and Beit Hanina before reaching further stops at new Jewish settlements at the end of the line.[6]

The tramway is the centrepiece of a 'Master Plan' drawn up by the city municipality in 1999 whose aim was to ease traffic congestion and generate new development in and around the city, by building roads, tunnels and overpasses. From a population of 730,000 in 2013, Jerusalem is expected to grow to nearly a million inhabitants by 2020, placing pressure not just on its transport infrastructure, but on all public services, land and other scarce resources such as water.[7] The tramway route allowed the Israeli authorities to present an alternative view of Jerusalem as a unified, modern metropolis, rather than a divided and contested city. The plan with its centrepiece of a clean, environmentally friendly means of transport, ignored the city's fractious politics.[8] In a parallel world of warm rhetoric and glossy brochures produced by the city planners, the railway was an indispensable piece of urban modernisation. Others were more candid about its political message. In August 2005 Israeli prime minister Ariel Sharon signed the contract between a private consortium, CityPass, and the Israeli authorities to begin work on building the railway. Sharon said: 'I believe that this [Jerusalem Light Rail] should be done, and in any event, anything that can be done to strengthen Jerusalem, construct it, expand it and sustain it for eternity as the capital of the Jewish people and the united capital of the State of Israel, should be done.' Palestinians were outraged at what they saw as a new means by Israelis to colonise the West Bank, and support expansion of the settlements. The bullet shape of the planned train seemed particularly prescient in firing up a new round of conflict between Jews and Palestinians.

The immediate effect of the tramway was to increase traffic chaos in Palestinian suburbs of East Jerusalem. A report by a Palestinian human rights network described how construction noise, congestion and air pollution were worse in Palestinian areas, where the tramway squeezed local road traffic into a small lane either side of the track and did away with parking spaces. In Jewish areas the railway was built with room for additional traffic.[9]

Out of twenty-three stations along the 14 kilometre route of the tramway's Line 1, only three serve Palestinian neighbourhoods, added after protests by local civil rights groups. Palestinians saw the tramway as overwhelmingly for the benefit of Jewish residents in the new settlements, a resource which they neither could nor would use.

Rayah Sbitany works for one of the few large-sized Palestinian companies that operate out of Ramallah in the occupied West Bank. She is against the tramway: 'It is taking up our roads—the 8 a.m. rush-hour is terrible and it doesn't provide a link to anywhere such as schools.' Her parents have asked her not to travel on it to work, because they are afraid it will be targeted by Palestinian suicide bombers attacking Jewish settlers. A description of an everyday journey on the tramway in 2012, a year after it was inaugurated, includes how the train would suddenly stop, the passengers would be forced to disembark, and Israeli Special Forces would board to search for suspicious packages. Travelling on the railway was tantamount to running a gauntlet of 'danger and fear'.[10]

Corporate complicity

Two European companies played a central role in this tangled tale of Middle East diplomacy, territorial manipulation and urban planning, crossing a line between business and conflict politics and finally unleashing a furious global backlash. Alstom, a French engineering company, and the French environmental and transport group Veolia invested in a one-quarter stake in the consortium that created the tramway. Alstom's role was to provide the engineering and the train cars, Veolia's to design and operate the tramway.

Palestinians claim that the companies made possible a project that entrenches discrimination against them, reduces their mobility, and will succeed in killing off their hopes of an independent state. Jamal Juma, head of the Stop the Wall coalition, says that Veolia's participation in the light railway amounted to an aggressive assault on Palestinian rights and a systematic squeezing out of the Arab population on the West Bank:

> When Veolia come and co-operate with the Israeli state and allow settlements to exist, they are contributing strongly to the destruction of houses and confiscation of property. Neighbourhoods that could benefit on the road from Jerusalem to Ramallah are now blocked and disconnected by the tramway. A road that was 10 metres wide has become 2 metres wide.[11]

The French companies were accused of 'complicity' in Israel's illegal occupation, and abetting a war crime. Palestinians described 'seemingly mundane acts of business [as] criminally tainted'.[12] International opposition to Israel's occupation of the West Bank had previously directed its efforts at diplomatic protests against the Israeli government. Now activists switched to showing how businesses that operated inside settlements, or traded with them, were helping Israel to tighten its control over the West Bank. Veolia found itself caught in the sights of grassroots protesters, organisations such as the UN and the European Union and international NGOs. As well as the tramway contract, Veolia operated bus services between Jewish settlements in the Occupied Territories along Road 443, often referred to as an apartheid road, because Palestinians are prohibited from using most of it. The bus service helps to make the settlements viable by providing transport links between them and East and West Jerusalem. Veolia subsidiaries were also granted permits to handle waste from factories in Israel, at a waste site on Palestinian land at Tovlan in the Jordan Valley, which Palestinians claim was built illegally, and only serves Israelis, in violation of international law.[13]

Unsettling facts on the ground

Veolia's decision to do business in the Occupied Territories coincided with the escalation of Jewish settlement activity in the West Bank. The settlement policy is central to conflict politics in the region. It paved the way for the light railway project and is at the crux of how violence, territory, business and livelihoods are connected in the Israeli–Palestinian conflict. Between 2001 and 2007 more than 10,000 residential units had been built in the West Bank in order to attract Jewish settlers to move out of Israel's overcrowded cities and suburbs. By 2015 there were more than a hundred Israeli settlements, home to nearly 600,000 Jewish residents.[14] Looked at on the map these small towns, typically consisting of residential blocks, and each with a synagogue, a school—even sometimes a university—and usually a shopping centre, appear like isolated pinpricks of habitation. Once linked by public transport, they become transformed into a string conurbation. This is the effect of the Jerusalem Light Railway—to connect the dots. So-called outposts penetrate deeper into the West Bank where settlements have been built without Israeli government approval, and often by the most politically radical or ultra-Orthodox Jews.

The settlements are opposed by Palestinians and most of the international community, because they create a new reality on the ground of Israeli presence in the West Bank. The settlement policy and the relentless increase in the number of settlements have become the most potent tools of war in the West Bank. On 31 August 2014 Israel announced that it was appropriating 1,000 acres of land in the West Bank near Bethlehem to eventually house a thousand Israeli families, in the largest single expansion of settlement activity in over thirty years. The move was in retaliation for the kidnapping and murder two months earlier of three Israeli teenagers, taken from outside the city of Hebron on the West Bank and later found buried in shallow graves.[15] Government ministers said that the appropriation was 'an appropriate Zionist response to murder. Building is our answer to murder.'[16]

In a congested and contested terrain with scarce resources and development challenges due to its hilly and arid nature, the issue of who controls land has always been central to the political struggle between Israel and Palestine, and has run through all attempts to bring peace to the region. The Oslo Accords, brokered by the Americans and signed by Israeli prime minister Yitzhak Rabin and Yasser Arafat of the Palestine Liberation Organization (PLO) in 1993, designated the West Bank into three named areas. Towns such as Bethlehem, Hebron and Ramallah, the headquarters of the Palestinian Authority (PA), are in two of these. The third area consists of land that was intended to be transferred from Israeli control to Palestinian jurisdiction. It contains most of the West Bank's natural resources, including water, as well as space for development. Palestinian building permits in this area are regularly refused, and Israel often demolishes developments that are put up. Yet it is on this third category of land that Israeli settlements have proliferated. More than twenty years after Oslo, most Palestinians feel that they have become worse off politically and economically, as a result of the 'peace agreement'. The opening of the tramway, running through this controversial third area, cutting Palestinians off from East Jerusalem while feeding the growth of Israeli settlements, came to symbolise the cause of their frustration and anger.

Boycott and backlash

A year before Veolia began construction work on the railway, Palestinian civil society organisations decided to try a new tactic to oppose Israel's steady annexation of the West Bank and the Gaza Strip. They created a mass movement with the aim of applying non-violent pressure on Israel, using economic, cultural and symbolic tools. The Boycott, Divestment and Sanctions (BDS) campaign was launched in July 2005 to claim Palestinian rights to live and work in the West Bank. BDS modelled itself on the South African anti-apartheid movement, stating that it was a 'rights-based not a solution-based' initiative. Its members included 170 different bodies from trade unions to refugee networks and professional associations. They demanded an end to Israeli occupation of Palestinian territories in Gaza and the Syrian Golan Heights as well as the West Bank, dismantling of the wall, and a return of refugees and guarantees of Palestinian rights within Israeli territory.

BDS's prime targets were not politicians and diplomats, but foreign companies, which they regarded as working on the frontline of Israeli occupation. Calling for commercial boycotts, a consumer and investor backlash, BDS geared up to force companies to withdraw from doing business with Israel in the West Bank. The resistance, which had previously been waged with stones and bombs, by diplomatic protest and political manoeuvring, suddenly stormed into company boardrooms, and chose to fight on the issue of business and human rights.

Omar Barghouti, the co-founder of BDS, is an intense, bespectacled, middle-aged human rights activist, who became Veolia's nemesis. A controversial figure, Barghouti was born in Qatar, where his parents were Palestinian refugees. He grew up in Egypt and studied in the USA before settling in Tel Aviv, from where he campaigned for Palestinians to be given full rights as citizens within one state of Israel. Barghouti's call for academic boycotts of Israel triggered insurrections on university campuses in the USA and Europe, and made him a thorn in the side of the Israeli authorities and Jewish critics, who have described him, among other things, as 'a red-necked propagandist of the worst order', and BDS as 'one of the greatest threats to academic freedom in the United States today'.[17]

In 2017 Israeli authorities arrested Barghouti for an alleged $700,000 tax fraud, and banned him from leaving the country. The ban was later lifted by an Israeli court, allowing Barghouti to travel to the USA, to collect a peace prize at Yale University. Describing BDS as a 'new battlefield', Barghouti expanded his sights from academic targets to Veolia and other French companies, understanding their importance to Israel for implementing its urbanisation plans.

Armed with the slogan 'Derail Veolia', BDS mobilised opposition to the light railway worldwide, attacking the French company's interests across Europe and as far afield as Australia, the USA and Iran. BDS lobbied passengers on Connex trains in southern England, local authorities in British and European cities that had contracted Veolia to run water and waste management services, European banks that had lent money to the company, and pension funds that had bought Veolia shares. Despite its relatively small—5 per cent—financial stake in the CityPass consortium, Veolia became the main focus of the boycott campaign. In comparison to its larger partner French group Alstom, Veolia's consumer businesses, and its reliance on numerous public authorities for utility contracts, meant that it had a higher public profile than other companies, and plenty of weak spots. It was particularly susceptible to media pressure. BDS issued press releases which linked rubbish collection on the streets of Camden in London with the plight of Palestinians in the West Bank, water-treatment services in Stockholm to the illegality of Israeli settlements. A succession of local authorities from Birmingham to Sweden and the Netherlands found themselves in the headlines and under public pressure to cancel their contracts with Veolia. Enough responded to that pressure for Barghouti to claim in an interview with the *Financial Times*: 'We are winning the battles for hearts and minds across the world, despite Israel's still hegemonic influence among governments in the US and Europe.'[18]

From Boston to Brighton, Palestinian activists heckled commuters at city stations, distributing leaflets that attacked the French company over its business in Israel. Even Jewish organisations criticised Veolia over its operation of bus routes in the West Bank. Artists joined in, mocking the company's involvement through sculpture and drawings. The wall along the West Bank line sprouted new graffiti of a struggling toytown train and the slogan 'Heavy Railway'.

A tale of two companies

Veolia ranks among the *Financial Times* list of Europe's top 100 companies with a turnover of $30 billion a year and over 171,000 employees. Its interests include energy services, water and waste management, and it directly touches the lives of millions, supplying drinking water to 95 million people, 56 million megawatt hours of energy, and collecting and recycling rubbish.[19] Until 2011 it ran train companies, such as Connex, the operator of Southern Rail in the UK. Its headquarters are in Paris, its shares listed on the Paris and New York stock exchanges, and its operations span seventy-two countries. By any measure, Veolia is the very image of a modern global corporation. It believes in corporate citizenship, emphasising its 'long-term' approach to progress, and its commitment to communities and sustainable development. It sets itself goals such as reducing greenhouse-gas emissions, preserving and restoring biodiversity and the recovery of materials and energy. It defines its relations with customers, employees and investors in terms of ensuring access to basic services and a fair distribution of resources. At the shareholders' meeting of 2019, chairman and CEO Antoine Frérot declared:

> At a time when many people oppose the actions of businesses and dispute their contribution to society as a whole, I think it is necessary to recall their usefulness, starting with that of Veolia. The more our business demonstrates that it is working for all its stakeholders, the more it will be accepted and recognized. ... Our business prospers because it is useful, not the other way round. Its usefulness is the source of its attractiveness for its customers and it is its usefulness which keeps its employees committed and which is the foundation of the loyalty of its shareholders, customers and partners.[20]

Like many corporations of its size and status, Veolia is a long-standing member of the United Nations Global Compact, a voluntary initiative to encourage companies to respect principles such as human rights, care for the environment and labour regulations. The Global Compact promotes the idea that business can be a force for good. Through aligning business strategy with a commitment to sustainability and universal rights, companies take responsibility for improving society across the globe.[21] Veolia is more than just a token member of the

Global Compact. It meets regularly with the Global Compact board, it submits regular progress reports to the Global Compact website, and has been closely involved in working with the UN on issues such as the 2015 and 2030 development agendas, access to basic services for the poor and climate change.

In 2008 Veolia published a document, 'Ethics, Commitment and Responsibility', which stated: 'Irrespective of the geographical area in which we operate, we must conduct our business in accordance with both national standards and the recommendations of international organisations.' The company has a distinguished record of humanitarian relief and development aid, based on its expertise in providing drinking water and waste-water services. Its charitable foundation organises a network of 500 employees with specialist skills ranging from plumbing to engineering, IT, finance and law, which can be mobilised at short notice to intervene in natural disasters and the aftermath of conflict. It has run more than a hundred emergency missions, including delivering emergency supplies to Indonesia after the 2004 Indian Ocean tsunami, working with the French Red Cross to give 50,000 Kurdish refugees in northern Iraq access to drinking water, and helping four villages in the Occupied Palestinian Territories to develop water and sanitation facilities. In 2019 France's Foreign Ministry asked the Veolia Foundation to send a humanitarian emergency mission into Mozambique alongside Médecins Sans Frontières and the French Red Cross in response to a devastating cyclone which had destroyed basic infrastructure.[22]

So how did a company that today proclaims its strong local roots and direct interaction with people's everyday lives stumble into a project in Jerusalem which not only appeared to contradict its ethical commitments, but resulted in it losing business and legitimacy worldwide? The answer lies partly in the gap between different aspects of Veolia's corporate personality, between the humanitarian aid Veolia and the commercial company.

Veolia attempts to manage both corporate faces, and enjoys the publicity from being seen to be doing good, but at the time of the Jerusalem railway contract there was no strategic co-ordination between them. 'Veoliaforce is totally disconnected from the business side. They are separate tracks,' explains Christian Pitavy, the engineer in charge of Veolia's business tenders in Lebanon, where the company had extensive commercial contracts for sewage- and water-treatment plants. In the case of the Jerusalem Light Railway, the ethical discrepancy between the company's principles of promoting human rights and helping disadvantaged communities and its decision to seize a business opportunity was to have dramatic consequences.

Uri Starkman was the CEO and founder of Veolia's business in Israel. On signing an early deal with the Israeli government to supply privately produced electricity from a power station in Mishor Rotem (not in the West Bank), Mr Starkman declared: 'We are happy to be part of this project. We could not have found a better partner. We are confident that it is possible to work in Israel and to profit from projects here.'[23]

I asked Veolia's then director of corporate communications, member of the group's ethics committee, and the CEO's adviser on international relations, Dinah Louda, why the parent company had become embroiled in one of the most controversial cases of human rights and conflict in the world, by participating in infrastructure and resource projects in the West Bank. She explained that the project was conceived in the atmosphere of optimism that followed the Oslo Peace Accords of 1993. The agreement gave the Palestinians limited self-governance for the first time over parts of the West Bank and the Gaza Strip, and paved the way for permanent status negotiations over issues such as Israeli control of the West Bank, the borders of Palestine and Israeli settlements.

Veolia believed that the tramway met a real need for projects to improve infrastructure, and that it would also help a rapprochement between Israel and the Palestinian Authority. It acknowledged that the project had been the 'subject of criticism', but Ms Louda said this reflected a lack of understanding of the actual situation. Veolia's statements claimed that the rail link would allow residents of East Jerusalem easier access to the city and its surroundings, while construction would benefit the Arab population in terms of jobs and improving their environment. The company also said that the tramway would operate on the basis of non-discrimination between religious affiliations, and that Arab communities were 'overwhelmingly in favour of the creation of this transportation system'.[24] When challenged as to how the project was consistent with the group's statements about corporate responsibility, Veolia said it was conducting an 'open dialogue with local stakeholders'.

Yet few people report having had any kind of conversation with the French company. A journalist who covered the story for *Globes*, the leading Israeli business magazine, said that he found the company 'very quiet'; he never spoke to them directly during the time they were involved in the light railway, and their public statements all focused on business issues to do with the tramway contract. The company appeared to ignore any of the political dimensions, or the idea that Palestinian opposition could have an impact on the business world. Stop the Wall coalition, a Palestinian rights movement, told a similar story of having had no direct contact with the French company. Veolia commissioned an opinion survey in Shu'afat, one of the Palestinian suburbs along the train line. The survey showed that the Palestinians living in this neighbourhood viewed the project favourably. There was no formal consultation with official representatives of the Palestinian population either by Israeli authorities or Veolia.[25]

Perhaps Veolia was persuaded by the lack of public debate in Israel about the tramway. The Jerusalem municipality displayed plans for the rail link when it was first proposed, for example visiting schools to present its plans, but hardly any Palestinians reported taking part. Another explanation is that Veolia approached the light railway project as simply a technical contract for an overseas customer. A contracting arrangement suggests that there is limited involvement between the company and local society. The principal relationship is with the buyer of the services—in this case the Jerusalem municipality—implying a limited degree of engagement compared to, say, an investment decision, the building of a manufacturing plant or the creation of a long-term workforce on the ground. While contractors need to take into account political risk, this is usually viewed in terms of what can jeopardise the project rather than in terms of the impact on the local population.[26]

Another reason why Veolia may have misjudged opposition to its role in the light railway is a breakdown in communications. In a large global group with many different subsidiaries, spread worldwide and run by small local management teams, senior executives may not pick up information that is obvious on the ground. Local managers may also play down potential problems in case they lose a contract. In Paris, Veolia may have just failed to see or understand how the railway had added a powerful new aspect to the grievances of Palestinians over the changes Israel had imposed on the West Bank.

With the train literally coming down the track, the signals for Veolia were flashing red. Consumers, trade customers and even investors reacted to the BDS boycott campaign. A Dutch council that attempted to award a €1 billion tender to a subsidiary of Veolia received protests from twenty organisations, while a former Dutch prime minister lent his support to the campaign. Students at Cambridge University pressured the university and local authorities to cancel their contract with Veolia Environment. In November 2008 passengers on the Stockholm subway, operated by Veolia, were asked to attach a red card to their clothes to show their opposition to the company's involvement in the Jerusalem railway. Norwegian pension funds announced that they were selling shares in companies working on Israeli settlement-related projects. The Dutch bank ASN, which described itself as an 'ethical bank' that upholds international law and human rights, decided in November 2006 to dissociate itself from Veolia Transport and other companies working in the Occupied Territories.

Veolia claimed that the spate of cancelled contracts was the result of commercial decisions, and that any disruption to its business was marginal. It was hard to prove the case either way in many instances, as local authority officials did not always want to admit they had been influenced by Palestinian demands. However, it was clear that BDS was winning the war of words and the battle of newspaper headlines, as public and private customers of Veolia suddenly found the company toxic to do business with. BDS claimed that in total the group lost over $20 billion of business as a result of the global backlash against its participation in the Jerusalem tramway.[27] Opinion is divided over whether BDS pressure targeting those who did business with companies that operated in the West Bank contributed to building peace in this intractable conflict. Even supporters of the movement say that there are more effective ways of persuading companies to change their behaviour than to engage in the kind of open confrontation that BDS has made its hallmark. Its tactics of public shaming and boycott are seen by many as blunt instruments for dealing with such a complex conflict.

Nonetheless, the worldwide protest demonstrated how economics and business had become a new frontline in the Middle East.

Confronting rules of law and war

Veolia's involvement in the West Bank had consequences beyond Omar Barghouti and the BDS boycott. In 2007 the Palestine Liberation Organization (PLO) and the Association France-Palestine Solidarité (AFPS) launched a combined lawsuit against Veolia and Alstom, claiming that the companies had violated international humanitarian law (IHL)—the so-called law of war—in helping Israel to build the light railway, and called on the French courts to annul the companies' contracts.

A key principle of international humanitarian law prohibits annexation by force, and is intended to prevent an occupying power exercising control over territory it has conquered. 'Control' in this sense means that the occupying state cannot transfer its own civilian population into the area. In the case of the West Bank, Israeli settlements in the Occupied Territories are seen as jeopardising Palestinians' right to self-determination.

International Humanitarian Law is made up of long-standing norms such as the 1907 Hague Regulations and the 1949 Geneva Conventions, which govern how states should behave when normal domestic and civilian law is overtaken by conflict. It is intended to provide protection for civilian populations even if they are on the losing side of a conflict. It establishes their rights, for example to the use of land and natural resources. IHL prohibits 'individual or mass forcible transfers' of protected persons within the occupied territory and the destruction of private or public property, and stipulates that water and other natural resources of the occupied territory may not be damaged or depleted.[28] In 2004 the International Court of Justice had issued an Advisory Opinion that Israel was occupying the West Bank illegally and that its building of the wall and Israeli settlements on occupied Palestinian land violated key principles of the Hague and Geneva Conventions. The AFPS legal action claimed that infrastructure and other projects which served the settlements or contributed in any way to perpetuate their existence were, by extension, also illegal.

UN Security Council resolutions and rulings by the International Court of Justice have also accused Israel of breaking international law over its actions in the Occupied Territories.[29] What the court case against Veolia and Alstom sought to prove for the first time was that the laws protecting an occupied people also applied to companies, and that a foreign state—in this case France—had a legal responsibility to restrain companies based in that state from conniving in any breaches of law.

This was unprecedented, and a legal minefield. Under international law, occupation had been defined as a temporary situation. Economic and corporate operations, likely to be long term, are not covered by its provisions. Lawyers for the Palestinian activists first had to prove that the case could even be heard in a French court. AFPS argued that as Veolia and Alstom were headquartered in France, the claim that they had broken international law should be examined by French judges.

The case not only put companies under a new legal spotlight of responsibility for their actions; it called into question the relationship between governments and companies, and sought to clarify whether a government could be held accountable for the behaviour of companies that operated within its jurisdiction, wherever that behaviour occurred. The case challenged the assumption of liberal economics that the role of government is to preserve the ability of companies to make profits. Instead, it proposed a higher duty to protect civilians, and in particular vulnerable people, even where they are not citizens of the state in question—in this case, France.

The French Foreign Ministry argued an additional point, which attempted to deny any responsibility on the government's part for the companies' operations in the West Bank, because their activities were not connected with the Middle East conflict:

> The participation of French companies in the construction of Jerusalem's light rail system falls within the framework of an international contract that is driven by business rationale. In our eyes, their participation in this project has no implications on the status of East Jerusalem. ... The fact that Alstom and Connex (Veolia) are private businesses *exonerates* [author's emphasis] the French government from this issue and disables any means it may have had with which to act.[30]

Yet there was evidence that the French government had not merely chosen to disregard or condone Veolia and Alstom's business in the West Bank, but that the railway investment was part of a systematic policy of encouraging French contracts in Israel. If this is true, then there are grounds for claiming that the French government incited the companies to break international law, and was morally and legally responsible.[31]

The French legal action led to other cases, in which lawyers and civil society activists sought to establish the principle and limits of corporate responsibility, arguing that, as subjects of international law, this was a legal obligation for companies. Lawyers argued it that this 'personality principle' had arisen because of companies' growing influence over political and social issues worldwide.[32]

In March 2013 the Versailles Court of Appeals confirmed that under French law corporations could be held liable under civil law if they are found to have contributed to activities that violate international humanitarian law. Two months later, in May 2013 in a separate case, the Dutch Prosecutor ruled that Dutch persons and legal entities were responsible for ensuring that they did not in any way infringe IHL. Even minor incidents could render a company liable to prosecution in the courts of its home country.[33]

While lawyers argued in European courtrooms, seemingly remote from the ground zero of the conflict in Jerusalem, precedents were being established that foreign companies could no longer assume that what they did in faraway places would go unnoticed. The laws of war and humanitarian principle, although never designed to apply to companies, were also relevant to business.

In the case of Veolia and Alstom, however, this was an argument that was never legally proven. After six years of rulings, appeals and protracted argument, the Nanterre court finally decided that companies are not the same as states or even international organisations such as the United Nations, and therefore they cannot be held liable, whether through their direct behaviour or by association, for laws that are made with governments and individuals in mind. In the lawyers' jargon, companies have no international legal personality.

By this time the Palestinian plaintiffs had run out of appeal options, yet the legal battle had played its part in putting the companies and the French government under the spotlight. Veolia and Alstom had withdrawn from the West Bank. By taking them to court, the opponents of the light railway had shown that whether or not companies have a legal personality, they do have a political profile. At the very least they inhabit a grey zone of uncertainty about their status and their role in international politics. The boycott campaign had proved that there were more effective ways of holding companies to account than the rule of law. The real judges of Veolia's behaviour were its customers and investors. Veolia had been challenged in front of worldwide public opinion for its attempt to separate commerce and business from the politics of conflict and humanitarian concerns, and for dismissing a duty of care to the people affected by its controversial contract. [34]

In 2009, with the light railway line still under construction, and only a few years into a planned thirty-year contract for the railway, Veolia announced that it was withdrawing from the CityPass consortium and attempting to find a buyer for its stake. In September 2013 the company sold its local bus services subsidiary to Afikim Company, and in April 2015 its water, waste and energy activities in Israel were also sold, along with the Israeli management, to a US-based investment firm for $220 million. In 2015, after trying for more than six years, Veolia also finally offloaded its 5 per cent stake in CityPass and sold Connex Jerusalem, the company that operates the light railway.

Omar Barghouti declared to the media:

That two international corporations (Veolia and Alstom) with multi-billion euro turnovers have been forced to withdraw from a project that they have funnelled considerable resources into defending, is an important signal of the strength and moral weight of the BDS movement. The fact that [Veolia is] being replaced by Israeli companies rather than more experienced international companies, who surely would have been preferable replacements in the eyes of the Israeli authorities, indicates that no international companies are willing to become targets of the highly effective and visible BDS movement. [This victory sends] a clear message that people of conscience all over the world will not stand by while corporations aid and abet Israeli war crimes. [35]

The global public relations and legal storm had cost the company business and caused it worldwide reputational damage. The crisis of legitimacy Veolia faced was one that few companies encounter, but it showed how even a business contract which appeared small in the scale of the group's global operations could trigger overwhelming public pressure. It demonstrated that even in places where a company might believe it could escape scrutiny, people were watching. If the light railway was a metaphor for Israeli oppression of the Palestinians, its builder and operator Veolia had become, briefly, a symbol of transnational corporate abuse.

Fight and flight

What could Veolia have done differently? First, it failed to assess the legal risks of operating in the West Bank where it knew that its actions would be governed not only by the terms of its contract with the Israeli authorities, but also international human rights law and international humanitarian law, because the railway project was taking place in a conflict zone. The decision to enter into a contract in a territory with unclear legal jurisdiction amounted to a potential breach of international law, supported institutions that had been deemed illegitimate, and undermined Palestinian authority in the disputed West Bank. The contract stipulated that Veolia would be bound by the laws of the Jerusalem municipality, even though under international law these laws had no force because Israeli sovereignty was not established along large parts of the rail route.

The company misunderstood the impact of participating in the railway project. It treated the project as a technical assignment, ignoring the reality that the railway had profound political meaning for both communities, Israeli and Palestinian, as Ariel Sharon's 2005 speech had made clear. Building a rail line through Jewish settlements created new 'facts on the ground', that disrupted the civic, political, social and economic rights of people living on both sides of the Green Line.

Since 2008 the international community has increasingly turned its attention to the capacity of global companies to commit human rights abuses, and the lack of measures for preventing this or compensating victims, because these companies act across borders and often fall outside clear jurisdictions of any one state. Companies are now required (although not legally compelled) to carry out, at the very least, due diligence to assess the likely effects of their operations on individuals, families and communities. Many companies have added a new type of accounting function, the social audit, to cover this type of non-financial consequence of their operations. When Veolia was planning the Jerusalem railway contract, even before 2008, it would have been aware of copious advice to multinational companies about how to adhere to standards of responsible business conduct. This guidance includes warnings of the need to observe both national laws and internationally recognised standards. The importance of ethical responsibility was underlined in Veolia's own commitment to initiatives such as the UN Global Compact. In the case of the Occupied Palestinian Territories, the situation is complicated by the fact that Israel itself is deemed to be in breach of international law by occupying the West Bank. However, there was plenty of evidence that co-operating with Israel amounted to abetting the illegal occupation and supporting a policy of illegal settlement. A succession of UN resolutions and reports on the specific theme of the occupation and the settlements made it obvious that Veolia was entering a political—and legal—cauldron.[36]

In 2014 a UN Working Group on human rights and transnational co-operation and other business enterprises emphasised that businesses connected to Israeli settlements 'need to be able to demonstrate that they neither support the continuation of an international illegality nor are complicit in human rights abuses; that they can effectively prevent or mitigate human rights risks; and are able to account for their efforts in this regard'. The report made it clear that if companies could not prevent or mitigate the risks of being involved with human rights violations they should consider halting operations.[37]

Veolia could also have reacted differently when the mounting opposition to its participation in the project became clear. Even if the light railway had not been so politically contentious, many infrastructure contractors routinely discuss with residents how the construction and operation of a project will affect them, and attempt to minimise disruption and possible grievances. Moreover, the light railway project was not an isolated and exceptional example of Veolia doing business in the Occupied Territories. Its other operations in the Occupied Territories, including the bus service between Israeli settlements and its waste landfill operations, gave the boycott movement further cause for their protests. The advice to companies that invest in conflict-affected areas is that they should be able to demonstrate that they have tried to avoid or deal with any adverse impact they cause.[38] Yet Veolia appeared to stumble into expanding its business dealings in a strip of land beset by intractable and violent confrontation, with little awareness of the damage it might do to the dynamics of the conflict, or its own reputation.

There was a mismatch between the ethical face of the global corporation run from Paris and the limited efforts it made to manage the effects of its operations in the West Bank; between its international profile and its near invisibility on the ground. My attempts to secure a meeting or have my telephone calls returned by the Jerusalem office were fruitless. Veolia's attempts to demonstrate that it had engaged with communities affected by the railway were of little use, either in helping to persuade opponents of the benefits of the railway as the company saw them or finally in limiting the damage of the international boycott.

The Jerusalem Light Railway represents many different things to those who have crossed its lines. For Israelis, the railway has improved transport services in a crowded metropolitan area, and made it easier to get around the city. Five years after the first line was inaugurated, it was apparent that the trains were crowded with a mix of Jewish and Arab passengers, young and old. The railway effectively created 'Greater Jerusalem' from a city previously divided between Palestinian and Israeli territory. As such, the municipal authorities have been able to claim it as a symbol of coexistence. Palestinians see it differently—as a benchmark of oppression, their hopes of an independent state and their own capital in East Jerusalem buckling beneath the railway's smooth tracks.

For companies the railway is a cautionary tale of the pitfalls of operating in the middle of conflict, and of becoming, unwittingly, a party to it. It showed how a paralysing combination of civic protest, legal complexity and politics at every level from high diplomacy and state relations to grassroots revolts could hit even the largest foreign corporation. Veolia's involvement will provide a textbook case of reputational risk in business schools for decades.

Veolia refers in its statements on corporate social responsibility to the importance of a 'right to operate'. This phrase recognises the need to do business with the support and approval of local people. The case of the Jerusalem Light Railway showed that this is more than just a technical licence, or formal commitment. Trust and legitimacy are assets that travel beyond boundaries and jurisdictions. They can slip through cracks in laws and regulations, be won and lost in places where the law is imprecise. Tainted legitimacy can infect business in different countries, and good standing can be hard and expensive to recover, as we shall see later in the book, in the case of BP. The Jerusalem Light Railway showed just how costly careless corporate behaviour in a fragile conflict environment can be.

7

STATE BUILDING IN THE BALKANS

From the arid and bitter political landscape of the West Bank, in the wake of Veolia's retreat from the Occupied Palestinian Territories, we turn to three years later on a cold, wet day in early November in Kragujevac, an industrial city two hours east of Belgrade. Two days previously Serbia had been basking in a late burst of autumn sunshine with temperatures of 19 degrees, weather that promised to extend a late summer. The leaves on the trees had been impossibly golden. Today everything has changed and the leaves are dripping. We pick our way through puddles in a down-at-heel residential area not far from the centre of town. It is miserable terrain. The Communist-era concrete apartment blocks are stained with damp. Dark doorways lead into gloomy stairwells, the stairs supported by rusting banisters. At the base of each tower block the paving stones are cracked or missing, weeds growing through them. We are looking for a group of people who have offered to explain what it is like to live in this city, exposed to the rain and cold, and sudden change, where jobs and prosperity are dependent on the fortunes of one industry and one company. We find the group—Slavica, Alexander, Zoran and Branislav—in the local community centre, where they are keeping warm with Turkish coffee and memories of Kragujevac in its heyday, when it was the beating heart of industry, energy and community in former Yugoslavia.

CORPORATE PEACE

This is a story of another global corporation that went looking for business in a country riven by conflict. Like Veolia, Italian car giant Fiat had little idea of all that its investment would entail, and how it would impact everyday life in Serbia. In this case, though, the consequences of Fiat's presence were less obvious, and certainly less damaging, than Veolia's. In the Balkans, as in the conflict politics of the Middle East, it is impossible to disentangle business and history. New investment might be about a new future and promises of change, but in conflict-torn societies it also has to deal with the past. The legacy of bitter civil wars in the 1990s as Yugoslavia disintegrated, decades of creaking socialist economies and chronically weak democratic institutions are a toxic mix, which seeps into even new beginnings. Companies have unique opportunities to play a role in transforming this legacy, but this fragile environment also offers scope for business to aggravate the weakness and deep-seated vulnerabilities of ordinary citizens and their communities. The stories of this chapter are about both kinds of possibility, negative and positive, in the Balkans.

On 23 December 2009 Fiat completed a deal to take a 67 per cent majority stake in a new company, Fiat Automobiles Serbia (FAS). FAS had been created out of Serbia's oldest and largest industrial conglomerate Zastava, located in Kragujevac. The government was to hold the remaining shares. Fiat paid €700 million for its stake, with promises of further investment to develop Zastava as a world-class manufacturing and export base for the Fiat 500 model. Its goal was to produce 200,000 cars a year. For Fiat, Serbia offered the chance to develop a new world manufacturing centre that could produce cars with lower costs than in developed countries, including its home base in Italy. Fiat promised to modernise the Zastava plant, introduce the latest technology and manufacturing processes and transform management standards. The government promised new infrastructure as well as subsidies to take care of workers, who had been laid off in the transition to the new plant. For their part the city authorities promised co-operation to accommodate municipal services to the needs of Fiat, from hotel rooms for visitors to land for a supplier park and vocational training of potential recruits.

From the outset, the deal was highly political. It created an alliance between a foreign company and government authorities in a country still finding its feet after the wars of the dissolution of Yugoslavia a decade earlier, a combination of political and business power, which promised progress and change. The creation of FAS was made public just one week before Serbian national elections in June 2008, which were won overwhelmingly by a liberal coalition that promised a pro-European future for the country. Fiat acknowledges that its investment was 'an important step' in manoeuvring Serbia closer to the EU, admitting what Serbian voters understood clearly: that 'the governing party won the election thanks to Fiat'.[1] The regeneration of Zastava was large enough to be deemed a project of national interest. Fiat's intervention would be the motor to accelerate post-war development.[2] For the citizens of Kragujevac, Fiat's endorsement of their city was a source of local pride which rivalled its other claim to fame as the home of the tennis star Novak Djokovich.

When I first visited Zastava shortly after the deal was signed in 2009, only part of the manufacturing site was usable. The river that ran through it was polluted, the roofs of buildings had fallen in, and the new owners were operating out of temporary offices in a Portakabin. The result of its deal with the authorities was that Fiat transformed this piece of post-war dereliction, building a state-of-the-art car plant, employee facilities and offices with Italian leather chairs, and created jobs—and an Italian lifestyle—for its workers. By the time of my second visit to the plant five years later, a new model was rolling off the production line, the workforce looked and behaved differently, and the site was quietly and efficiently busy. It was a shining example of World Class Manufacturing (WCM), a Japanese-designed system that Fiat follows, which standardises every aspect of production and plant management to ensure that the quality of a Fiat car made in Serbia is the same as one produced in Italy, Poland, India or Brazil. FAS had become the biggest exporter in Serbia, selling nearly €1 billion worth of cars.[3] It was a poster child for Serbia's new future.

But now it is 2016, and the global recession has reached Kragujevac. The city has the look of many industrial communities that fail to keep pace with changing economic circumstances. These changes begin elsewhere in the global economy, where the prices of steel and components are set, where the level of interest rates is decided and consumers demand—or not—to buy new cars. These changes are felt by local workers and communities although they have no influence over them. The new economic circumstances threaten to derail promises of modernisation, progress and prosperity made in better times. Even with Fiat's investment, Kragujevac has not been able to shake off the decay of state socialism, much less its exposure to a cruel world economic cycle. Production targets are abandoned, employment prospects are re-evaluated and the engine of economic growth splutters. Meanwhile, a new kind of uncertainty and poverty has crept into life in Serbia, revealing the disadvantages of such a rapid transition to a market economy. What makes a difference in this recession, compared to countries with developed economies and settled societies, is that foreign investment was meant to offer more than economic growth. Global production was part of a political project to build a state out of the ruins of conflict and authoritarian rule. The arrival of Fiat in post-war Serbia represented a peace dividend, a route to a democratic, free-market and European future. Serbs hoped that, as well as delivering tangible material benefits, Fiat's decision to back Zastava would also bring about social, political and cultural change.

Transition trouble

When Yugoslavia broke into pieces at the end of the Cold War, seven new states—Croatia, Slovenia, Bosnia-Herzegovina, Serbia, Kosovo, FYR Macedonia and Montenegro—eventually and painfully appeared in its place, each one triggering fresh waves of violent conflict. The forceful dissolution of a single country ruptured lives and entire villages and towns, but also cut old production and supply chains, and destroyed local markets for goods and services. Physical infrastructure such as transport links and power lines, already in a poor state after decades of Communism, was destroyed beyond anything experienced by other countries in the Communist bloc. In each successor state in former Yugoslavia the economy had to be reinvented for the free market—a process complicated by violent nationalism, ethnic tension and a lack of basic governing structures.[4] The wars of former Yugoslavia, coming on top of a generation of decay and arrested development, required a project on a massive scale to build modern democratic societies.

The international community, which had intervened, albeit belatedly, with military force to secure peace in this Balkan break-up, mobilised resources to rebuild government institutions, write new laws, oversee democratic elections and keep the peace between belligerent factions. The creation of a modern economy in the new states was an integral part of an unprecedented international peacebuilding project. It depended on privatising production and carving out a new role for the state, which, rather than owning and organising manufacturing, was required to provide an environment conducive to foreign investment. The sale of factories to global companies was seen as the best way of reviving production capacity, improving competitiveness and introducing modern managerial and technological standards. Tax breaks and new laws to welcome foreign money were the priorities of government policy. In Serbia, a wave of privatisation after the fall of the authoritarian regime between 2002 and 2011 saw over 2,300 companies sold, to new, often foreign, owners. The companies that changed hands were responsible for over 330,000 jobs.[5]

Fiat Automobiles Serbia (FAS) is the flagship example of this model of transition by privatisation. Zastava's history dates back to 1853 as a cannon foundry. In Tito's Yugoslavia it had been a typical state conglomerate, a linchpin of the socialist economy. From a vast, sprawling site dominating not only the city of Kragujevac, but also industry in the surrounding region, Zastava made Yugo cars as well as railway rolling stock, trucks, tanks and light weapons. The factory was the cornerstone of a social system of employment, housing, education and welfare. It started to disintegrate during the Balkan wars of the 1990s, and was hit further by UN sanctions, which affected output and the import of technology. In 1999, when Western allies reacted to President Slobodan Milosevic's ethnic cleansing of Albanians in Kosovo, NATO bombing destroyed most of the plant: what was left was polluted from the use of depleted uranium bombs.[6] People remember how workers repaired the bomb damage after each raid without being paid.

After the fall of Milosevic in 2000, Zastava rebuilt production partly through assembling Fiat models under licence, using foreign technology to develop new versions of the Yugo. Fiat had a long-standing presence in Zastava going back to the 1960s and 1970s. As part of Tito's efforts to modernise the Yugoslav economy, Fiat had helped design the production line at Zastava and started car production there. By the 1980s the company was making up to 200,000 cars per year, including small exports to Africa. When the Serbian government decided to sell a majority stake in the company in 2008, the choice of Fiat as the buyer because of its previous history represented a form of continuity as the plant and the city headed to an otherwise unknown future under private ownership.

Building a new model

Slavica Stepojevic is a small, bird-like woman in her sixties with children and grandchildren. She first went to work for Zastava in 1980, straight from school; that is what all her friends and family did. Despite her tiny frame she worked as a welder in the body shop, building the front chassis of the cars, making thousands of components a day and lifting heavy weights. She remembers everyone working under one roof—those like her who worked in the tin shop, mechanics and paint-shop workers, turning out 1,000 cars a day, in a packed and claustrophobic factory. There were nine other women on her shift, although she describes it as men's work, and men got paid more for making the most complicated component parts. 'It was a difficult job but I got to like it. It was a responsible job and we were not allowed to make mistakes.'

The plant employed nearly 25,000 people, and often up to four members of the same household. People were given quick training courses on the assembly line, so they could begin work immediately because the demand for labour was so high. For every set of workers employed on a shift in Zastava, there were over 3,000 children of employees who were connected to the factory, including directly through school lessons that trained them for eventually joining their parents in the factory. Even children with learning or physical disabilities were trained for specialist jobs that they could do. Such jobs no longer exist. In the old days, workers were given subsidies to buy houses in the city with plots of land. The company contributed to civic events and local sports teams, and it was part of a welfare system which spread beyond the city and the region, throughout the whole country. When there was an earthquake in Skopje (now the capital of neighbouring Macedonia), part of the company's revenues were sent to help victims. Other causes included donations to the military, and loans to Kosovo in the 1980s to help offset the effects of economic recession. The company was not so much an enterprise as an entire civic system of solidarity, loyalty and protection.

Slavica remembers that times were good until the war in the 1990s:

> The whole city and the Yugoslavia itself depended on the cars. Then the war came. There was an embargo [by the West], but we worked on as if nothing had happened. We were subsidised by the state so half the people were sitting at home doing nothing. Then there was inflation, and with the salary we had, we couldn't buy anything. I left in 1999 when NATO bombed the factory. I wanted to find another job as my state pension is just €100 per month. I made pizzas for a time and I look after my grandchildren. My son does not work at Zastava. He is thirty-three and he is washing cars now.

When Fiat took over the bombed-out company in 2009, it agreed a deal with the government to retain just one in five jobs at the plant. Fiat handpicked those it decided to keep on, hiring mostly young workers under forty. Many were sent to Fiat headquarters in Turin for training. The company paid €2 million into a solidarity fund for the remainder of the workforce, and €700 of the €4,999 price of each new Fiat car was earmarked to compensate workers who had been made redundant.

For the citizens of Kragujevac, even those who had held onto their jobs through the takeover, ownership change at Zastava quickly proved a bumpy ride with few shock absorbers. Employment levels fluctuated as Fiat cut the workforce from 1,700 to 1,000, but then took on local construction workers to build the new factory. The financial crisis of 2008 forced the company to revise its original output and job targets agreed in the deal it had made with the Serbian government. Temporary production halts were introduced, so that even those in work found that their employment was precarious, and their pay packets not guaranteed. By 2014 only 500 of the original cohort of Zastava employees remained. Fiat management explained that its human resources policy was common practice in the industry. Variable employment terms would allow the plant to continue working even during downturns in the economic cycle. The company insisted that it was aware of the necessity of maintaining jobs and its importance to the economy of Kragujevac and Serbia as a whole. It reassured the city and the nation that it was committed to acting as a socially responsible employer.[7]

Nonetheless, these were harsh demands for people who until recently had been used to a quite different model of business. While Serbs saw Fiat as part of their state-building project, the company was following other priorities. Its investors demanded profit increases; consumers wanted cheap cars. The requirements of World Class Manufacturing meant maintaining production standards, as well as meeting financial and environmental regulations. The drivers of the new Serbian economy were coming from far beyond Serbia and a world away from Kragujevac.

The story of Zastava's downturn as a result of shifts in the global economy is no different from that being played out in many communities in Western Europe or the United States, where heavy industry, and car manufacturers in particular, face competition from cheaper labour in developing countries. They are prone to violent swings in customer demand, which undermine profits and often lead to plant closures. Fiat's investment in Serbia was itself part of this pattern. The Zastava plant was intended to be a European manufacturing hub, which could take advantage of Serbia's low wage levels, to produce budget cars for a new market of consumers in Eastern Europe, and improve the company's profit margins on sales to Western Europe. The template for this low-cost production plant existed in similar factories that Fiat had developed in Brazil and Poland. The first CEO of the new Zastava plant was a young manager whose previous job had been managing Fiat production in India. Fiat believed it knew not only how to build budget cars, but also how to operate low-cost manufacturing facilities, and get them to work to world-class standards and increase export sales.

However, the story of Fiat and the citizens of Kragujevac was different in one important respect from what Fiat expected from its long experience, both in pre-civil war Yugoslavia and elsewhere in the world. Zastava was part of a country emerging from conflict and authoritarian rule, trying to navigate widespread political and economic transition, and dealing with deep social tensions. In Serbia's fledgling democracy there was limited protection for workers, and weak social and government institutions such as trade unions, civil society organisations or laws to provide a bulwark or safety net for those affected by the workings of a global business. In 2016—when a further 900 jobs disappeared at the plant, plus 600 in supplier companies that provide parts for Fiat cars—Serbian citizens, lacking places to turn to to provide them with protection, talked of taking their protests onto the streets.[8]

Relying on foreign investment to modernise the economy had left ordinary Serbs vulnerable in the face of business interests that were largely focused on the needs of international investors and foreign consumer markets. When recession forced Fiat to revise its production targets, Serbs also noted that the group's Italian factories faced less swingeing cuts in jobs and output.

Within five years of its takeover of Zastava, Fiat had achieved a remarkable transformation of the plant, and had contributed to reviving Serbia's post-war manufacturing base. However, reconstructing an entire state and its civic and government institutions is an enterprise that even Fiat found demanding. The economic effects of operating in Serbia were only one part of the picture. The investment also had implications for Serbia's post-war recovery that were less visible, but equally significant in terms of its road to peace. Moreover, it became clear that there were two different agendas—the company's, on the one hand, and that of the government and people of Kragujevac, on the other. Exposed to the pressures of a changing global business climate, these agendas began to conflict.

Alexander is an electrician who worked at Zastava for twenty-three years until he was laid off in 2016. He remembers how things changed for the better when Fiat took over the plant. Obsolete equipment was replaced with new technology. Instead of always being called on to fix broken machinery, Alexander got to work with robots and the latest digital equipment. Management systems were introduced that ended the quixotic oversight of the Communist and post-Communist era, when many supervisors were political appointees or ran independent businesses with machinery they had cannibalised from the assembly line. In the city, Fiat gave money for sports facilities. It encouraged the Serbian passion for water polo. It supported the local basketball team, and deals were made for new players. Hotels and restaurants opened to cater for new expatriates and overseas visitors. A supplier park was developed for companies producing the component parts required on Fiat cars, and new businesses sprang up. The city had an air of expectation and revival.

Inside the Fiat bubble

Like all modern car plants, most of the assembly tasks at Zastava are performed by robots. The floor of the factory is quiet and ultra clean. Employees wear Italian-designed overalls in pristine white. For safety, they move around the factory on marked pedestrian lines. There are safety 'captains', designated by managers, to make sure their colleagues are following safety procedures. They are identifiable because they wear green bracelets, and are rotated weekly. The first thing that strikes a visitor touring the plant is not only that the employees are young—the average age is just thirty-one—but that inside this manufacturing 'bubble' a certain kind of person has the highest status: someone youthful, healthy, well-dressed and active, both socially and physically.

Roberto Cristiano was in charge of human resources at Zastava in 2014. He said that hiring younger workers was a way of modernising the working culture of the plant and accelerating change. His policies included providing new facilities for workers' families, such as a playground, kindergarten places, scholarships for older children and open days, where employees are encouraged to bring their families onto the site. Rather than using local doctors or hospitals and strengthening public facilities, healthcare is provided on site by a company contracted from Belgrade. Plant director Francesco Ciancia explained that in many ways, such as providing kindergarten places for workers' children, the company has filled gaps in public services. It has also negotiated directly on behalf of the city residents with the authorities over improvements in public services. For example, the high school in Kragujevac reorganised its curriculum to meet Fiat's requirements, offering Italian as a foreign language and engineering courses in robotics. Local schools introduced classes on road and occupational safety procedures.

Inside the Fiat bubble there are rules that not only protect workers from safety hazards, but also ensure the confidentiality of research and commercial know-how. There is a 'parliament' inside the plant, where 'opinion leaders' debate issues, and a punishment and reward system. According to Roberto Cristiano, this is not about corporate philanthropy but rather a deliberate business strategy designed to raise standards, guarantee worker loyalty and improve the quality of the present and future workforce.[9] The separation between this island of globalisation and the surroundings of the plant is underlined symbolically by the river that runs through the site, which cuts it off physically from the city. There is tight security on the entrance gates, and controls to deter any chance visitors. Life inside the bubble looks and feels different from the city outside. This is standard practice for a transnational company, the equivalent of the perimeter fence that featured at the start of the book. However, the existence of two different and parallel worlds is a source of tension, with consequences for Serbs' sense of their own identity and well-being.

Dilemmas of dependency and democracy

One consequence of the inside-out world of the Fiat plant, and in particular the company's preference for recruiting younger workers, is a change in social relations in the city. As older employees have been laid off and their places taken by those aged between thirty and forty, there is a noticeable generational divide. One former worker explained: 'An old guy loses his job as an accountant in the plant, but he then opens a bar which his son, now hired by FAS, can go and drink in.'[10] Older citizens feel they have less of a stake in the future of the city and, as employment has shrunk at the plant, even their children cannot expect jobs there.

There was a feeling that local people had limited opportunities for advancement in Fiat, to the point where they were discriminated against, with one-third of management jobs originally going to Italian expatriates.[11] Workers speculate that to get promoted you need personal connections and friendships with people in senior positions. Zoran and Alexander tell me that Fiat's human resources policies were not the kind of international management techniques they had expected. They felt that they were based on the advantage of knowing someone senior in the company. These kinds of suspicions echo an earlier era when connections to the party counted for everything. Whether or not they are justified, the perceptions of favouritism and a privileged elite show how difficult it is to wipe the slate clean in a country with recent memories of political corruption and civic distrust.[12]

Slavica, Alexander and Zoran say things have changed in the city since the worldwide recession. The company now keeps its distance, and has even withdrawn progressively from engaging with civic life.[13] Economic downturn put an end to the generous support of sports teams. The water polo pool is no more. The best welfare services are now only available to those on the inside of the plant.[14] While director Ciancia says that the company continues to work with the city authorities, it has restricted integrating with the local community in favour of establishing new practices and institutions that will not be 'contaminated' by local contacts:[15] 'We didn't want to be so close to the old institutions of Kragujevac, because we are a private company. We didn't want to be interconnected with local communities or politics. We don't want to be seen as a patronage system.'[16]

Inside the plant, Alexander was one of 900 workers who held onto their jobs after the takeover, until it became clear that only younger staff were being employed. He says workers had to take IQ tests to demonstrate their competence, and undergo medical checks. At fifty years old, he became anxious in case his age put him at a disadvantage. With every round of redundancies he lost colleagues who did not pass the tests. Friendships and acquaintances became strained. While national leaders and the international community urged reconciliation as an essential step in the country's recovery from civil war, economic developments in Kragujevac seemed to be creating new divisions between people.

Hiring policies at Zastava changed. Fiat uses national employment agencies located far away from Kragujevac, so new recruits who, for the first time, were from outside the region, have joined the workforce. Alexander and Zoran tell me that Serbs from Kosovo (who were expelled after the war in 1999, and went to live in Serbia itself) now get the best jobs. The two men are both from the minority Roma community, and they believe that there is discrimination against Roma who apply for jobs at the plant. Other changes have happened: services such as catering and waste management have been put out to tender, outsourced to firms from outside the city because they offer the best value

for money. A long-standing custom at Zastava of hiring disabled workers and adapting parts of the factory to their needs has also disappeared. Zoran tells me he knows this because he has a disabled child:

> In the early days we were told by managers it was going to be milk and
> honey. Technicians used to have to improvise to do their jobs, then
> they were told they would get everything they needed. In the begin-
> ning this was true. We had good salaries and bonuses, but the honey-
> moon only lasted a year. The problem was people took loans from
> banks. Particularly the young workers, they wanted to buy things
> against their new salary. Then their salaries dropped and now they
> cannot repay the loans.

Three months ago Alexander, who was already on a reduced-hours
contract, was made redundant. He says it will be difficult to find
another job, since only younger people get retraining schemes. 'I didn't
expect this. It is as if they [Fiat] want to close the whole thing down.'

There is fear in the city that Fiat's commitment to the new Serbia
is only as strong as its profit and loss account, and that global recession means that the company will move elsewhere. The city's dependence on jobs, contracts and the investment that outsiders such as
Fiat bring, fuels a sense of insecurity across the region, where other
foreign companies have taken over local manufacturing facilities,
partly encouraged by the initial Fiat investment. Rather than Fiat
delivering a European future as they expected in 2009, Serbs feel that
they are still on the fringes of Europe, with few benefits from being
part of a global production line.[17] Local wage levels are lower than
those in other European car-production centres—for example,
workers in Fiat's Polish factory earn a third more, and Italian workers
20 per cent more.[18]

The air of uncertainty and insecurity is magnified by a lack of transparency that surrounds Fiat's plans for Kragujevac. Because Fiat's purchase of a stake in Zastava was deemed of 'national interest', it was
negotiated directly between government ministers and the company's
management. This was unusual—normally such deals are concluded
between the executives of the companies involved. The Serbian government owns a third of the shares in the new company, and FAS has two
out of seven seats on the board, although it has limited operational
control of the plant. Meanwhile, the contract between the state and

Fiat, although technically public, has always been shrouded in secrecy. Fiat has been highly sensitive to speculation about production plans and financial targets that circulate in local and national media, in case this reaches investors, damaging its share price and jeopardising formal disclosure requirements for a company listed on the New York Stock Exchange. When a Serbian government minister proudly let slip at the Geneva Motor Show that Fiat was planning to build a new model at Zastava, the company humiliated him by publicly denying the claim and organising a damage-limitation exercise with the international media to dismiss the story. In fact, Fiat had decided not to build the car. It is not clear whether the minister knew this and was trying to force the company's hand by 'announcing' a different decision. The episode shows the complicated political games that continue to be played around the presence of the Fiat plant in Serbia.

Journalists' attempts to investigate the company's finances, disclose wage negotiations or speculate about the introduction of new models have often been blocked. Fiat's efforts to control local media interest in the plant conflicted with a recently liberated and newly independent press, hungry for information. Misunderstandings between eager journalists and the local management led to rows between the company and news outlets.

As the largest exporter in Serbia, Fiat enjoys a privileged status among the country's other foreign investors. Fiat has accompanied government ministers on trade and investment promotion trips abroad. Its influence can be seen in the powerful Foreign Investors Council, which operates parallel scrutiny mechanisms of key Serbian parliament decisions through sub-committees on legal affairs and human resources. As a result of Fiat's involvement in Zastava, Serbia was invited to join the European Union Automotive Committee—despite not being a member of the EU—which sets competition, production and environmental standards for all European car makers.

Although Serbia has acquired new status among EU decision makers, this has mixed implications for the country's fledgling democracy. It has brought the government increased influence within the EU, but, by allowing the company a say in key decisions over economic and labour policy, politicians have also ceded some of their domestic powers. The embassy network has become a second track of communication on commercial matters, and Fiat uses diplomatic channels to gain information, and shape the government's policy agenda.

Building cars or building a state?

Despite changes of government and president since Fiat helped secure electoral victory for a pro-European coalition in 2008, governments of all colours have seen the Fiat joint venture as the flagship project of attempts to build a modern economy that will help Serbia move closer to the European Union. Zastava is a magnet for attracting other investors. The Fiat plant demonstrates that Serbia can play host to the demands of global capital, and be a world-class manufacturing base. Aleksander Ljubic, the government official in charge of crafting the joint venture, says of Zastava: 'It sends a message that this country can offer production for a European market and [that] we are capable of producing European quality. Politically it is very good for the country because it is important for people here to be able to drive good cars.' In 2016, leaving the plane at Belgrade airport on arrival in Serbia, passengers see their bags delivered through mock-ups of open luggage compartments of Fiat cars. The message is clear: Fiat *is* Serbia, a national symbol, part of the country's new image.

Yet Fiat's project to rebuild Zastava as a global manufacturing centre is not the same as the political project to build a state and cement the peace. The two parties—the company, on the one hand, and the government, on the other—have interests that are different and occasionally diverge. Fiat's willingness and ability to be a peacebuilder in the Balkans is limited by its corporate vision, which sees its investment in Serbia as primarily a financial and economic affair. Its effects on Serbia in terms of influencing social, political and cultural life, and guaranteeing the country's turn to democracy, are second to its business goals of manufacturing cheaply, being close to growing consumer markets and the potential of gains in productivity from operating in a developing economy. Another factor that has caused the political and business agendas to conflict and limits Fiat's commitment to Serbia's democratic project has been a global recession, which has cut short some benefits of the investment, created new uncertainties and deepened the vulnerabilities of citizens in an already fragile country.

In 2012 Fiat began assembly of the new 500L car—the one whose rear end is displayed in Belgrade's baggage hall. Locals were proud that Serbia was to produce a car that would sell all over the world. Their pride was tempered when they realised that the 500 model does not contain the 70 per cent locally produced components originally envisaged, but in fact has very little local content at all. Fiat's most popular current model is not, after all, a 'Serbian' car. Buying a 500L is also beyond the means of most workers who produce it, affordable for relatively few people in Kragujevac.[19] Slavica tells me that she has a Fiat car, but it is an old model—anything else is too expensive for her. Does she think that Fiat is a Serbian company? 'No, not today. It has great marketing, but [their investment] has been like going back to the future. We are a post-conflict country and we get exploited because we have no other choice.' In this region, this is a refrain that is not unique to Serbia.

Patriotism and progress in Kosovo

Next door to Serbia—and part of it, before a bloody fight for independence was helped to victory by a NATO air war in 1999—Kosovo is approximately the size of Wales. Twenty years after the war it remains politically, economically and socially damaged, but not short of building projects.

Kosovo's Highway of the Nation runs for 77 kilometres between Morine, on the border with Albania, and a point north of the capital, Pristina, bisecting the country. It was completed in 2013, and like steel braces on a wobbly set of teeth, it is intended to clamp Kosovo's economy in place, providing critical infrastructure that will allow trade and commerce to grow.

The project was undertaken by a joint venture between US contractors Bechtel and Turkish conglomerate ENKA, which won a €400 million public tender from the Kosovan government in 2010. Construction work was completed within three years, and won an industry award.[20] The project partners committed to hiring 3,000 local workers, a significant employment boost to the struggling Kosovan economy, where over 63 per cent of the working-age population were recorded as not 'economically active' and every other young person of under thirty-five was officially without work.[21]

The project was notable for several reasons. It had symbolic value as an example of modernisation, and was a rare case of major international companies operating in a country that has largely failed to attract foreign investment, and whose traditional industries were languishing twenty years after the end of the war, and more than a decade after independence.[22] Many large companies are still state owned, and Western corporations have declined to move in. Kosovo is one of the few countries in Europe, for example, where in 2019 you cannot find a McDonald's or a Starbucks.[23]

An exception to the lack of foreign interest is Turkey. Kosovans joke about the 'new Ottoman Empire', as Turkish companies have taken over running the airport, and bought up companies in the food and banking sectors. Turkish imports have overtaken those from Germany to become the second-largest source of foreign products, after Serbia. As a result, Turkish companies are in a strong position to influence change in Kosovo, through bringing new skills and standards as well as money for development. ENKA, a world leader in building infrastructure projects, which works in many conflict-affected countries including Iraq and Libya, is no stranger to this context of political fragility and economic underdevelopment. The group has built a number of major roads in the region, including motorways in Romania, Croatia and Albania.

The second reason the highway project was remarkable was how expensive it was. From an initial tender price of €400 million for 102 kilometres, building costs more than doubled, while the length of the highway was cut to 77 kilometres by the time of completion. The final bill put the price per kilometre at €10.65 million, which is up to four times more than the cost of similar-length roads built around the same time in Finland and Bulgaria.[24] The cost of the motorway over three years was equivalent to over half Kosovo's entire public expenditure in just one year, 2012, and ate up nearly two-thirds of the tiny country's budget for capital spending. By any measure, the Highway of the Nation was an expensive way to use public finances to promote traffic flow.

Peter Feith, a former head of the International Civilian Office, the body established by the international community to oversee the country's independence, was one of the most vocal critics of the motorway, not only because of the burden it put on Kosovo's resources, but for the lack of transparency surrounding the tender: 'Information was withheld, and all of a sudden we were presented with a fait accompli of this contract being concluded and being a liability on the budget.'[25] Other eyebrows were raised by the role of the US ambassador at the time, Christopher Dell—the most powerful diplomat in Kosovo—who promoted Bechtel to win the tender and subsequently accepted a retirement position as a regional director of the group in Africa.[26]

As in the case of Fiat's deal with the Serbian government, the contract between the government and the companies has never been published. In 2014 Bechtel–ENKA won a further €660 million tender for an additional 64 kilometre stretch of motorway between Pristina and the Macedonian border. A Kosovan newspaper published a notice that information about the contract could be viewed, but curious parties had to be quick: the information window was shut after only two hours. A Kosovan think tank reported that it was not allowed to take a copy of the document, which only existed in English and not in the local language. Its attempts to view the original contract through invoking part of a Law on Access to Public Documents failed.[27] As in Serbia, this lack of transparency matters because it creates suspicions of improper conduct, and undermines efforts to build democratic and accountable public institutions. The American Chamber of Commerce in Kosovo said that it fuelled public suspicion of politics: 'The public thinks that this is clear evidence of corruption particularly relating to public procurement.'[28] The highway contract was not the only example of obfuscation. A survey by the Chamber of Commerce in 2014 showed that over half of respondents had not been given access to public documents they requested relating to procurement projects, urban planning, property registry and registration.

The motorway project was also controversial because it led to allegations of human rights abuses, infringement of labour laws and irregularities concerning the hiring and employment terms of construction workers. Media reports uncovered problems with workers' salaries and unpaid overtime after fifty workers were laid off.[29] Bechtel–ENKA was accused of exploiting workers through long hours and inadequate rest periods, and of violating contracts.

Some of these claims derive from the testimony of former workers, collected for a study by local activists.[30] The workers told of poor site conditions, inadequate training—particularly when using hazardous equipment—and above all, injuries suffered, which were ignored by company management, and not detected or monitored by public officials. Many reported or witnessed injuries to hands and feet, and said people were told to drive trucks and handle equipment with no training or proper safety supervision. They claim that there was pressure to minimise injuries, and they were frequently referred to doctors who sent them straight back to work. Payslips produced by the employees are evidence of excessively long hours and low pay.

Adem is a whistle-blower who is suing Bechtel–ENKA after an injury to his hand. He clutches it as he explains:

> My hand got clenched the moment I tried to remove a cowl. A colleague of mine came immediately and took me to the nearest ambulance, which was near the workers' kitchen. They gave me an injection and did an X-ray scan. I did not work the next day, but I worked the day after that. I had to work. I had no other choice because I have four children to take care of. They all go to school.

Adem says that he and others bribed supervisors €300 each to be hired onto the project. At least one female employee was seen by her co-workers being subjected to extreme sexual harassment.

Not all the allegations of mistreatment made by employees can be substantiated. When I tried to talk to Bechtel–ENKA in Kosovo about the claims, they declined to be interviewed or respond to allegations by Kosovan NGOs or to newspaper reports. The government has also refused to debate the claims of disgruntled workers or to address the allegations of activists, and Adem and other alleged victims of the motorway project are angry that the Kosovan authorities did nothing to intervene. Government officials questioned have dismissed media reports criticising the project as 'false arguments and half-truths', and warned that such criticism deters future investors.

At the time of the motorway contract, Kosovo's parliament had passed new safety legislation governing accidents at work,[31] but with little public funding there was limited money to enforce it, and few mechanisms such as inspections and safety audits, or judicial procedures to handle complaints that resulted from the lax safety culture.[32] Adem says: 'Someone must do something because Bechtel–ENKA is here today, but might be gone tomorrow. We are the people of Kosovo, we are those who will continue to work, live and die, and contribute here. It is not fair to make invalids out of us.'[33]

A beautiful road

ENKA's corporate mission statements talk about the company having three strategic 'value' pillars: safety; being a good member of the community; and concern for people. Its records show that there were 3,950 hours lost to accidents on the Kosovo project.[34] The project produced limited benefits in terms of training local workers and providing them with new skills. Although nearly three-quarters of workers hired were from Kosovo, supervisory roles went to the pool of labour and managers that ENKA already had or could draw on from Turkey. Neither is it clear that this costly project contributed to the extensive efforts by the international community to build peace in the region by reforming government institutions and reinforcing a system of law and regulations. Politicians refer to the road as the 'Highway of the Nation'—a way of giving it status and rallying public support behind it. The meaning is clear: the road is so special to the future of Kosovo that it is a patriotic undertaking, which should be beyond criticism, or even accountability.

The motorway was a one-off construction contract rather than a long-term investment in industrial capacity such as Fiat's intervention in Serbia. There were no incentives for the foreign contractors to contribute to a state-building agenda, or provide progressive benefits that would help Kosovo's post-war development. It was simply a case of fulfilling a contract and getting the job done. However, like Fiat, the construction companies could take advantage of operating as a privileged foreign business, with few restraints on their behaviour, and special access to Kosovan government ministers and officials. The state's strategy of privatisation and public works to deliver economic development led many ordinary Kosovans to look at the private sector as just another channel for elites to make money and gain political power. With few role models among other global corporations operating in the country, and no history of dealing with private business, this meant that foreign companies were in the driving seat, able to influence a weak government, which had limited resources to insist on quality controls, or enforce laws that might protect its citizens.

Andrea Capussella is an Italian who worked for the International Civilian Office in Kosovo, the body set up to supervise the country's transition from a persecuted province in the former Yugoslavia to an embryonic state seeking independence. Capussella was put in charge of economic development, but found that his misgivings about the road project were brushed aside—not only by the Kosovan government, but by his international colleagues too.[35] He believes the international community has failed the fledgling country:

> The [motorway] project illustrates the reasons why the international state-building largely failed in Kosovo: weak legal and political accountability (which allowed the government to commission the motorway on questionable commercial terms), and weak supervision. EU member states, which have an interest in the long-term development of Kosovo, because they have committed large amounts of money and political will to protecting the interests of ordinary Kosovans, and continue to monitor the country closely in every sphere from politics to economics and even culture, had to watch as the government inflicted a huge opportunity cost on a still poor and rather fragile country. Schools, hospitals, rural roads, water pipes and other critical facilities could have been built with 26% of GDP, that instead went on the road project. The most remarkable aspect of this story is that it happened in the world's most closely supervised nation.

Criticisms of procedural irregularities with the tender, that attacked the wisdom of diverting such a large proportion of the state budget to one infrastructure project, have been swept aside. The most frequent remark about the motorway today is not about the missed opportunity for it to improve the chances of peace in Kosovo. It is about its feat of quality engineering: 'At least it is a beautiful road.'[36]

The motorway project showed that if government and international supervisors could not or would not rein in the power of the foreign contractors, there was even less opportunity for civil society, trying to emerge from decades of an authoritarian regime, to influence corporate behaviour. Trade unions were ineffective in documenting reports of workplace injuries and abuse, and challenging the decisions of contractors. Although international and local media reports drew attention to the project's irregularities, there is no tradition in Kosovo of investigative journalism to uncover and challenge companies if they commit abuses. When NGO activists called a public meeting in autumn 2014, to discuss safety concerns in the construction industry revealed by the motorway project and challenge unregulated privatisation, not a single journalist replied to the invitation to attend.

For nearly a quarter of a century the Balkans has been a real-time laboratory for the twenty-first-century project to rebuild states and ensure peace, through supporting free markets and democratic institutions. In Serbia and Kosovo foreign investors and contractors have promised to bring jobs, technology and international standards of behaviour to put back together a society fractured by violence, community divisions and the legacy of authoritarianism. Symbiotic alliances between global businesses and local governments are forged amid the turbulent transformations that are under way, with business and politicians needing one another, but often divided by distinct and competing interests. Governments in post-conflict states, with few resources and weak authority, do deals with foreign companies but find themselves unable to enforce their terms. Companies enter markets that open up fresh opportunities in the aftermath of conflict, and are expected to help smooth the transition to peace, yet they can disrupt the complex process of building a new society out of conflict and chaos, and stir up fresh tensions instead. Companies rely on traditional management practices that often prove insufficient to deal with the profound and wide-ranging implications for human welfare created by investment and commercial projects in fragile societies. Local communities not only see foreign companies as a source of jobs and new livelihoods; they also expect them to act as bulwarks against weak and dysfunctional state bodies, unable to protect their own citizens. The price of transition is a new form of citizen insecurity made up of temporary jobs, shocks from the global economy, tainted benefits, new forms of social discrimination and no power to gainsay powerful foreign money. However well-intentioned and apparently successful, the impact of global business on ordinary lives in such fragile settings demonstrates how vital companies are to the complexity of modern peacebuilding and yet how inadequate they sometimes are to the task.

8

BEYOND THE PIPELINE

REPUTATION RECOVERY IN GEORGIA

There is not much visible to the naked eye to mark the route of the longest and most controversial oil pipeline in the world. An occasional yellow triangle stuck into the grass is all that indicates that, 2 metres beneath the surface, more than a million barrels of oil flow each day between the Caspian Sea in western Asia and European homes.

The Baku–Tbilisi–Ceyhan pipeline (BTC) is a $ 4.1 billion strategic investment by Azerbaijan, Armenia, Georgia and Turkey, and oil giant BP, which built and has operated it since 2006. According to BP, the pipeline is one of the great engineering feats of the millennium. But its real value is not as a technical achievement on the part of architects, diggers and welders of this steel snake, but as a sign of geo-political necessity. The pipeline is a fuel-filled umbilical cord linking the Transcaucasus region, one of the world's most unstable hotspots, to Europe and Asia.

Half of the borders of the Caspian Sea are conflict zones, the sites of vicious civil wars in Chechnya and Dagestan, and so-called frozen or unresolved conflicts in Azerbaijan and Georgia. The umbilical cord attaches Georgia and its neighbours to the European Union and the USA, which depend on oil from the Caspian Sea to keep their way of life secure. In return, the West provides a security blanket for countries along the route of the pipeline, against aggression from powerful neighbours such as Russia and Iran, guaranteeing a market for the region's oil, which contributes to their economic and political stability.

Georgia is at the centre of a 3,294 kilometre web of steel pipelines which criss-cross this conflict zone. The country's 70,000 square kilometres are necessary territory for energy companies attracted by its commercial and strategic importance.

For BP, the pipeline is not only about making money from supplying oil to the EU market, or dealing with the region's politics, or even the technical challenge of managing a linear object of over a thousand miles, which has sixty crossing points, any of which could present a safety and environmental hazard. It is also about the company's ambition of creating a new model of large-scale investment by major, multinational enterprises in developing countries, transitioning from war to peace, from authoritarianism to democracy.[1]

Building and managing an engineering project that would directly affect nearly a million people in 450 communities in Georgia became a test of BP's credibility and reputation, demonstrating that a foreign corporation could deliver protection and prosperity which far outweighed the commercial rewards at stake. This is the story of how BP dealt with communities, many of them isolated and rural, which found themselves caught up in a game of international energy politics as the pipeline was laid underneath their villages and farms, against a backdrop of revolution, war and change in Georgia. It is about how BP sought to go beyond the pipeline, to address issues of everyday security and welfare for people living in a country emerging from conflict and authoritarianism. It is also a story about a company defining its obligations and responsibilities when operating in a dangerous and fragile country. In the Caucasus, BP sought to create a new role, doing the right thing in a faraway country. Its story illustrates how a company can learn lessons from past mistakes and behave in ways that defy traditional management thinking. At the same time, BP's experience in Georgia shows how difficult and risky the challenge of corporate peace can be.

BP is the world's third-largest energy company and eighth-largest company in any sector in the world, with revenues of $249 billion.[2] It traces its origins to the 1908 discovery of oil in Iran, and until the middle of the twentieth century it was an arm of British foreign policy in the Middle East. Today, it is no longer British Petroleum but a global group that happens to be headquartered in London. Its subsidiaries include some of America's oldest oil companies, and its operations span six continents. BP is a classic example of a corporation that works across national borders and is powerful not only because of its sheer size, but also because it owes no allegiance to any single country. Governments like to talk about a country's 'flagship enterprises', but being British is no longer critical to BP's identity or success. It has long outgrown its national heritage: its executives, employees and investors are from all over the world. It has no natural home market. It is accountable to many different bodies from financial markets to government regulators, as well as being the target of international pressure groups and public opinion.

Reputation blow-out

For all its size, spread and power, at the turn of the twenty-first century BP had a problem. It faced mounting pressure from the environmental lobby and a growing perception that oil companies in general were 'dirty' business.[3] It was attacked in the press, and its shareholder meetings were barracked by activists.[4] To head off public hostility, BP embraced the issue of climate change. It coined the slogan 'Beyond Petroleum'—a sleight of hand on the company's acronym. It unveiled a new logo of a yellow and green helios and invested in alternative energy, putting solar panels on petrol stations, and supporting projects to build clean cities. It joined emissions-trading schemes and financed the development of non-fossil fuels.

Despite its efforts to create a new image as a green, clean company, between 1994 and 2010 BP found that public opinion was still fixated on its oil wells, and that this was affecting its attempts to diversify, including into renewable energy. From Colombia to Alaska, from refineries in Texas to drilling rigs in the Gulf of Mexico, the company was dogged by claims that it was contributing to climate change, and by accusations of negligence and bad practice. In Latin America BP was accused of fuelling civil war, being responsible for fatal accidents among its workers, and causing major environmental damage. Then, on 20 April 2010, the oil-drilling rig Deepwater Horizon, operated by BP in the Macondo Prospect in the Gulf of Mexico, exploded and sank, resulting in the deaths of eleven workers on the rig and the largest spill of oil in the history of underwater drilling. Four million barrels of oil flowed from the damaged well over an eighty-seven-day period, damaging a thousand miles of shoreline around the Gulf, before the well was capped on 15 July. Six months later the US government filed a complaint against BP Exploration & Production and several other oil companies it alleged were responsible for the spill.[5] The verdicts from six inquiries into the accident by public agencies in the USA, including a Congressional investigation, concluded that the accident was caused by multiple errors made by a number of companies including BP and its partners on the Deepwater Horizon rig. As the corporate partners traded accusations over who was most responsible for the explosion, it was BP that found itself at the centre of the global public, legal, political and environmental storm. Chief executive Tony Hayward was forced to resign. An independent report, published in 2011, criticised BP's *laissez faire* management strategy as well as poor oversight by government regulators. It also concluded that the cause of the accident lay in the culture of the offshore oil and gas industry: 'While this particular disaster involves a particular group of organizations, the roots of the disaster transcend this group of organizations. This disaster involves an international industry and its governance.'[6] The report noted that BP's system 'forgot to be afraid'. The company had forgotten the lessons of previous problems in exploring for oil, failed to draw the right conclusions from safety signals or develop an information and learning culture across the organisation that might have prevented the accident. In concentrating on how to produce, BP had ignored its responsibility to protect.

The costs of the Deepwater Horizon blow-out were huge. The clean-up bill was $17.7 billion in 2010, forcing BP to write off $40.9 billion to cover its liability, which was likely to stretch years into the future. The company sold off $23 billion worth of assets, and tried to reinvent itself all over again.

A 'dividing line between good and evil'

BP had first entered Georgia in 1996, as the leading shareholder in a consortium to build and operate energy pipelines. Asia's rich oilfields had boomed after the collapse of the Soviet Union in 1991 as outside investors poured in. A pipeline that would link Baku, the capital of Azerbaijan on the Caspian Sea, to the Mediterranean was a way to access their oil and gas resources. It would also free countries such as Germany, Austria and Poland from persistent threats by Russia to cut off oil and gas supplies through interfering in other pipelines, which passed through territory it controlled. In 2006 and 2009 a third of homes in Eastern Europe faced a chilly winter as Russia turned off the taps. In a virtual war of energy politics, the Europeans vowed 'never again', and scrambled to come up with new ideas for guaranteeing energy supplies.[7]

The 1,768 kilometre BTC pipeline was a way of winning this new 'cold war'. It would deliver the largest new supply of oil in fifteen years, outside OPEC.[8] However, deciding the exact location of the pipeline involved a complex strategic calculation, as the USA and the European Union tried to avoid sending it through potentially hostile countries along the route. Nothing less than the security of the West was at stake in siting the pipeline on friendly territory. President Nursultan Nazarbayev of Kazakhstan, one of the regional powers involved in the debate, commented: 'You could get the impression that what is to be built is not a purely civilian structure, but something that constitutes the dividing line between good and evil.'[9]

Georgia was centre stage in this delicate geo-political dance. The country had regained independence in 1991 as part of the break-up of the Soviet Union, but had suffered a turbulent two decades since, increasingly distancing itself from Russia. The 'Rose Revolution' of 2003 overthrew the vestiges of Russian influence and sought to install a democratic regime. Five years later Georgia was invaded by its neigh- bour as Moscow dispatched troops to the border areas, with the declared aim of protecting ethnic Russians living on the Georgian side. The short summer war of August 2008 ended in stalemate, but Russian troops had advanced within a hundred miles of the capital and captured Gorky, Georgia's second-largest city and the birthplace of Stalin. Russia withdrew in the face of international outrage at its invasion, but maintained control over two autonomous provinces, South Ossetia in the Caucasus Mountains, and Abkhazia in the west bordering the Black Sea. It was a piece of territorial opportunism, to be repeated six years later when Russia annexed the Crimea in a bid to control another former satellite, Ukraine.

Russian hostility was motivated by its determination to protect a sphere of influence in the region and prevent what it saw as Georgia's turn towards the West. An application for Georgia to join NATO and the European Union had been much discussed by the post-revolutionary regime of President Mikheil Saakashvili. Russia was fiercely opposed. The proposed oil and gas pipelines added to the strategic importance of the Transcaucasus, reinforcing Georgia's position at the crossroads between oil producers in western Asia and consumers in Europe. It also reflected the precariousness of the country's position on the fault line between Russia and Europe. With 1.3 per cent of world oil consumption estimated to pass through its pipelines daily, not only Russia, but also the USA, the European Union and regional powers had a stake in what happened to Georgia. As one commentator remarked: 'Energy is the basement level of what Georgia is about. It is a transit country with powerful neighbours and in the short and medium term the pipeline means that Georgia feels secure.'[10]

Dismantling the perimeter fence

Oil and war have been linked since the beginning of the twentieth century. As with conflict diamonds and other minerals in Africa, oil reserves can prop up dysfunctional governments, encourage greed and political patronage, and provide the fuel that feeds conflicts by aggravating social and ethnic tensions and giving armed groups access to illegal revenues, which sustains the fighting.[11] The black gold of the Caspian Sea was a prize which Russia and other international powers vied to control, and which drove the domestic politics of countries in the region.

Next door to Georgia, in Azerbaijan, the discovery of large oil and gas reserves had created a petro-state, where revenues and royalties account for a third of the government's revenues, and oil is used as a tool of political control, the source of the state budget, and a well of patronage that government officials can dip into. So-called rentier economies depend predominantly on the revenues, or 'rents', from selling commodities such as oil while having no industrial base of their own. Rent seeking distorts normal economic conditions, gearing a country exclusively to one commodity and to a market ruled by external consumption. One result is that these types of economy are highly susceptible to swings in demand. They also breed political weakness, and high levels of corruption.[12] Foreign oil companies have to navigate this toxic terrain. It creates tensions between global standards of conduct companies are expected to observe and their relations with local governments. BP's efforts to promote human rights, transparency and security in Azerbaijan had been criticised as inadequate by international NGOs. They claimed that the oil giant was using 'social responsibility' to avoid addressing conflict politics inside Azerbaijan, or the complex causes of instability in the country. By choosing not to use its influence over the Azeri government, or to work on conflict resolution, and above all by treating energy as an issue of geo-politics rather than individual human welfare, the company was seen to be undermining chances of achieving peace in the region.[13]

BP has been part of the story of resource curse in other parts of the globe, with devastating consequences. It had been heavily criticised for its operations in Casanare in north-east Colombia, where oil reserves had generated a bonanza of royalties, and where politics was reduced to a struggle for personal enrichment and the accumulation of power. Until it arrived in Colombia, BP had had little experience of drilling for oil where there was a history of local violence and a negligible state presence. The area was in the grip of armed groups in Colombia's civil war, and between 1990 and 1998 BP was accused of making a number of critical mistakes, which allowed these groups to benefit from the sudden wealth of the region, effectively funding the civil conflict.[14]

By the time the company arrived in Georgia to build the BTC pipeline, its history in Colombia had dealt yet another blow to its declining reputation, particularly in the eyes of the environmental and anti-globalisation lobbies. BP's chief executive John Browne decided that the company had to change tack. In a lecture at St Antony's College in Oxford in 1998, he professed to have learned from the mistakes the company had made and offered a new interpretation of BP's global role: 'One of the things we have learned is that we can't stand aside from the problems of the communities in which we work. We can't try to operate in splendid isolation and cut ourselves off from local realities behind a security fence.'

As a result of this new attitude BP decided to invest in what it called 'local realities'. In Georgia the company allocated an initial $124 million for social improvements in villages that would be most affected by the pipeline. It hoped that local development projects would help to reduce hostility to the pipeline, and make it easier for the company to operate, reducing incidents of accidental or deliberate damage. The spending budget was a fraction of the nearly $4 billion cost of building the pipeline, and was easily justified by BP executives as the price of managing a business risk. Yet the programme that BP undertook was also risky. The combination of political, social and business costs the company faced in such a troubled country was considerable. It meant that BP was taking on problems of safety and welfare at grass roots, in a more profound way than it had ever previously contemplated.

Breaking ground

About an hour's drive south of the capital, Tbilisi, the countryside is wide open, with rich, fertile volcanic soil, ripe for growing vegetables, fruit, flowers and corn. The region boasts twenty-two different microclimates which allow for easy cultivation and a long harvesting season. These conditions had made Georgia the wine and produce backyard of the former Soviet Union, and agriculture was essential to Georgia's post-independence economy.

The pipeline cut a swathe through this farmland, snaking through villages and settlements, along river valleys, and across family plots. Locals regarded it as a threat to their way of life. Fears spread about safety and the risks to those living on top of it. Villagers were unconvinced by BP's assurances that the land would be returned to normal after construction had finished. The company set up a Community Investment Programme (CIP) to address what it called 'non-technical' risks—the kind that might damage its global reputation, unnerve investors and customers and jeopardise its licence to operate in Georgia. To begin with, avoiding these risks meant making efforts to minimise the impact of construction in terms of noise, dust and disruption to people's livelihoods. As one employee explained, the early goals of the programme were simple: 'We just didn't want locals to throw stones at us.'

Villagers saw the arrival of the pipeline not only as a threat, but also as an opportunity to make money. The first arguments arose over who should receive compensation for the use of their land. Before any turf could be turned and holes dug, the company had to negotiate with more than three thousand individual landowners, sometimes arbitrating in disputes between families over who was entitled to compensation, trying to conciliate those disappointed at finding they were not eligible. Where BP needed to buy additional land, many of the 100,000 'land owners' who came forward to negotiate had no title and no means of proving ownership. The company had to rely on locals verifying neighbours' plots. These were then marked out by hand and registered. For the first time, a rural land registry was created. BP's steps to protect property rights and set up a complaint and grievance mechanism were important, not only in how it managed construction of the pipeline, but also because it fell to the company to define the rights of Georgian citizens, and in part their relationship to the government in Tbilisi, as land ownership and tenure were an important element of that.

The process of deciding who would receive money became tangled up in deep-seated grievances and long-standing feuds which had simmered within communities and between families.[15] BP, the outsider, was exposing internal wounds, stirring up envy and having to deal with historical resentments, which it could barely understand. One family prospered, another lost out. The pipeline was bonanza or bane depending literally on which side of the line you found yourself—and in many cases depending on your gender. Women rarely participated in consultation meetings with the company, and they had little say in negotiations for compensation. The only person authorised under Georgian law to engage in dispute resolution was the named owner or user of the land, who was generally the male in the family. Compensation was paid into a bank account in the man's name, or directly to men in cash. International standards about equal rights or due process were abandoned in managing the stampede for BP's money. In 2003 an article in the *Financial Times* reported: 'Money is already flowing to landowners in Georgia ... the sums are paid in cash ... because no one trusts the banks. In one example a landowner carried (away) $35,000.00.'[16]

The compensation boom sometimes had farcical consequences. Under the scheme BP had proposed for determining compensation payments, villagers with land directly on the pipeline route received the most money, and they could claim additional compensation if their land was cultivated in some way, with trees or crops. A sudden outburst of nature resulted: new trees sprouted overnight on bare patches of earth just as assessors were due to arrive. Many of these trees were concreted into position.

Unrest also ran high, and on a couple of occasions BP vehicles entering villages were attacked by disgruntled locals. In rural parts of Georgia, where the state was a faint and remote presence, farmers were used to relying on their own resources to manage community affairs. BP's arrival risked dividing communities over the distribution of its funds, but at the same time uniting locals in their opposition to what they saw as outside interference that was colluding with a distrusted state regime.

BP decided that it needed to change tactics. Rather than an administrative approach using outside auditors and government regulators to draft agreements with land owners, settle compensation disputes and hand out funds, the company expanded the Community Investment Programme. The CIP became a way of organising the company's dealings with local communities, and it meant that BP itself, rather than delegated officials from local or national government, was present and visible in villages to decide on and oversee the investments made by the programme. 'Communities were used to having big expectations and nothing being met. The company had to manage those expectations. That is where the CIP played a big role in establishing trust. It was the tool to create a trust environment,' explained Temur Gazhonia, site controller at BP's Pumping Station Number 1.[17]

By calling in local NGOs and representatives of community groups to help spread information and carry out training programmes, the CIP made it a priority to let people express views and be listened to. The hope was that debate and rational argument would crowd out aggression and violence. Largely it worked: as one local commented to BP two years into the programme: 'We are now explaining to you, not screaming at you.'

Promise in the pipeline

Uzein Guseinov, Chesminaz Shapieva and Ali Sadikov are farmers in Kvemo Kartli, a region of wide open green spaces punctuated by fields of fruit and vegetables, and in the spring by a profusion of wild flowers. At harvest time when I visited, the fields were teeming with ripening sweetcorn, wheat was being dried and milled in the farmyard, fruit trees were weighed down with apples and plums. The farms are family run, mostly using traditional skills and techniques, and simple in their layout. Like many of their neighbours along the construction route, Uzein, Chesminaz and Ali feared the disruption that would be caused by construction workers, and the unseen hazards of oil and technology spoiling the beauty of the area and threatening their traditional way of life.

They were sceptical of the development benefits being promised by BP's social investment programme. Nonetheless, swayed by the promise of money, Ali had helped organise a group of Azeri farmers to dig an irrigation channel. The Kvemo Kartli farmers were typical of the minority ethnic groups scattered throughout Georgian communities, which have deep family and cultural ties to other countries in the region, such as Azerbaijan. Ali and his friends saw the irrigation channel as a way of improving their chances of growing early spring vegetables, which they could export to Russia, and replace produce that was being imported from Turkey. In this way, what BP encouraged in Georgia had repercussions far beyond the local neighbourhood and out into the entire region.

The farmers went from house to house, canvassing support for the project. The irrigation channel was dug and the water began to flow. Buoyed by their success, the group began to organise other activities. They talked about introducing new crops and trying different farming techniques. In 2009 the original band of farmers, now organised into a co-operative, bought their first tractor. Other machinery followed, as well as investment in fertilisers. The growing size of the project, and the conditions set out by BP for receiving its funding, meant that the farmers had to learn to use spreadsheets setting out what they spent, and the outcomes in terms of agricultural yields. By 2010 the co-operative had grown to include nearly seventy families in the district. Ali said that during the Soviet Union era they had waited to be told by the local party official what to plant and when. Now he took pride in showing me the new collection of seeds he had chosen himself, and would begin sowing once the fields had been ploughed. The farmers were experimenting with new growing methods so they could take on competition from other districts in supplying green vegetables to the capital, Tbilisi.

It was a story I was to hear again and again around kitchen tables and in farmyards along the length of the pipeline. Uzein and Chesminaz took up the challenge of adopting new techniques using BP's money to grow tomatoes in a greenhouse for the first time. Chesminaz worked with Care International, one of BP's NGO partners, experimenting using fertiliser to grow early cabbages. Speaking through the Care representative he explained:

> For many years after the collapse of the Soviet Union nobody created a seed bank so there were no improvements in quality; in fact, the seeds degraded. Previously there was no maize in the village, we also did everything manually. Then one day, one farmer agreed to accept Care's help and he started using the new technology. The whole village was sceptical, but then this farmer also started to write poems. The rest of us could see that he suddenly had the time to do this, so we started to follow his example and this inspired the organisation of the group.[18]

Local hostility towards the pipeline softened, oiled by a steady flow of money which went to building roads, shops and schools as well as directly into the pockets of villagers. A 4 kilometre-wide zone was established along the length of the pipeline. Within this core zone farms and villages were eligible to receive benefits from the development company.

The social investment programmes relied on creating bonds between residents and organisers, within farming communities, and across districts. The common link was that all stood to benefit in some way from BP's handouts and development support. Projects worked by people spreading information among their neighbours, colleagues and customers, while money was mostly channelled to lots of small-scale schemes, rather than a few grand initiatives. The effect was, in the words of one of BP's partners, to 'create small islands of good practice supporting professionals as well as the introduction of different, better standards'.[19] The long-term effect was to unleash a wind of change, which transformed the way those who received funds earned their living, and influenced the futures of many more in the ranks of small companies, contractors, neighbourhood co-operatives and community organisers.

More than just an environmental restoration scheme, the CIP became the umbrella for hundreds of different social and economic schemes, worth more than $15 million. The emphasis on protecting the environment in rural areas, for example, rewarded individuals who set up local food, renewable energy and conservation projects, including eco-tourism. But BP's programme also provided support for groups such as Georgia's Scout movement, which expanded with company money and set up units in forty-three schools in over forty villages, where its 1,300 members would discuss topics such as conflict resolution, environmental protection and leadership skills. Irina Pruidze, the Scouts secretary general, explained:

> The youth we work with are people who are starting to become citizens. Particularly in villages in the high mountains, they are so isolated and there is nothing to do, so they were happy to see something happening. There are a lot of ethnic and economic issues and if people don't communicate with other ethnic groups we risk having conflicts in future. This [programme] encouraged participation in social and political life.[20]

BP's initiatives were doing more than mitigating the impacts of its commercial activities. They amounted to a wide-ranging and integrated attempt to transform the welfare of everyday life across large parts of Georgia.

The social investment drive began to pay off in terms of the company's image in Georgia. According to Irina Pruidze, Scouts came away from the meetings with new, positive attitudes towards business. Youngsters from agricultural communities saw opportunities in working for a company to help them earn a living. In the capital, cultural initiatives linked BP to a flourishing of international arts. A theatre partnership, brokered by the British Council in Tbilisi, brought theatre, opera and ballet contacts with the National Theatre in the UK, which expanded into a regional project involving Armenia, Azerbaijan, Northern Ireland and Georgia to develop plays that could be performed in each country.

Reputation risk or recovery?

BP's impact was being felt in many different ways, as the company's spending extended to projects that supported entrepreneurship, encouraging alternative livelihoods and promoting Georgian culture. Its presence was changing social life, particularly in the countryside where life in communities was adapting not only to the money BP brought, but also to new ways of earning a living and using free time. These different kinds of effect moreover had symbolic significance in a country struggling to establish its independence from Russia and create a new national identity in a turbulent geo-political context, which included outside powers trying to influence Georgian politics. The CIP began to have a say in how communities, districts and regions ran their affairs. In rural areas as well as Tbilisi, the approach was on educating for change, rather than simply building infrastructure or handing over funds for development schemes. The programme used training and learning as tools to drive a movement that attempted to shift Georgia out of its conflict trap. There were language and professional courses for journalists, a management college for contractors, courses in public administration for officials, training in business methods, and graduate-level economics at a new International School of Economics at Tbilisi State University (ISET). Members of school boards were offered training to help them regulate teaching standards and manage school budgets. Many of these schemes had no direct connection with the pipeline. A programme to increase the use of renewable energy was delivered by an 'Energy Bus' which toured towns and villages giving advice and subsidised loans on energy-saving products.[21] A scheme to teach women about setting up small businesses was intended to stop the illegal trafficking of young women and provide them with alternative ways of making a living. BP was later approached by men asking for the company to give them similar training so they could become mechanics.

Not everyone was comfortable with the extent of this corporate influence, or how BP behaved. The company was criticised for not doing more to promote human rights, uphold the rule of law and develop good governance in a country that was trying to establish democracy. BP was accused of avoiding key political issues and condoning questionable practices.[22]

The task of managing the pipeline itself was also sensitive, and had political ramifications. The safety of the area around the pipeline depended on a system of security, which either involved private guards hired by the company or required BP to work with state security forces, with the risk of becoming involved in confrontations between people and police that could turn violent. The pipeline was a potentially hazardous structure, liable to accidents from construction work, the handling of waste created by digging the trench and other environmental hazards, such as water, pollution and increased traffic around the construction sites. In neighbouring Turkey the pipeline had led to eleven attempts by locals to tap oil illegally, and there were constant reports of sabotage. Pipeline security was a very real concern, and meant that BP had to resort to using varying degrees of force and detention of trespassers. Security guards hired by BP were trained in human rights principles in an effort to handle any trouble responsibly, but sometimes the company had to call in state security forces, which often led to heavy-handed treatment and human rights abuses.

Partly to avoid the security dilemma, BP introduced a system of horseback patrols and set up community liaison offices, which were supposed to help avoid problems of sabotage or unintended accidents. Surveillance operations were put in place around the pipeline, and were to be run locally in order to maintain good relations with communities. The system included a 'hierarchy of responses', which varied from simple deterrence to the use of armed force.

The pipeline safety regime in Georgia was more sensitive to avoiding violations of human rights than equivalent systems along stretches of the BTC in Turkey and Azerbaijan. Nonetheless, the company attracted criticism from NGOs for concentrating on compensating for abuses rather than trying to prevent accidents and attacks in the first place. The pipeline investment programme was more about ensuring that there were economic benefits for the project, and about conflict prevention in Georgia. Any physical and political damage caused by the building and, later, the operational phases of the pipeline was not the main point of BP's initiative. Critics claim that BP failed to get the balance right between its social and economic investments, which were unusual and ambitious, and offsetting the negative effects of its commercial operations, which represented a more traditional form of corporate responsibility.[23] However, the extensive safety regime the company installed around the pipeline, combined with a series of checks to monitor environmental consequences, were themselves evidence of how wide ranging BP's efforts were to protect local people. They were unusual if not unprecedented for a modern global corporation.

At the end of the pipeline

By 2006, with construction finished and the pipeline buried beneath 2 metres of grass, mud, rock and forest along its length, BP's business in Georgia changed. It became primarily a provider of energy services, operating two pumping stations, employing 400 people, and supplying jet fuel to airlines at the capital's airport. All this was run from a small office in Tbilisi, and while its contribution to the Georgian economy was still significant, it was no longer critical to the country's development. However, the company's social influence continued to spread. In providing public goods and services, particularly in rural areas, which had been overlooked by the central government, BP increasingly appeared to be offering a substitute for many state responsibilities. Yet the company had no popular mandate or official authority for this. Its role expanded incrementally and without particular design, and helped place BP in a powerful position at the heart of Georgian life. Compared to conventional development organisations such as UNDP, the World Bank or many NGOs, BP was often extremely influential. Many local organisations found it easier to deal with the company than with other donors such as the EU, which was particularly active in Georgia at the time. Although BP's schemes were many and varied, the company appeared to have a defined agenda, even if it was not certain how long its commitment would last. Programmes were criticised for providing only short-term funding, and projects were sometimes stopped without reason, as priorities changed. BP's intervention came with no clear method of accountability. If there were local objections to its plans, the strongest form of leverage over the company was the threat of opposition to the pipeline. BP was susceptible to any suggestion that building the pipeline might destabilise an already fragile society.

The company became known as a shrewd investor: its spending was targeted on particular goals, it insisted on value for money and was careful to demonstrate that it rejected any form of corruption and favoured transparency. This made BP programmes look quite different from interventions and donations from other foreign organisations that arrived in Georgia with overseas aid and development projects.

Ketevan Vashakidze, Georgia director of the Eurasia Partnership Foundation, which works on developing Georgian civil society, describes the company's impact as significant because it represented a novel form of strategic philanthropy, which was quite different to the fragmented small and personal initiatives that had existed previously and were typical ways in which rich individuals or businesses supported public works.[24]

To demonstrate its accountability and responsibility as its role became increasingly sensitive, particularly in relation to security, BP brought in third-party organisations to monitor its activities. They were supposed to flag up environment, safety and human rights issues, and audit the money the company spent on development. Local bodies were trained to check the finances of projects and measure BP's behaviour against international standards in order to ensure that it was consistent with what it had promised to do. In 2004 the company set up the Caspian Development Advisory Panel (CDAP), a watchdog body with the task of monitoring and reviewing impacts of the pipeline. In one sense this was a tame watchdog: the panel reported to then chairman John (Lord) Browne. While its reports detailed every aspect of BP's social, safety and environment programmes, and ensured that all documents relating to the pipeline were publicly available, accompanied by citizens' guides on how to read them,[25] the result of this transparency initiative was no less than fifteen different layers of monitoring and oversight. These had the opposite of what BP intended, and made it hard to work out who was responsible for what. Moreover, although BP set benchmarks to show that it was complying with international standards—for example, on human rights—it also created a number of strategic opt-outs that would preserve its room for manoeuvre. The system it instituted was an odd mixture of Georgian law and international regulation, leading critics to claim that BP's watchdog system worked on the company's terms. It not only insulated the company from national laws on human rights and environmental protection; it also had the effect of undermining the authority of the Georgian state, and setting BP up as a parallel form of governance inside Georgia.

If BP lawyers had made sure the company was able to operate in a grey zone of accountability, there was still the risk of political confrontation over its social initiatives. BP used its position to lobby for changes to government policies, tax regulations and food-safety standards,[26] and highlighted issues the government had ignored, but which mattered to Georgians to improve their daily lives.

In 2010 a programme to train recruits in public administration and policy brought the company close to a row with the authorities over labour rights. The government moved to limit trade union influence in schools. This put BP, in its role as an important educational donor and reformer, under pressure to support union rights. Yet the company chose to remain silent. Civil rights groups, which regarded this confrontation with the government as a key political issue in Georgia's emerging democracy, were shocked by BP's behaviour, and disappointed not to find an ally for their opposition to the government crackdown.[27] It seemed that there was after all a limit to how far the company would go to provide an alternative to the state.[28]

In fact, a mutual arrangement had developed between company and government in which the state was happy to claim the credit for cultural and infrastructure improvements, funded by BP money, while the company settled for a relatively low public profile. The company co-operated with the state, while at the same time deliberately bypassing it, declining to bring it on board as either a co-funder or a project partner. The pipeline contract had obliged BP to commit $8.8 million a year to environmental improvements, yet the company resisted pressure to donate these funds to the government, via the Environment Ministry. Instead, BP distributed it directly to communities and civil society groups.[29]

BP's attitude was to keep the Georgian government close but not lose sight of what ordinary citizens needed, either as a consequence of the pipeline construction or because they were affected by the upheavals caused by government reforms. Political theory suggests that the relationships between companies and governments in their host countries are critical, collaborative or complementary. Human rights activists often point to complicity between governments and big foreign businesses.[30] BP's approach in Georgia did not fit into any of these categories. It was an awkward coexistence, but it recognised that the company and the state also depended on each other. The company's insistence that its programme remained independent of the state was both a symbolic imperative and a practical working arrangement.

Gia Gvaladze, BP's external relations director in Georgia, is frank about its relationship with the government:

In the construction phase our presence and the level of engagement was enormous because we needed the government's support. We could go very close to a 'risk area' with the government because their understanding of what we can do [was] high, but this does not mean they have completely lost their appetite for rent seeking ... they know that anything we do has to be well justified and within legal and logical limits.[31]

BP played the part of 'good citizen' within Georgia, but its story is also about it being a good pupil, learning from its involvements in other conflict zones that had stirred local and international opposition. One indication of the success of the pipeline programme in helping to restore its global reputation was that in 2010, when BP became engulfed by controversy as a result of the Deepwater Horizon disaster in the Gulf of Mexico, it suffered no side effects in Georgia. Local experiences of BP were markedly different from the company's image in the USA, and the tide of opposition to BP worldwide did nothing to damage its Caspian operations. BP continued investing in Georgia long after it finished construction of the pipeline, and this created a bedrock of trust and confidence which did more than just allow the company a licence to operate in the region. It meant that BP was regarded as an active partner in Georgia's transition to peace and democracy. The company's presence was also a catalyst that encouraged communities and other organisations to act. Communities had to agree to maintain the roads and camps that BP built and which were returned to local users after construction workers finished with them. The monitoring systems that BP put in place to ensure protection against spills or malicious damage to the pipeline had to be maintained and updated by local people. A form of shared responsibility emerged between the company and citizens as both confronted the risks as well as the opportunities the pipeline presented.

BP's own assessment of what it had achieved in Georgia was set out in the final report by the CDAP advisory panel in January 2007, which applauded the 'breadth and ambition' of BP's social and environmental investments, but cautioned that the commitment had to be not only maintained but enhanced: 'BP [has] laid a good foundation in their effort to establish a new model but that sustained effort will be required in many areas for the duration of pipeline operations if that vision is ultimately to be fulfilled.'[32]

As the report pointed out, BP faces a long-term commitment in Georgia and an ongoing role in contributing to peace and stability in a country that is still in conflict with Russia over parts of its territory, and with a programme of internal democratic reforms still unfinished. The unusual breadth of the company's involvement in this process means that its Georgian strategy may not be easily replicable in other conflict zones, although the company has adopted a similar approach in post-war Iraq. There, it is working with local people in the Raumaila oilfield in southern Iraq to manage development, and build community reconciliation as well as mitigate the impacts of its operations in order to avoid violence and intimidation. As in Georgia, the decision to go beyond minimal safety and prevention measures requires a delicate and long-term partnership alongside community and government leaders. Both situations reflect a recognition that even the largest global business can only prosper if it gets things right at ground level.[33] The pipeline project had shown that a corporation could behave differently when faced with a complex combination of safety, political, social and environmental risks, and that learning how to manage the insecurity of ordinary people in a volatile environment was a valid strategy for a progressive business.

Extractive companies in the oil and mining sectors have been guilty of some of the worst abuses of social, political, labour and environmental rights on every continent. As we have seen, they can be implicated in driving conflict, because natural resources are crucial to the economics and political dynamics of modern wars. At the same time, these companies are proof of the paradox at the heart of this book: that enormous economic and investment power can also be applied to unlock positive change in some of the most fragile societies on earth, when it is deployed from the grass roots upwards. Corporate peace can be spread through small villages as well as in government circles.

Resource and mining companies are now at the forefront of novel thinking about how to use their power to manage the volatile and dangerous situations they find themselves in, and how to seize the opportunities that commercial operations offer as well as deal with the risks they pose in fragile countries. What BP did in Georgia was a sign of a growing awareness by some businesses of the possibilities of using their power in a different way. Other companies, their reputations also on the line, would come to the same realisation, as we will see in the next chapter.

9

THE POWER OF PROTECTION IN LIBERIA

The ruts of red earth are hard and unforgiving to any vehicle on the road with normal tyres. It is the dry season, so they are compacted solid. In a few weeks' time the rain will soften the ruts, and deep pools of dark water will pose a different kind of obstacle to human, animal and machine traffic, making large tracts of the country inaccessible. With few tarred roads, trucks carrying foodstuffs and other essentials will get bogged down and block the passage of others behind them. Farmers will find it difficult to get their goods to market. Travel becomes unpredictable, demanding patience, a flexible body able to absorb endless jolts as the vehicle bumps from one water-filled pothole to the next, and a flexible schedule, as arrival may be days away.

It is late May 2014, Liberia, West Africa. Two executives from the steel-making conglomerate ArcelorMittal are on a routine trip in the capital, Monrovia. Even in the country's largest city, travel is haphazard and uncomfortable, and the journey time usually a best guess. As well as the normal urban hazards of heavy traffic, pedestrians spilling out into the road, kamikaze motorcycle drivers and overcrowded buses labouring slowly, belching out petrol fumes and holding up cars in their wake, Monrovia presents other challenges to mobility: even here proper roads are scarce. Turn off the main drag and you are quickly into unpaved, unmarked, unlit tracks which, depending on the time of year, are dusty, rock solid, with ruts baked by the equatorial sun, or sliding

153

lakes of mud and rainwater. Sometimes the hazard has more human form: turn a corner and you drive into an angry crowd of demonstrators, protesting at government corruption, someone having been detained by police, or the effects of a new law. At a moment's notice, the demonstration can ignite into a riot; best accelerate quickly and move on, if the road and its ruts allow.

All this is normal. The passengers in the back seat of the white Toyota SUV do not give it a moment's thought. For the country manager it is part of the daily routine. For his fellow passenger visiting from the London office, it is by no means his first trip to Liberia, so he knows what to expect. Yet on that May morning, all is not normal in Liberia. The date is significant, because for the past two months reports have been accumulating of an outbreak of the Ebola virus in rural areas. People are dying in their homes and in the streets. Where the disease will strike is unpredictable, yet it is spreading steadily across the country, lethal and apparently unstoppable. Also spreading is fear and uncertainty of when and where it might strike next.

The vehicle moves through the traffic along the potholed road, and the passengers become aware of a new development. On the radio there are reports of Ebola deaths in the capital. The virus is no longer a distant menace of the countryside. On that late May morning, news of the discovery of four bodies in Monrovia causes the passengers a jolt more powerful than any rut in the road.

Alan Knight, ArcelorMittal's general manager for corporate responsibility, was one of the two men in the back of the Toyota:

> It was obvious at that moment that a lot of people had come into contact with the disease. It was a game-changer—not because they were dead, but because they were in the middle of Monrovia. I went home to London thinking that as a business we were prepared for problems, but over the next few weeks it turned into a disaster in slow motion.[1]

What Knight and his colleagues did next was unusual, and unprecedented in its scale. They turned ArcelorMittal into a protective force to combat the spread of Ebola in Liberia. Facing what they saw as failures in national and international action to address the crisis, ArcelorMittal mobilised a swathe of private companies and public agencies in a co-ordinated response to the epidemic. The Ebola outbreak was eventually to infect more than 27,000 people, killing more than 11,000, with widespread disruption and damage to the physical, mental and economic well-being of millions across West Africa.[2] The death toll was less than international disease experts initially predicted. It is impossible to calculate how many casualties were avoided through the action of foreign investors such as ArcelorMittal. However, one result of their intervention was to alter the mind-set of a group of global companies. The crisis influenced how they understood their obligations to local populations, and it changed the perceptions of traditional security providers, such as government and aid agencies, regarding the role of corporations in an existential catastrophe. To borrow Knight's term, the Ebola crisis was a game-changer for the idea of corporate responsibility:

> We knew we could not run a business successfully with this happening in the country. It was both a commercial and a human reaction. You could say it was commercial and we were driven to protect our operations, or it was done out of pure charity. It really doesn't matter—the intervention was the same.[3]

What the private companies did was more than a humanitarian response. Their concerted action changed the way the crisis was managed, and established an important precedent for business to become more aware, engaged and effective in tackling Liberia's chronic welfare and governance problems and promoting its chances for peace. More than any other story in this book, the Ebola epidemic highlighted the potential for companies to exercise a critical role by connecting local action to their considerable international influence and resources.

Fear and contagion

The 2014 outbreak of Ebola Virus Disease (or EVD) in West Africa turned out to be the largest case of a disease that had been seen periodically in the region's rainforests in the three decades since it was first identified in 1976 in a village on the Ebola River in the Democratic Republic of Congo. EVD is transmitted to people from wild animals. Fruit bats are thought to be the source of the virus, but chimpanzees, gorillas and small forest mammals are also likely carriers. Village populations come into contact with the virus through hunting and eating infected animals. Once in the human population, Ebola spreads through personal contact, and specifically through bodily fluids. Everyday gestures such as handshakes, embraces and kisses become deadly manoeuvres. During the outbreak people had to abandon normal modes of greeting; they didn't touch each other, but kept their distance. Physical contact became taboo—or medicalised, as only masked and suited health workers risked human touch.

For foreigners, Ebola has always conjured up a mythical terror as the stuff of science fiction and horror novels and films, thanks to its extreme symptoms and its deadly nature. Victims suffer a sudden onset of fever, muscle pain, headache and sore throat, followed by vomiting and diarrhoea, internal and sometimes external bleeding. Blood can ooze from the gums and appear in faeces. Death can be painful and rapid.

The 2014 outbreak has been traced back to late December 2013 when Emile Ouamouno, a two-year-old boy living in the equatorial forest village of Meliandou in Guinea, died, followed in quick succession by his sister and mother. Emile was later to be identified as the so-called Patient Zero, the source of the disease, which then spread to Sierra Leone and Liberia.[4] One reason for the rapid spread of Ebola was the local custom of washing dead bodies before burial using a communal bucket of water. Relatives and neighbours who came into contact with Ebola victims then contracted and passed on the disease, up to two days after the initial victim had died.

Throughout the late spring and early summer of 2014 ArcelorMittal, like other companies, government officials and civil society organisations, noted with increasing alarm the spread of the EVD contagion. Three months after Emile and his family died in Guinea, governments in the region and the World Health Organization, the UN agency responsible for combating the spread of infectious epidemics, had identified the disease, yet the outbreak received relatively little attention in the outside world. Aid agency Médecins Sans Frontières (MSF) was on the frontline, offering treatment and diagnosis, as the number of cases mounted inexorably, but the response by the international community at large was subsequently described as 'criminally late'.[5]

The WHO's situation reports on Ebola in West Africa showed little sense of urgency about the situation until three months after Alan Knight had first learned of corpses in the centre of Monrovia.[6] At that stage there were 1,546 recorded deaths, out of more than three thousand confirmed and suspected cases across the region, an alarmingly high fatality rate. Liberia, Guinea and Sierra Leone were classed as countries with 'widespread and intense transmission'. The WHO's report of 29 August noted that cases were increasing in the epicentre in Lofa county and also in Monrovia, and that those infected by the virus had only a 50–50 chance of surviving. In most areas of Liberia the treatment system of referral centres, laboratories, tracing of contacts, safe burial and 'social mobilization' to tell people about the disease and teach them how to limit the risk of contagion was classed by foreign experts as partially or totally non-functional. 'The capacity to cope with the increasing caseload remains dramatically low,' stated the WHO.[7] With this prognosis, the pace of international alarm quickened. At the end of September an article in the *New England Journal of Medicine* by scientists from the WHO and Imperial College, London predicted that the number of cases in the region could escalate to more than 20,000 within eight weeks. The warnings from the influential US health institute the Centers for Disease Control and Prevention (CDC) were even more dire, claiming that if trends continued without intervention or changes in community behaviour, cases in Liberia and Sierra Leone alone would reach between 550,000 and 1.4 million by the end of January 2015.[8]

The risk was more than the uncontrolled spread of Ebola in West Africa. Of even greater concern to the international organisations was that EVD could spread internationally if undetected carriers boarded planes and crossed borders. UNICEF said it expected that 80 per cent of those who contracted Ebola would die. As one international observer put it, these were figures on the scale of a plague.

Epidemiologists struggled to understand the behaviour chain of the disease, and its social as well as its pathological effects, in order to stop further transmission. Health workers could not be trained fast enough. An initial network of 450 nurses and doctors, which the British Red Cross thought it could rely on, proved insufficient to handle all the diagnostic, preventive and curative tasks that were required just to keep abreast of the disease.

By September the international response had speeded up, but it was not until the end of the year that a clear system emerged in which different actors and organisations identified their responsibilities, combined their capacities, and the response was co-ordinated. It was five months later still, in January 2015, that authorities and aid workers got on top of the disease 'cycle' and were able to prevent transmission, transfer new cases to treatment centres and finally reintegrate survivors back into the community.

Containment efforts were hampered not only by a lack of facilities, but also because healthcare workers were among those who were becoming infected and dying. It also became clear that the true scale of the outbreak was much worse than the official figures suggested. Victims were being abandoned, with the dead left to rot behind closed doors as neighbours and families feared being either contaminated medically or ostracised socially. People were not reporting cases of Ebola, both in order to avoid the consequences and because they did not trust the authorities to deal with the sick.

To those on the ground it was clear that the Ebola outbreak was not just a biological phenomenon but, above all, a social and political crisis. The epidemic was exceptional not primarily because of the virus itself, but because the worst-affected countries, such as Liberia, lacked proper health systems; populations mixed freely across poorly defined and porous national borders; and efforts to halt the spread of infection were woefully inadequate.[9] One international aid worker described the situation in non-medical terms as 'simply chaotic, out of control because systems were overwhelmed. It was that way until Christmas 2014.'[10]

The Ebola epidemic broke on a country weakened by two decades of civil war, which had left public institutions in Liberia shattered and had destroyed national infrastructure and basic social services. Health facilities in particular were chronically under-equipped. There was a shortage of qualified doctors and nurses, few clinics to provide treatment, no system of public information, almost no laboratories for testing or to provide accurate monitoring and information. Those that did exist were only in urban areas. There were few ambulances or other kinds of emergency transport, and shortages of electricity and water. Health workers were poorly paid, and a lack of public confidence in the health system meant that, when Ebola appeared, victims had to rely on their own forms of treatment. If you live in the USA, an average of more than $9,000 per year will be spent on keeping you healthy. The average Liberian citizen will have less than $45 a year spent on them.[11]

Liberia had more than simply an impoverished healthcare system: its whole economy was teetering on the brink. Its society was as fragile as the axle of a vehicle navigating the ruts in the road, and just as liable to break. Liberia is one of the poorest countries in the world, with an average life expectancy of fifty-seven years. Nearly two-thirds of the population live below the poverty line, nearly half are hungry and lacking food security, and out of 187 countries in the UN's human development index, Liberia sits fifth from the bottom.[12] Two ruinous phases of civil war from 1989 to 2003 had killed an estimated 250,000 people, as one murderous dictator was ousted by another, each with his own militias and support from neighbouring states, in a conflict that drew in next-door countries Sierra Leone and Guinea. Thousands more Liberians fled their homes, particularly in rural areas where marauding troops perpetrated atrocities on villagers, and allegiances changed regularly from one side to the next. The population of Monrovia doubled to a million by the end of the war, as refugees crowded into makeshift mud and tin shacks in search of food, jobs and safety from tribal militias. A quarter of all Liberians live on the fringes of this urban sprawl, with few public services and little infrastructure, poor sanitation and overcrowding.

In 2003 a peace agreement was signed. Charles Taylor, who had been president since coming to power in a bloody coup in 1997, resigned and was subsequently found guilty of war crimes including murder, rape and terror by the International Criminal Court in The Hague. He was sentenced to fifty years, which he is currently serving in a British prison. The UN deployed 15,000 peacekeepers to Liberia, and in 2006 Ellen Johnson Sirleaf became Africa's first female president, with the daunting task of rebuilding the country.

Liberia's economy is propped up by a crutch of enormous outside aid budgets, remittances from the diaspora in the USA and foreign investment. It is a country that, even for Africa, has an unusually high level of foreign interference. Its political elite, its culture and its financial lifeblood are generated overseas, from the USA in particular. The country is the oldest independent republic in Africa, created as a haven for freed African-American slaves by abolitionists before the American Civil War. The country's name means 'Land of the Free', but in fact most things come at a high price in Liberia, including the foreign

159

investment that is the economy's lifeblood. Global companies such as Firestone Rubber, a Japanese-owned tyre giant, and Malaysian-controlled Sime Derby, which produces palm oil, as well as international mining companies, dominate an economy geared to resource extraction, and organised via concession agreements between foreign investors and the government. Firestone's rubber plantation in Liberia is the largest single one in the world, and its concession agreement dates back to 1926, when the company was granted a ninety-nine-year lease over a million acres of land.[13] The concession gives the company extensive power and privileges, such as the right to run its own system of law and order through its Plant Protection Department, including powers of arrest and detention, in order to safeguard its property and technology.[14] A 2016 World Bank draft report described Liberia's natural-resource economy as a site of contest and conflict. Concessions to foreign companies have long been regarded as a means of economic gain for local elites, and are a source of grievance among the rest of the population. The unequal development of the country, high poverty levels and a lack of employment opportunities were part of the combination of factors that explain the country's long civil war, and why that conflict was so protracted and intractable.[15]

The investment concessions require foreign companies to make annual contributions to local social development funds.[16] However, the system for enforcing such commitments is weak, and there are claims that concession companies persistently under-deliver payments.[17] Fluctuations in world commodity prices mean that companies often claim they cannot afford the costs of financing the social benefits they have committed to. If forced to pay, they threaten to withdraw their investment.[18] Heavily reliant on revenues from foreign resource operations, the government responds by tolerating a range of negative company behaviour, from failure to pay social dues to more serious human rights infringements.[19]

Between 1989 and 2003 civil war killed off foreign investment and Liberian development. Even after the war inward investment was as little as $3 million a year. While it has begun to return, there has been a dramatic deterioration in relations between companies and local communities. Hopes that foreign companies would bring improvements to everyday life have been eclipsed by grievances over labour conditions, social rights and environmental damage that their operations entail. Unrest, riots and even violence are commonplace as sites of foreign concessions periodically erupt with tensions. The atmosphere around operating sites often brims with mistrust and suspicion. The election of former international footballer George Weah as president in 2018, on a populist platform that included making the private sector pay more, has stepped up tensions. Foreign companies have been publicly singled out as part of the reason why ordinary Liberians remain so poor.

Digging deep in Liberia

ArcelorMittal is an integral part of Liberia's concession economy. It is the world's largest steel and mining company, with nearly 200,000 employees in 60 countries across the globe, producing 113 million tonnes of crude steel for cars, construction, household appliances and packaging. It is a classic example of a modern transnational corporation (TNC). The present conglomerate, the world's first 100 million-tonne-plus steel producer, was created in 2006 through the merger of Luxembourg steel maker Arcelor and Mittal Steel, the family company of Indian businessman Lakshmi Mittal, who is group chairman and chief executive. Although technically headquartered in Luxembourg, ArcelorMittal's global operations are managed out of a modern steel-and-glass building in London's Berkeley Square, and its shares are listed on eight different stock exchanges. It is famous in the UK for having commissioned Anish Kapoor to design the twisting red spiral sculpture made out of recycled steel, the ArcelorMittal Orbit, which was the landmark symbol of the London 2012 Olympic Games.

In 2006 ArcelorMittal established its position as the global industry leader, expanding in thirty-five countries, including an agreement with the Liberian government to reopen a derelict mine in the north of the country with the intention of eventually producing 15 million tonnes of iron ore.

Headquarters in Mayfair and cutting-edge sculpture are a universe away from the gritty reality on the ground which generates the $6.3 billion profit that ArcelorMittal made in 2016.[20] The group is no stranger to environments where there is chronic underdevelopment, political tension, even conflict. Its Liberian business consists of two separate parts, physically connected by a single-line railway track. In the north where the country merges into neighbouring Guinea and Ivory Coast, and the Nimba Mountains rise in steep green peaks up to 4,500 feet, is the Tokadeh mine, next to the town of Yekepa. There has been an iron-ore mine near Yekepa for over fifty years, since foreign investors arrived in the 1960s to exploit a discovery of iron-ore deposits, which were particularly rich and pure. They built a prosperous town of 20,000 people who thrived on the jobs, economic output and attention generated by the mine. Amateur film footage by one of the foreign managers at the time shows a Rolls Royce being transported to the town on a river barge, for a visit of international dignitaries. European families with fair-haired children play on the streets, visit shops, enjoy the golf course, go to the cinema and bathe in the large, blue company-built swimming pool. The dark side of this idealised existence in the Liberian rainforest was a disfigured landscape where the red, iron-rich earth is exposed amidst the natural green canopy, the peaks are deforested and deep cuts are slashed into the mountain, streaking it with black, the colour of the mined ore. Local workers, then and now, are housed in flat-roofed white blocks in orderly rows on the plateau in the shadow of the mountain. Half a century later the houses are still the same, along with the only communal road, still unpaved and liable to be clogged by construction trucks stuck in its ruts.

About 250 kilometres away on the coast is the second part of ArcelorMittal's operation, where iron ore is shipped out from the Atlantic port of Buchanan. On a good day—meaning when there is no rain or the delays of getting stuck behind a logging truck—the journey from the mine to the container port takes six hours by road. At the beginning of the 1960s the foreign mining company built a 273 kilometre single-gauge railway connecting the mine to the sea, providing the country's most reliable piece of infrastructure which connects its coast to the interior. One option for making the tortuous journey to the mine is to ride shotgun in the cab of the locomotive, no less uncomfortable and backbreaking than by pickup truck, but one hour shorter, and the only viable method during the rainy season.

Company staff describe Yekepa as 'a difficult environment' to operate in, both physically and ethically. Government and administration here is in the hands of local tribes who exercise their own forms of authority and norms, including by secret societies, whose rituals remain largely hidden to outsiders but feature hierarchy, initiation, fear and violence, according to the rare documentation that exists.[21] The rule of law penetrates the thick jungle canopy only partially; land ownership is unclear and undocumented, leading to persistent disputes between locals and foreign investors.

The mine has seen some of the worst cases of unrest around foreign company concessions in Liberia as the local community became disillusioned with the slow pace of development after the war ended. In July 2014, as the Ebola threat was building, rioters armed with hunting rifles occupied the mine area, holding staff and contractors hostage for a number of hours, and destroying buildings and facilities. The riot provoked a presidential statement reassuring foreign investors that the government would protect their lives and property. The perpetrators were quickly rounded up, and eleven were subsequently convicted and given fifteen-year prison sentences. Reporting the incident, Reuters quoted one demonstrator as saying that ArcelorMittal had not fulfilled the terms of its concession agreement with the Liberian government. It had not compensated local people for crops, nor had it paid wages or renovated houses.[22]

What constituted responsible behaviour by a foreign company changed significantly between the 1960s, when the Tokadeh mine was first developed, and the 2000s, when ArcelorMittal arrived. The modern equivalent of the 1960s hand-held cine film shot by expatriates is a corporate video of 2012 in which ArcelorMittal managers enthusiastically demonstrate the company's social and environmental investments. Instead of the fair-haired children of 1960s expats, the video shows local schoolchildren in smart orange-and-black uniforms at one of the three schools supported by the company. Safety training is provided to limit accidents caused by people straying onto the railway line. Hospitals treat up to 12,000 patients, 66 kilometres of new road have been built, and 746 different species of butterfly identified as in need of preservation. 'As a responsible company I would say we want to maintain peace. We want to work in harmony and employ as many people as possible,' the chief executive of ArcelorMittal mining in West Africa tells the cameraman.

Encountering Ebola

Two years later this piece of film footage began to look as quaintly dated as the home movies from the 1960s. Ebola was about to move ArcelorMittal's sense of corporate responsibility to a new level. The first alert came from the company's risk manager, who was troubled by increasing reports of small-scale outbreaks of the disease, two counties away to the west, along the border with Guinea. The company brought in heat-seeking scanners to test for fever among employees and visitors, and head-to-toe protective clothing resembling spacesuits, with built-in respirators. Sets of the protective gear were distributed to hospitals on company sites as well as to other hospitals and clinics in the counties where ArcelorMittal was present. The company built isolation units at the port and the mine. Handwashing facilities became a standard feature at the entrances to offices. A South African expert on infection control was brought in to help company managers understand how the virus spreads, and what might be effective in containing it. Gradually, ArcelorMittal was erecting a protective fence or *cordon sanitaire* around the mine, the township and its shipping and administrative operations. Communities that had been slowly rebuilding links to their neighbours which had been cut off during the war suddenly found themselves isolated again.

ArcelorMittal was not alone in trying to hunker down behind barricades. When the wife of one of Firestone's employees fell ill and died after looking after relatives outside the plantation area, the company used churches and its own radio station to issue information about Ebola symptoms and treatment in a bid to protect its staff. The outpatient health centre was turned into a secure hospital with access only from the outside. A new septic tank was dug to treat waste.[23]

It was less easy to provide this level of containment in the rest of the country, especially in urban centres, where workers were at risk of passing on the disease before they showed any symptoms. It became clear to aid workers that companies such as ArcelorMittal and Firestone were able to do better in containing the disease, not only through controlling infection around their own operating sites, but by exploiting the close connections they had with communities and their knowledge of how people worked, lived, moved and behaved around their sites.

The companies were at the centre of a network of daily life and movement that the public disaster response could tap into. While the government and the international community struggled to develop a coherent plan to address the spread of the disease, companies found themselves functioning as the first line of protection against the epidemic, particularly in the countryside.

Knight's next move was to speak to the Mittal family, the wealthy industrialists who ran the steel conglomerate:

> I told them we have put a metaphorical fence round our business to stop Ebola but it won't stop the problem, which is becoming horrific. People in the country were very frightened and they were right to be, it wasn't that they were overreacting. It made me question what we were doing. At that stage we were being defensive, we weren't acting with others. I wasn't exactly asking for their permission, and I am not sure what they would say no to, because what we were doing was so day to day. We weren't even spending a huge amount of money. A cynic would say it was a good bit of public relations.[24]

Lakshmi Mittal, the company CEO, once described as the world's third-richest man, owns more than a third of ArcelorMittal shares as well as London's most expensive house, on Kensington Palace Gardens' 'Billionaire's row'. He has shares in Queens Park Rangers football club, the Escada fashion brand and boasts the usual list of must-have accessories of the super-rich, such as yachts and cars. The sixty-eight-year-old self-made magnate personifies the complicated and paradoxical relationship between global business and the rest of society: Mr Mittal has been publicly attacked for decisions to shut steel mills in struggling industrial towns in Europe. He is also frequently voted among the most influential individuals in the world, praised for his charitable initiatives, which have set up universities, funded national sports teams and donated generously to Britain's Comic Relief charity. Like other company leaders, Mittal navigates a fine line between financial success and social sensibility.

What Knight proposed to the Mittal family was low cost and commercially prudent, yet socially savvy. However, it propelled the company into a world of international politics and diplomacy that many executives usually try to avoid, and it wasn't what the company set out to do. Knight decided to invite a handful of representatives of other foreign mining companies with business in Liberia to a meeting at ArcelorMittal's London headquarters in Mayfair. As he gave them coffee, everyone began talking about Ebola, exchanging stories, sharing notes. The feeling in the room was anxiety, but also a growing anger that the international community—governments and public bodies— were not doing enough to combat the epidemic. Their frustration was directed particularly at the UN World Health Organization, for its lack of public statements, and for leaving aid agencies and governments in the affected countries to confront the crisis on their own. The reaction of those at the Mayfair coffee meeting was more personal than commercial. As individuals, their concern was that Liberia's plight was being ignored and that the scale of suffering was much greater than outsiders realised. 'We had to shout really loud to be heard,' recalls one participant.

At the same time, many of the companies did not want to be part of a lobby group. They preferred to work quietly on their own. Finally, the meeting decided that the CEOs of nine of the companies present would send a letter to the WHO director general Margaret Chan, politely asking: 'Where are you?' Two weeks later Chan responded, asking to speak to them. A conference call was arranged from the ArcelorMittal office. During that call, not only companies but international health officials, ambassadors and ministers spoke to each other for the first time. More than a hundred people took part. Knight heard later from Chan's office that the letter that had led to such an unprecedented gathering had been received with astonishment by the WHO. This leading international organisation was unused to being approached by the private sector. Business leaders were not on their radar for responding to this kind of emergency. The WHO was also taken aback by how organised the private companies were, and the business leaders' level of logistical and strategic thinking on the issue.

From a handful of companies, the initial group quickly drew in many more who saw the chance to make a practical contribution to the growing crisis. ArcelorMittal's London headquarters developed into a 'war room', manned twenty-four hours a day, seven days a week, receiving updates and co-ordinating company responses to the unfolding disaster. Thus began the Ebola Private Sector Mobilisation Group (EPSMG), a virtual information system and communications hub with its own webpage, www.epsmg.com. 'No-one was expecting it would be so huge,' recalls Ewa Gebala, ArcelorMittal's head of mining communications. 'We had colour-coded emergency plans and trigger points. Every day when I came to the office I did not know what would happen.'[25]

What the companies put on the table was not cash as much as information, logistics and practical resources: the offer of emergency transport where it was needed, an extra vehicle mobilised as an ambulance, a motorbike transferred from Monrovia up-country and a constant stream of data from villages, townships and communities. It was, according to one corporate executive, like running a dating agency, pairing suitable partners who had things to offer each other. Agencies like the World Food Program and MSF would draw up lists of resources and goods they needed. If they could not get them from the government, they turned to the companies. The EPSMG became a way of pooling and exchanging goods and services, as well as a support group for those caught up in a threat that not only challenged their commercial and financial interests, but also touched their personal sense of humanity and obligation.

It was, in many respects, a naïve undertaking. The mining giant Rio Tinto, which operated in neighbouring Guinea, assembled health packs for distribution to affected communities, only to find that they were intercepted at customs and the food in them thrown away because the company had not realised that they infringed customs rules.[26]

The companies' approach was different from the way in which traditional actors such as the government and aid agencies were working with communities affected by Ebola. Education and public information programmes tended to patronise local communities, the companies felt. 'The tone and language were all wrong,' remarked one ArcelorMittal employee. The public announcements ignored the fact that communities knew how to fight Ebola, through word of mouth, working together and using their own customs for staying disease free. They had lived with Ebola long before this outbreak, but the foreign experts often behaved as if only they knew how to control this epidemic.

The companies, which had also in some cases a long history of working with Liberians, recognised that local people had skills, knowledge and resilience, which would combat Ebola more effectively than the response systems imposed by outsiders. ArcelorMittal believed the disease had to be defeated from inside villages and communities, and by using local resources. Moreover, the government response had to rely on state institutions that had been weakened by civil war. They were no match for the rapid and relentless spread of the disease. Even international aid agencies struggled to adapt.[27]

Particularly in the early days, the private sector represented one of the most coherent and effective channels for organising a control and rescue operation. Companies could quarantine workers to keep their estates Ebola free. They could introduce tracking protocols which included hourly handwashing, no-touching policies, passing out gloves and facial masks, and carrying out mandatory temperature screenings every few hours. Any employees who showed a range of up to five symptoms could be quarantined immediately, and later transferred to a secure treatment unit. Companies also had access to resources such as trucks, money and communications to reach beyond their own premises and provide emergency assistance to the wider public. Everyone else needed to generate resources from scratch. The companies were one step ahead.

There was another difference between how companies responded to Ebola compared to other internationals: they refused to leave. On the morning of 8 September, with global news of the epidemic starting to spread as fast as the disease itself, British Red Cross worker David Luke arrived from London on a plane whose only passengers were other aid workers. A month earlier the US government had ordered the families of its officials to leave because of the lack of adequate health facilities. Most of the passenger traffic at Monrovia airport was a one-way tide of departing expats. The US Peace Corps withdrew hundreds of staff. Luke remembers being picked up from the terminal building and driving past dead bodies on the street on the way into Monrovia. The WHO had declared an international public health emergency as the risk of contamination carried by airline passengers materialised. There had been casualties as far away as Europe and the USA. At the beginning of August British Airways, then Kenya Airways, cancelled flights into Liberia, Sierra Leone and Guinea. The government declared its own state of emergency. International borders were shut and the region became a contamination ghetto.

ArcelorMittal had a 110-seater plane on standby, but its evacuation plans were never implemented. Part of the reason was that if the company withdrew, the mine at Tokadeh would fill with water and quickly become unusable. Health experts criticised what they saw as 'questionable decisions' by companies to continue operating. It was felt that they were putting their own interests before public safety.[28] Just one encounter with one person could lead to twenty different individuals being exposed to Ebola.[29] 'We had to ask ourselves constantly whether we were doing the right thing in continuing to operate, and asking employees to work,' remembers Ewa Gebala.[30]

Most public offices and private businesses did close their doors, which was one reason why Ebola did not in the end generate the hundreds of thousands of casualties originally feared. By late 2014 there was an important shift in companies' strategies. 'We began to think what more we could do,' says Gebala. 'We realised we were not alone, so we thought maybe we should find out what others were doing and learn from one another.' Companies that until then had been largely reacting to the epidemic began to mount collective efforts, creating partnerships of unlikely bedfellows—aid workers, middle managers and local officials—in order to pool resources and information to mount a more active response. Gebala again: 'Someone would suggest they had ambulances and other equipment, which they could give to NGOs to access villages more quickly. We realised there was potential and possibilities in working together.'[31]

The mobilisation group became a multiplier, corralling third-party resources and coming up with new ways to identify cases early, in order to contain infection. Based on its success at company level, ArcelorMittal realised that replicating its own systems nationally could make a difference. It moved from protecting assets to protecting employees and their families, and the communities around the mine. From there, the corporate effort morphed into a mission to rescue Liberia as a whole. As well as influencing what was happening on the ground, companies realised they had the power to, in the words of Gebala, 'shake the world' and galvanise action globally.

Why did the company do it? It was certainly in the company's interest to stabilise the crisis, tackling specific flashpoints of the disease and safeguarding the economy as a whole. Even if it could afford to put its assets at risk, it couldn't afford to have the country fail.

At its high point the Ebola Private Sector Mobilisation Group con-vened 500 people across the world, from governments to companies to international health experts, on a conference call to discuss the state of the disease and pool resources to combat it. It was more than the ArcelorMittal phone system in London could cope with. Alan Knight remembers sitting cross-legged on the bed in his hotel room in the middle of the night, preparing to chair the teleconference—the unwit-ting conductor of a virtual global orchestra while he was still learning to read the music.

Even those involved in the mobilisation effort describe it as clumsy and ad hoc. Yet it helped galvanise and co-ordinate international action in the vital initial stages of the epidemic. In a country with minimal levels of public goods and services, with no strategic significance, which meant that it was likely to be overlooked by the rest of the world, foreign investors stepped in to plug a gap and build a network of public action, not just in Liberia but worldwide.

Lessons of Liberia

The Ebola crisis revealed a different face of the global investor. Foreign companies could be more than just motors of economic development on the one hand, and drivers of conflict in fragile countries on the other, in the classic duel between the good and bad corporation that the world recognised. The crisis in West Africa showed that there was a third dimension. Business could also act to help villages and communi-ties mobilise, build their own resistance and resilience, and fill gaps in critical public services. As ArcelorMittal and others demonstrated, companies could offer protection in a storm, but they could also assist local people to protect themselves. This was a novel aspect to the pri-vate-sector presence in a developing country, and it was a new twist in the story of global public opinion, which had focused overwhelmingly on the troubled and abusive relationships between foreign corporations and local people.

The Ebola Private Sector Mobilisation Group showed the ability of companies to command critical resources and use their access to peo-ple on the ground to serve as a bridge between the international com-munity and the local context, opening up a new channel for protection, action and change. Companies had proved to be a vital, unexpected link in a chain of emergency assistance which attempted to combine a mixture of urgent needs and many different players.

The ultimate impact of the corporate effort in Liberia is difficult to assess, in terms of how many lives were saved, who received care, and which communities were held together. One consequence was to make companies, and those they worked with among government officials and humanitarian agencies, understand that traditional responses were no longer adequate. Companies proved they could work with their competitors as well as those who had been among their fiercest opponents and critics. The government's tendency to regard companies simply as cash cows for development was overtaken as novel working alliances emerged between foreign investors, government ministries and civil society. All involved had to learn new skills and ways of working.[32] Corporate power had been bent to a new purpose.

In September 2014 the UN Security Council had unanimously passed Resolution 2177 to address the Ebola outbreak in West Africa, declaring the epidemic a 'present threat' to international peace and security. The resolution attracted the highest ever number of co-sponsoring states, and was only the second Security Council resolution to deal with a non-conflict issue.[33] The vote was an indication of a shift in what was deemed a security risk in an era where climate change, health pandemics and migration have added to the international agenda for action, alongside terrorism and armed conflict.

Global companies had, with sharp elbows and a strategic use of resources, imposed themselves onto this new agenda, and shown their ability to shape global action from the ground up. The Ebola outbreak questioned not only the nature of international security in the modern era, but also who was responsible for ensuring it. The humanitarian effort delivered by aid agencies could tend the sick and provide emergency relief; but the epidemic, and the risk it posed to regional stability and global welfare, was rooted in failed government systems, chronic lack of public healthcare and the effects of years of conflict.[34]

In rising to the Ebola challenge, could companies simply be said to have engaged in an extreme form of humanitarian philanthropy, or did their contribution break new ground in terms of imagining a corporate role in global security? Among the lessons for humanitarian actors was the need to work more closely with communities themselves, something that the companies, for all the mistrust and confrontation with local populations that they engender, proved quicker to realise.

ArcelorMittal describes its responsibility in terms of a duty of care towards vulnerable communities, which were the ground zero of its commercial operations. It simply took leadership in shaping that duty of care into a coherent response, which spread to the whole country. Over the course of the nearly two years that the EVD epidemic lasted, the companies' aims of protecting their assets and their ability to operate in Liberia morphed from private interest into a public good. Ewa Gebala sums it up: 'In this situation you have to be bold. You decide to operate in these countries and you owe something to the people in good times as well as bad. What we did showed what our values really were, and I was really proud of my company.'[35]

Ebola was an exceptional situation in which normal behaviour was suspended by the urgency and scale of the threat. After the outbreak subsided ArcelorMittal and other members of the EPSMG tried to find ways of continuing the spirit of the coalition, and using their experiences to improve the relationship between business and communities in Liberia. Most members agreed to maintain the group as an informal coalition of interest, rather than try to institutionalise it. Alan Knight draws a parallel between Ebola and the HIV-AIDS epidemic in southern Africa. He believes that companies should continue responding to Ebola as an ongoing semi-permanent threat rather than a natural disaster or humanitarian emergency requiring emergency intervention. In this, ArcelorMittal's experience is similar to BP's in Georgia. Both companies have realised that responsibility, and a closer involvement with the problematic conditions that exist in troubled countries, is a long-term commitment.

Many of the members of the EPSMG recognise that they need to move away from patterns of resource extraction and exclusive benefits, which cut off most Liberians from the benefits of foreign operations, and ultimately left them more vulnerable to the EVD crisis. The legacy of Ebola includes the problem of survivors who are ostracised by their own communities, with women in particular unable to find jobs. In 2019 another serious outbreak of the disease in the DRC demonstrated that while healthcare systems remain impoverished, and governments in the region struggle to provide public services after decades of war, health pandemics will be persistent threats that require co-operation between many actors, including the private sector.

The future of democracy, prosperity and peace in Liberia and its neighbours, and the health of its people, depend on transforming the triangular, often fraught relationships between global capital, government elites and local communities. It would be unrealistic to hope that Ebola has improved trust between business and society or day-to-day relationships between local people and international investors. Incidents of unrest around corporate sites continue. There are still fundamental problems to do with social exclusion, poverty, underdevelopment and an unequal distribution of benefits from foreign business operations. These problems remain unresolved. In many cases they have been made more pressing by the collapse of the Liberian economy, and the deep wounds, material and psychological, that the epidemic inflicted on an already troubled society. The role of international companies in West Africa will remain a subject of controversy, and civil society campaigns to hold them accountable will continue.

It is February 2016: arriving at Roberts international airport in Liberia, I decant along with 150 others, from the plane from Europe. It is just a month since the World Health Organization finally declared Liberia Ebola free, and nine months after the government celebrated the end of the worst of the epidemic. On this occasion the airline passengers are the usual mix in any developing country of aid workers, UN officials, businesspeople and Liberians returning home. We have made a brief stop in Freetown, the capital of Sierra Leone, to pick up and drop off extra passengers, another sign that traffic across the region is back to normal. But before we are allowed in the terminal building, we queue up to have a gun pointed at our heads. A pistol of white plastic touches my temple to check my temperature. A momentary flutter of anxiety, as I have brought a cold with me from the English winter. Like the second before the immigration officer stamps your passport, my heart rate climbs, fearing an official refusal of admission. Then I am directed towards a bucket of disinfectant to wash my hands. Welcome to Liberia, Ebola free, but still nervous, traumatised and vigilant.

10

FINDING NEW GROUND

A decade after my original encounter in a London boardroom, listening to foreign investors shrug off problems beyond the perimeter fence in the Democratic Republic of Congo as not their concern, I am back inside another corporate sanctum.

The first-time visitor entering the headquarters of the global mining giant Rio Tinto in London's St James's Square goes to reception to receive a security pass, deposits their coat and is then handed an iPad with a short presentation about health and safety. The video details the fire escapes and drills, and recites the company's commitment to ethical principles. It feels like sitting through a safety demonstration on an aeroplane: necessary but also perfunctory. Once performed, and not a moment before, the ritual permits the visitor to pass through the electronic gates to the offices beyond.

This mundane procedure reflects two preoccupations of our time: being safe and corporate responsibility. The reception routine is a microcosm of these concerns intersecting, a moment in which business and security behaviours fuse.

The story of this book, told in different settings and with various protagonists, is how the global company is increasingly important in efforts to create a safer world in the face of persistent conflict and multiple forms of crisis and insecurity. The places where business and global security routinely confront each other are not headquarters in capitals, but villages, towns and cities where individuals and families rely on the power and possibilities of companies, including foreign corporations, to keep them safe from conflict and instability. Here instability, violence and chronic need come together with the workings of the global economy. Companies have the ability to change facts on the ground and impact life chances in these settings. This also gives them the chance to create conditions for both local and global security.

Companies that invest in the world's most fragile societies are part of how people experience insecurity every day. Sometimes foreign corporations in hotspots of chaos, change and violence are themselves drivers of instability and tension—even conflict itself. Whatever their business, they are often seen as extractive, taking resources such as minerals, crops, water, land, labour and often dignity from communities, and creating conditions for unrest.

Yet companies are also part of what is needed to stabilise fragile societies and build peace through supporting decent and legal livelihoods and the functioning of local communities, by respecting people's rights and providing them with the means to build better lives.

Our understanding of what global security means has expanded in the last two decades, from worrying about foreign invasion to caring about human well-being, ensuring the basic needs and dignity of ordinary people and guaranteeing rights to jobs, housing, food and clean water. Companies are central to delivering this modern vision of security at the local level. They can act as bulwarks against deprivation, social divisions and the complex forms of vulnerability that people experience as a result of conflict and crisis, whether from disease, natural disasters or ethnic violence. Because foreign investment contains the promise of a future that can counter the most chronic and intractable of these risks, global companies are also in a position to help fulfil the aspirations for a good life that are at the root of a stable society.

Conditioned over centuries to think of security in terms of what diplomats, armies and politicians do, the paradigm shift that has been taking place since the end of the last century is to reimagine security in terms of the fears, hopes, capabilities and actions of ordinary people at grass roots. What happens in streets, houses and local meeting places is not determined exclusively by governing elites, militaries and defence chiefs. What we have come to understand is that security is about a million seemingly insignificant personal experiences, sometimes in places far removed from national and international policy, or the attentions of mass media. Poverty, oppression and vulnerability in these places are ingredients that ignite localised conflicts which can spread and turn into global instability.

Flows of migrants and refugees from Africa and Asia into Europe, across borders in Latin America and from Central America into the United States, or from South East Asia to Australia, are examples of how local conflicts can become global problems. The repercussions of civil war in Syria and Iraq were felt not just within the Middle East, but also in murderous attacks on European cities. Illegal trafficking of drugs and people, and pandemics such as the Ebola crisis in West Africa in 2014, illustrate how underdevelopment, war and natural disasters become concerns that preoccupy us all and can affect us directly.

In the preceding chapters we have seen glimpses of how companies confront crises that are rooted in these forms of daily insecurity. The way corporate operations can impact ordinary lives and shape local risks and opportunities has implications for how we can do better to manage a troubled world.

In Mexican cities, plagued by drug violence, and in Liberian villages in the grip of a health epidemic, foreign companies provided protection for local people against overwhelming threats, using their resources on the ground, and their contacts and influence with international policy-makers and other companies, to find novel ways of addressing crises. In the Caucasus, the Balkans and the Middle East global companies had an effect on how people lived together inside communities. They changed relationships between local people and government officials in ways that were both beneficial and disruptive. These stories demonstrate how a foreign investor or contractor can alter the fabric of a society, particularly at moments when that fabric is most delicate or threadbare. This power can be negative, but positive contributions to peace also flow through channels of business activity, as much as human rights abuses and predatory behaviour.[1]

One conclusion from these stories is that treating business as separate from questions of public security no longer makes sense. The interests of companies and the stability and well-being of communities are closely enmeshed, and need to be looked at side by side and as part of the whole picture of what makes people afraid, unsafe and prone to conflict, but also in looking for how to improve their, and our, security.[2]

Seeing how companies are connected to people as they struggle to find stability, peace and development reveals a different picture from the evidence documented by business and human rights activists. Looking through a lens of human well-being, rather than simply human rights, we see ways in which companies are an essential part of building peace. Corporate power and individual powerlessness are two faces of fragile societies, which are often the distinguishing features of the hotspots of a turbulent world. Understanding what makes people vulnerable allows us to see how business power can change powerlessness. How creating opportunities to earn a living, to build better systems of governance and restore personal dignity that may have been eroded by crisis may depend on how a company behaves. Business power is also diffused and spread through supply chains and business networks. Global corporations have connections to the highest echelons of government, and are part of international webs of communication and influence that include consumers, employees and media. How companies behave at ground level can be magnified through these networks of connections, as we saw in the case of Veolia in the Occupied Territories, when a seemingly simple local commercial decision triggered a furious reaction among customers, investors, governments and media worldwide.

These illustrations of what can happen when business power confronts individual vulnerability, suggest that global corporations ought to become an integral part of tackling the challenge of global insecurity. Will business respond? Can companies live up to the proposition that they can make a positive difference to our hostile world? What does it take for a company whose principal aim is to maximise profit, cut costs, preserve its competitive advantage and guard its reputation with investors, customers and employees, to actively address the problems of a struggling society, trying to save itself?

Building peace through improving daily life requires more than obeying universal rules, and respecting minimum standards of good behaviour and human rights. It involves companies going beyond the management mantra of 'do no harm'. What we can see from stories of companies caught in the midst of instability and vulnerability is that they have to start by recognising and understanding their influence. Across the world there is evidence that companies are already reaching ever further into people's lives and, in doing so, breaking down some of the previous barriers between business and security. Without always planning it, companies are increasingly agents of human welfare, particularly when they, rather than governments, are the most important outside presence on the ground. The competences of the state as the traditional source of protection to citizens are starting to merge with those of companies.

However, the potential and limits of what companies can and should do to protect people are still unclear. The question of how global businesses respond to a spectrum of physical, material and psychological threats in crisis-affected societies, and whether they can contribute to preventing them, is only just starting to be talked about. Mostly it is a conversation confined to universities, think tanks and a few progressive company boardrooms.[3] Companies themselves remain mostly unaware of the critical role they can play in these circumstances, or their potential to create the conditions for peace. Becoming partners in government efforts to fight terrorism, combat health pandemics, deal with the problems surrounding forced migration, or work actively on conflict prevention and crisis management has proved until now to be a red line that many companies fear to cross.[4]

Although the idea of corporate social responsibility has become part of the modern management mantra, it does not adequately describe what companies can do or what is expected of them. It is particularly unsatisfactory in defining how companies tackle the dynamics of countries in chaos or conflict. Fashionable labels such as sustainability, resilience, shared value and prosperity attempt to persuade companies to do more.[5] The difference between the modern company executive and philanthropy capitalists or paternalistic corporations that built houses and provided civic amenities and schooling in the nineteenth and twentieth centuries on the basis of an 'enlightened self-interest' is that discretionary acts of welfare are no longer enough to deal with the risks such as environmental damage, social unrest and violations of international laws that arise in many of the most difficult locations where companies operate.

According to one senior executive it is becoming 'socially unacceptable *not* to do certain things. Things people didn't think about before the financial crash are much more visible to the broader base of consumer citizens. The message is that everyone has to play their part.'[6] Another executive describes the challenge thus: 'We know we have to comply with basic requirements such as due diligence on human rights, in reporting and being good citizens. At the other extreme we do not want to become development actors. But a lot of our time goes into thinking where we want to be between these two positions and what the territory in between looks like.'[7]

At the end of this book I want to think about this still-uncharted territory, what it might look like, and imagine how business power can be harnessed more directly to address the concerns of an insecure world. Global drinks company Diageo describes this new ground in terms of diminishing degrees of separation, or the distance between the company and the people who depend on it. In the first degree, the company might do things it believes could lead to change, such as business-skills training. A second degree might see the company provide washing facilities in the community, along with advice on disease prevention or how to use water economically. Here the company is moving beyond strictly commercial activities. In the third degree of separation, the company might carry out projects that have no direct business connection, but that meet community needs. Here is the new terrain of corporate responsibility and contributions to human welfare. It is also where the majority of companies begin to feel uncomfortable.

To illustrate why companies feel this is shaky ground, Diageo told me about a new brewery they planned to build in the province of Kisumu in Kenya. The project will provide income for 20,000 smallholders, create up to 100,000 new jobs, and increase government tax revenues. At the same time it will attempt to change local cultural habits, by making available legally brewed beer instead of bootlegged alcohol. It could also put pressure on local health facilities if there is a rise in alcohol-related illnesses. Four months after the agreement was signed in June 2017, violence broke out in Kisumu over the disputed results of Kenya's presidential election. Diageo had to make decisions on how to preserve the security and welfare of the communities it had invested in while also maintaining a good relationship with the government.

As trade and investment grow across borders, companies increasingly find themselves in places suffering acute and complex forms of insecurity, such as Kisumu. Being there means facing difficult operating dilemmas. Companies can find themselves inadvertently thrust into the role of protectors and guarantors of human security. Unsurprisingly, even the most progressive companies hesitate to go where governments and aid agencies fear to tread.

The idea of the global company as a new kind of Leviathan, as set out in Chapter 3, suggests that business can act as a substitute for governments in protecting people and helping them to improve their lives. The corporation's presence in many conflict zones is influential precisely because there is a lack, if not a complete absence, of state authority. Without a social contract between people and their government, companies sometimes provide the nearest thing in terms of delivering basic goods, and offering physical protection and other kinds of safety nets through underwriting incomes, health services and infrastructure.

Those who worry that corporations already possess too much power will object to such an idea. The proposition that we look to companies to provide security against violence and uncertainty is to allow them licence to manipulate states and usurp roles that rightly belong with governments. Private commercial authority is less accountable than government power, even in countries where democracy is frail and governments do not necessarily act in their citizens' interests. Commercial motives mean that companies cannot be relied upon to provide public goods, including security and welfare, freely to everyone, regardless of the economic and profit cycle. As one academic commentator put it, asking companies to protect us is like putting the fox in charge of the hen house.[8]

Stories of companies in the Balkans, Caucasus, Africa and Latin America show that a three-way alliance between business, people and governments is the most effective way to guarantee human well-being and stable societies. Coca-Cola, in assessing its 'contribution to stability, growth and optimism' (sic), refers to a Golden Triangle model in which the company's initiatives have complemented the role of officials who were formally responsible for citizens, and were also supported by NGOs. The company's efforts to influence a range of issues from the empowerment of women and youth to ensuring clean drinking water and creating jobs came from a global initiative that was also multi-local, 'leveraging universal human traits with high relevance in individual markets'.[9] As Coca-Cola found, the terrain of the good corporation requires companies to work from the boardroom down to the smallest local operation, and with different partners.

Most often, though, this Golden Triangle is less than glittering. The relationship between the main actors that are responsible for protecting ordinary people is frequently missing, or troubled. Visiting remote communities in the north of Liberia in 2018, it became clear that foreign investors spoke to government officials, and held direct discussions with communities. There was also formal communication between local government officials and people in villages. However, none of these different discussions was joined up. As a result, the fate of people who relied on these actors for different aspects of their overall welfare fell between the cracks. The failure of combined and comprehensive action to address grievances and aspirations, risks and opportunities, undermines the chances for real and effective peace and prosperity.

This is the peacebuilder paradox outlined in Chapter 1. Foreign corporations that are able to address core problems of local insecurity, in order to prevent them reverberating outwards and jeopardising the stability of whole nations and regions, are not routinely included in political efforts to build peace and security. Although business and security are the two most dominant features of the era of globalisation, they remain curiously disconnected. Companies are confined to financial and commercial silos, seen as simply purveyors of investment and economic gain. Not enough thought is given by those who make policy, or channel humanitarian efforts to crisis zones, to using companies' presence to mitigate or prevent conflict.

With companies relegated to the margins of policy debates about welfare and security, people who live around mines, plantations or manufacturing plants fall through the cracks in terms of protection. At best, companies are encouraged to contribute funds to areas such as education and health, constructing schools and clinics, without making them part of an overall plan for building communities and keeping them safe.

Meanwhile, companies themselves are reluctant to take on responsibility for the physical or material welfare of local people. 'Once you start doing that, you also become liable for any failure of services,' explains one mining company.[10] According to another: 'We build roads and we contribute to education but what we are clear about is that we do not want to be the state even if we are doing things that are state duties. In many places we are supplanting the state, but if you don't have a state to guarantee services and rights for citizens, it is meaningless.'[11]

As well as needing more cases of companies such as Diageo in Kenya or the experiences of BP in Georgia and Iraq to help map out the ground for corporate responsibilities, a public conversation is required to overcome companies' reticence and set out the terms for a corporate peace. The bulk of evidence of how companies affect fragility and welfare tends to show how they conspire with governments to pervert human rights in their quest for contracts for minerals or construction, tax concessions and other forms of preferential treatment.

What we can glimpse from the tales in this book is that while this perverse type of relationship does occur, for example in the West Bank and the Balkans, there are other cases where companies stand up for local citizens and against government weakness, joining citizen efforts to rebuild a Mexican city devastated by drug violence and chronic poverty, or bypassing state policy to bring economic, environmental and cultural benefits to poor populations in post-Soviet Georgia.

Mapping new ground in Colombia

In Colombia an unprecedented, real-time and highly public experiment is under way to encourage a new kind of corporate behaviour and address the relationship between business, government and communities affected by conflict. A peace deal signed in 2016 between the government and the FARC guerrilla movement called on the private sector to help implement the agreement, to end the world's longest-running civil war. Business was asked to contribute to creating a 'territorial peace' that meant extending basic infrastructure and public goods into areas once dominated by FARC. In many of these areas private companies were the only sizeable presence apart from the guerrillas, the government having been absent during the half-century of conflict. However, a peacebuilding contract between companies, government and people is proving difficult. Public expectations of companies are high. At the same time, many are not trusted by local citizens because of past behaviour, while companies fear they will be compromised for supporting a peace agreement seen as controversial and politically partisan, because it is associated with a previous presidential administration.[12]

A conversation with the new CEO of one of Colombia's largest mining groups revealed his dissatisfaction with government efforts on peace and development, and the opportunities for companies to do more:

> We have not impacted the well-being of the people and we should. It's everyone's responsibility: communities and companies for not insisting on long-term gains, the state for not coming in to occupy the space they are meant to. The private sector should not only generate value for shareholders, but also generate social and environmental value and value for employees. Companies already have logistical chains, we are experts in civil works. We need to step in, but we have to find the right way to do it.[13]

It is not only in Colombia that grounds for an enlarged business role are emerging, however painfully. Another sign of change is the United Nations Sustainable Development Goals (SDGs) agenda, which proposes a set of seventeen objectives to be achieved by 2030. The goals range from ending poverty and hunger to ensuring employment and economic growth and delivering peace, security and justice. The SDGs are an ambitious platform to co-opt business power to change the world by inviting companies to choose from a menu of different kinds of social investments. The UN and national governments need business money to meet a bill for achieving these objectives, which is estimated to run to $24 trillion over the next fifteen years. Instead of being vilified as predators by activist lobbies, companies are suddenly being courted to finance an end to poverty, address climate change, and bring about peace, security and justice. The SDGs have given big companies a seat at the table—nationally, internationally and locally—to discuss how to change societies on a scale that has never been done before and which governments alone could not contemplate. Meanwhile, it is also true that many companies see the SDGs as a chance to polish their social reputations.

Yet not all are comfortable with this sudden shift, which has dramatically increased expectations of what the private sector can do. A delegate at a meeting to discuss what business should do towards achieving the 2030 goals complained that there was no mention of the practical issues facing companies that want to contribute to achieving these goals, only the resources they can provide. The SDG agenda is an example of the mixed messages and confused public attitudes towards big business. The international community of governments and organisations sees company money as an alternative to public budgets, which can be tapped for the rocketing cost of ensuring global stability.

Many NGOs, particularly those that specialise in topics such as human rights and transparency, believe that the pursuit of profit makes companies a menace, particularly to fragile societies, although leading aid agencies such as Oxfam have notable partnerships with big corporations on issues such as poverty, education and health. Against this backdrop, one question for the future of peace and security is whether the global corporation will be accepted as the means to improve equality, development and stability across the globe.

Anyone looking for straightforward answers, or ready recipes for business contributions to peace, has to confront several difficulties. First, the private sector is not a single entity.[14] Even reducing it to transnational corporations involves different kinds of companies, across a range of industry sectors, and a variety of management styles.[15] In trying to define a new terrain of responsible corporate social action, even progressive companies do not act systematically. There is as yet no pattern or blueprint to help them actively confront chaos and crisis, and use their power creatively, although there is increasing guidance on how they can avoid behaving badly.

Second, we do not yet know enough about how precisely companies produce peace, or how building people's welfare at the grass roots can ripple upwards and outwards through chains of value which connect companies to suppliers and customers, investors and policy-makers and through many layers of social and political activity, in order to create national and global—as well as local—security.

What this book has done is place under a microscope situations where companies come into contact with conflict and crises, and reveal some of the fine-grained patterns of how companies manage to mitigate these circumstances. Here the focus is not on corporate strategies, ethical commitments or warm words, where companies promise to respect human rights in order to ensure their licence to operate. It is about the daily traffic between corporate power and resources and people on the ground. What happens in this interaction is determined by local know-how, time-tested ways of surviving, bonds between families or within tribes, and customs which shape personal, family, neighbour and community relations. Here is the fabric of society, and sometimes global companies manage to weave themselves into it, with all its frayed edges and its strong threads, and work with it to achieve results that can benefit the company and local people. Often companies' ability to do this, and to make a real difference to everyday life, comes down to individual initiatives by company managers on the ground with a sense of what it takes to deliver profits and lower risks, and at the same time work for the good of local people.

One executive, discussing my observations of corporate behaviour, suggested that there is a danger of seeing companies in black-and-white terms as either sinners or saints, or, as one writer terms it, 'pro-peace entrepreneurs or conflict profiteers'.[16] Sometimes companies do good inadvertently, while they are more intent on protecting their own reputations, prompting activists to claim that business is simply 'whitewashing', making superficial gestures of social commitment.

Business motives for confronting insecurity are rarely clean-cut. Their reasons for providing protection and welfare, whether by busing workers into guarded factories, providing essential services which have been neglected by government or detecting early symptoms of a fatal disease, are a mixture of wanting to minimise commercial risks, preserve their ability to operate and manage reputations and brands, as well as an instinctive human response or caring reflex to help those in need.

While there are interesting studies that look at motives as a way of predicting corporate contributions to building peace,[17] it seems to me that knowing what drives corporate behaviour is not sufficient to understand how business shapes a hostile world or the chances for peace. The effects of company actions, both deliberate and unintentional, on the ground, where personal security is in jeopardy, are more telling. Here we see companies at moments and places of high stakes, where people's lives are most exposed and a company's ability to do business is most compromised. The conditions for creating meaningful and lasting peace processes—what has been called 'positive peace'[18]—

and preventing violent conflict are most likely to be found in how these interests and challenges combine. The dependence of companies and communities on each other, and the fact that both face complex and connected risks and threats, suggest that the path to sustained peace is through a collective effort that involves both.

One pattern in how business confronts insecurity is the difference between initial corporate intentions and the actual effects of a company's presence. In the case of Veolia, its failure to calculate the impact of its decision to invest in the Jerusalem Light Railway aggravated the chances for peace and had disastrous international repercussions for the company. The risk calculus proved much higher than it expected. When it sought to sidestep the political issues involved in building a railway on Jewish settlement land, civil rights activists inflicted financial and reputational damage on the grounds that it was Veolia's responsibility to protect Palestinian rights.

In Serbia, Fiat's investment led it to play a significant role in the country's post-war reconstruction, a project that was often at odds with the company's economic goals. In both cases, how the outside world viewed the companies' impacts turned out to be different to what the companies thought they were doing in these locations.

We can also detect a trajectory in the different stories of how companies react to insecurity and crisis. As the Colombian CEO commented, companies are realising that they have to rethink ideas and geographical zones of responsibility, learn new roles and recalibrate their commitments to communities. BP learned from mistakes in Colombia and the Gulf of Mexico, and brought a new sense of obligation to the politics of the pipeline project in Georgia, later applying the same duty of care to communities in post-war Iraq. Its project to mitigate the environmental damage of an oil pipeline in the Caucasus turned into a long-term initiative to encourage economic development, as well as programmes to plug gaps in public goods and governance that resulted from Georgia's difficult transition from an authoritarian past. While nation-states in the Caucasus and the Middle East were focused on a struggle for influence in regions of strategic geopolitical significance, BP's intervention addressed a different set of challenges to do with everyday living, which affected the prospects for regional stability, but less visibly.

187

The companies that contributed to the Ebola Private Sector Mobilisation Group in West Africa understood that they needed to take a lead in responding to the health crisis that was enveloping the region, and that their special resources and knowledge could make a difference to the outcomes of the pandemic. These are examples of companies coming to realise the power that they have to protect people and shape the course of crises and transitions from conflict, and not shrinking from using that influence.

In this emerging puzzle of how business can ensure a safer world, public attitudes to corporate power will play an important part. Investors in multinational corporations are starting to realise the need for companies to act responsibly and do something about the welfare of local populations they work alongside. They increasingly understand the financial benefits (or losses) that come with certain types of corporate behaviour. However, the mixed messages towards companies that take part in the SDG agenda are just part of a much larger picture of continuing public hostility to the idea of global business power.

The private sector has not shaken off the pervasive distrust that motivated first anti-globalisation demonstrations, then the Occupy movement, and subsequently the Extinction Rebellion protests. Hostility to big business is fuelled by claims and evidence that companies such as Facebook and Amazon have violated privacy, under-paid taxes or engaged in dubious labour practices. If people need protecting, it is more likely to be from these Leviathans, rather than by them.

Human welfare and security represent a new benchmark for judging corporate behaviour. We criticise companies that pollute and violate human rights, but we could also assess them in terms of how they safeguard individuals and communities that are exposed to downturns, violence and chaos. A human welfare standard should reflect that vulnerable people in fragile countries face a whole range of different threats to everyday existence. Encouraging companies to meet that standard and demonstrate how they can mitigate those threats is a means of holding them accountable for how they operate in remote locations. It also becomes the grounds for challenging contemporary capitalism to operate in new ways.

For a millennial generation not prepared to accept untrammelled corporate power, and a worldwide public, which saw its trust in business crumble in the face of corporate scandals and the 2008 financial crisis, the idea of human security—making people safe when they are most at risk—opens up a new agenda for scrutinising business action. In this sense, the experiences of global corporations in different contexts of insecurity described in this book, help us to build a picture of contemporary corporate power and influence, and provide new insights into the purpose of business itself.

My sense in writing this book was that understanding how companies affect the welfare of communities in crisis could help to suggest new possibilities to rethink the terms of global peace. As changes in the multilateral world order, the decline of *Pax Americana* across the world, new dynamics of international politics and new types of disaster combine to reshape our security imaginaries, we have to find new ways to stay safe and new solutions to crises across the globe. Looking at how corporations operate at ground zero of insecurity and underdevelopment could help us, as bystanders, to decide whether their contribution to those challenges is part of what we should expect from today's business leaders. Between regarding companies as threats to the public good, and wanting their money to help fix global problems, is there a space for companies' and society's interests to combine?

In the last two decades, while we have become more critical of big business, we are also aware that companies are themselves complex ecosystems consisting of customers, employees, unions, suppliers, even government and civil society partners. This ecosystem includes those who are independent of them, but who experience their impacts. This means that in these different dimensions of a company, there is a part of all of us in what corporations do. For that reason, we can no longer regard them as separate from our concerns about security, or maintain artificial distinctions between the interests of companies, communities, government, social movements and activists. The story of this book is how these divisions break down in circumstances where these different interests are all threatened by crisis. Companies, and the rest of us too, must decide whether a path to peace is one we are ultimately bound to travel together in order to build a safer world.

NOTES

1. CONFLICT AND THE CORPORATION

1. David Van Reybrouck, *Congo: The Epic History of a People*, London and New York: Fourth Estate/Ecco, 2015, p. 39.
2. 'The Impact of Mining in the Democratic Republic of Congo: Performance to Date and Future Challenges', Oxford Policy Management, October 2013, available at https://www.academia.edu/1337 2247/The_impact_of_mining_in_the_Democratic_Republic_of_Congo_Performance_to_date_and_future_challenges.
3. Jason Stearns, *Dancing in the Glory of Monsters*, New York: Public Affairs, 2012, p. 299.
4. T. Gambino, 'Background Case Study, Democratic Republic of Congo', *World Development Report 2011*, 2 March 2011.
5. International Alert, 'The Role of the Exploitation of Natural Resources in Fuelling and Prolonging Crises in the Eastern DRC', January 2010, p. 10.
6. B. Coghlan, R. Brennan et al., 'Mortality in the Democratic Republic of Congo: A Nationwide Survey', *The Lancet*, January 2006.
7. Estimates of the death toll vary. While the *Lancet* survey counted over 4 million, the International Rescue Committee claimed that between 1998 and 2007 5.4 million Congolese died as a result of the fighting.
8. Source: International Crisis Group; figures for internally displaced persons are estimates by OCHA and relate to October 2006: UNDP, 'The Human Development Report 2005', available at http://hdr.undp.org/en/content/human-development-report-2005.
9. Georges Nzongola-Ntalaja, *The Congo from Leopold to Kabila: A People's History*, London: Zed Books, 2002.
10. Filip Reyntjens, *The Great African War: Congo and Regional Geopolitics, 1996–2006*, Cambridge: Cambridge University Press, 2009, pp. 284–6.

11. M. Kaldor, *New and Old Wars: Organized Violence in a Global Era*, Cambridge: Polity Press, 2012.

12. World Bank, *Conflict, Security, and Development*, World Development Report 2011, p. 7, available at https://siteresources.worldbank.org/INTWDRS/Resources/WDR2011_Full_Text.pdf.

13. The Conflict Trap thesis was made famous by Paul Collier and Anke Hoeffler, culminating in their book *The Bottom Billion*, Oxford: Oxford University Press, 2007. Collier (p. 22) tells the story of then rebel leader and later DRC dictator Laurent Kabila boasting that he only needed $100,000 and a mobile phone to seize the state—the rest of the money needed to finance his civil war came from $500 million of deals with foreign capitalists that he contacted on his phone.

14. P. Le Billon, *Wars of Plunder*, London: Hurst, 2013.

15. 'Protect, Respect and Remedy: A Framework for Business and Human Rights', United Nations,7 April 2008, available at http://www.business-humanrights.org/SpecialRepPortal/Home/ReportstoUNHuman RightsCouncil/2008; 'Guiding Principles on Business and Human Rights', available at http://www.business-humanrights.org/Special RepPortal/Home/Protect-Respect-Remedy-Framework/Guiding Principles; 'Business and Human Rights in Conflict-Affected Regions: Challenges and Options towards State Responses', United Nations 2011, available at https://www.business-humanrights.org/en/pdf-business-and-human-rights-in-conflict-affected-regions-challenges-and-options-towards-state-responses.

16. UNHRC, Report of Working Group, 10 April 2012, Section II, para. 11, available at http://www.ohchr.org/EN/Issues/Business/Pages/Reports.aspx.

17. Doris Fuchs, 'Commanding Heights? The Strength and Fragility of Business Power in Global Politics', *Millennium—Journal of International Studies* 33 (2005), p. 771.

18. M. Pugh, 'Corporate Peace: Crisis in Economic Peacebuilding', in T. Debiel, T. Held and U. Schneckener, eds, *Peacebuilding in Crisis*, Abingdon: Routledge, 2017, p. 177.

19. M. Berdal, *Building Peace after War*, Abingdon: Routledge, 2009, pp. 172–3; R. Paris and T. Sisk, eds, *The Dilemmas of Statebuilding: Confronting the Contradictions of Postwar Peace Operations*, London: Routledge, 2009, p. 14; M. Doyle, 'Three Pillars of the Liberal Peace', *American Political Science Review* 99:3 (August 2005), pp. 463–6.

20. M. Martin and V. Bojicic-Dzelilovic, '"It's Not *Just* the Economy, Stupid": The Multi-Directional Security Effects of the Private Sector in Post-Conflict Reconstruction', *Conflict, Security and Development* 43:2 (2017); Peter Davis, *Corporations, Global Governance and Post-Conflict*

Reconstruction, Abingdon: Routledge, 2012; G. Millar (2016), 'Local Experiences of Liberal Peace: Marketization and Conflict Dynamics in Sierra Leone', *Journal of Peace Research* 53:4 (2016).

21. See https://www.worldfinance.com/infrastructure-investment/democratic-republic-of-congo-becomes-africas-unexpected-success-story.

22. G. Kell, 'The Global Compact', *Journal of Corporate Citizenship* (September 2003).

23. For examples of a growing academic literature see A. Wenger and D. Mockli, *Conflict Prevention: The Untapped Potential of the Business Sector*, Boulder, CO: Lynne Rienner, 2003; V. Haufler, *A Public Role for the Private Sector: Industry Self-Regulation in a Global Economy*, Washington, DC: Carnegie Endowment for International Peace, 2001; B. Ganson and A. Wennmann, *Business in Fragile States: Confronting Risk, Preventing Conflict*, London: IISS, 2016; J. Oetzel, M. Westermann, C. Koerber and T. Fort, 'Business and Peace: Sketching the Terrain', *Journal of Business Ethics* 89:2(2010); J. Miklian and P. Schouten, 'Broadening Business, Widening Peace: A New Research Agenda on Business and Peacebuilding', *Conflict, Security and Development* 19:1 (2019).

24. J. Miklian and P. Schouten, 'Business for Peace: The New Paradigm of International Peacebuilding and Development', *SSRN Electronic Journal* (2014), 10.2139/ssrn.2538113; B. Leisinger and M. Probst, eds, *Human Security and Business*, Zurich: Rüffer & Rub, 2007.

25. 'Hijacking the SDGs: The Private Sector and the Sustainable Development Goals', Global Policy Forum, Analysis 78, July 2018.

26. Anthropologist Severine Autesserre has described the transnational community of expatriates who devote their lives to working in conflict zones as 'Peaceland'. These inhabitants share a common identity, similar and familiar relationships between themselves and with local populations, and common ways of working (S. Autesserre, *Peaceland: Conflict Resolution and the Everyday Politics of International Intervention*, Cambridge: Cambridge University Press, 2014).

27. Juan Carlos Echeverri, *Las claves del futuro: Economía y conflicto en Colombia*, Bogotá: Editorial Oveja Negra, 2002, quoted in A. Rettberg, 'Business-Led Peacebuilding in Colombia: Fad or Future of a Country in Crisis?' *Crisis States Programme Working Paper* 56, LSE, 2004, p. 2.

28. 'Civil society' usually refers to organisations such as NGOs, community associations, charities and labour unions among others, which act autonomously from policy-makers and business.

29. J. Holmes, *The Politics of Humanity: The Reality of Relief Aid*, London: Head of Zeus, 2013.

30. J. Ford, 'Engaging the Private Sector in Post-Conflict Recovery: Perspectives for SADPA', Institute for Security Studies (South Africa),

17 October 2014, available at https://www.issafrica.org/iss-today/the-business-of-peacebuilding-what-role-for-the-private-sector.

31. A. Abello Colak and J. Pearce, '"Security from Below" in Contexts of Chronic Violence', *IDS Bulletin* 49:1A (2018).

32. M. Kaldor and S. Beebe, *The Ultimate Weapon is No Weapon*, New York: PublicAffairs, 2010. See also chapters by Des Gasper and Amartya Sen in M. Martin and T. Owen, eds, *The Routledge Handbook of Human Security*, Abingdon: Routledge, 2014.

33. J. Ford, *Regulating Business for Peace*, Cambridge: Cambridge University Press, 2015, pp. 15, 16.

34. http://www.irinnews.org/analysis/2013/08/26/what-future-private-sector-involvement-humanitarianism, 26 August 2013.

35. John McMannis, 'Making the Case for Private Sector Engagement in the Fight against Malaria', The Global Fight.org, 29 August, 2017, available at https://www.theglobalfight.org/making-case-private-sector-engagement/. https://www.theglobalfight.org/making-case-private-sector-engagement/https://www.theglobalfight.org/making-case-private-sector-engagement/https://www.theglobalfight.org/making-case-private-sector-engagement/the Case for Private Sector Engagement in

36. Giles Hutchins, 'Futureproofing: The Regeneration Game', The Ethical Corporation, 18 August 2016, available at www.ethicalcorp.com.

2. A DOUBLE CRISIS AND A TURNING-POINT

1. 'An Agenda for Peace: Preventive Diplomacy, Peacemaking and Peacekeeping', Report to Security Council S/24111, 31 January 1992.

2. The humanitarian imperative to intervene was not entirely new for a British audience. Blair's speech had echoes of Gladstone's rhetoric over atrocities in Bulgaria by the Ottoman Empire in the late 1870s, when he called upon the government to join with other European states in forcing the Turks out of Bulgaria: 'I entreat my countrymen to require and insist that the government apply all its vigour to concur with the states of Europe in obtaining the extinction of the Turkish executive power in Bulgaria. Let the Turks now carry away their abuses in the only possible manner, namely, by carrying off themselves': William Ewart Gladstone, *Bulgarian Horrors and the Question of the East*, London: J. Murray, 1876, p. 31.

3. United Nations (2000), *Report of the Panel on United Nations Peace Operations* (Brahimi Report), UN General Assembly Security Council, 21 August 2000, New York: United Nations, p. 3; D. Chandler (2017), *Peacebuilding: The Twenty Years' Crisis, 1997–2017*, Basingstoke: Palgrave

Macmillan, p. 6; for a critique of the expansion and imprecise under-standings of intervention see also chs 1–3 in E. Newman, R. Paris and O. Richmond, eds, *New Perspectives on Liberal Peacebuilding*, Tokyo: United Nations University Press, 2009.

4. Remarks to author, London School of Economics, 29 October 2007.

5. R. Caplan, *Exit Strategies and State Building*, Oxford: Oxford University Press, 2014.

6. J. Stiglitz and L. Bilmes, *The Three Trillion Dollar War*, New York: W. W. Norton & Co., 2008.

7. Anna Fifield, 'Contractors Reap $138 Billion from Iraq War', FT.com, 18 March 2013; Sean McFate, *The Modern Mercenary*, New York: Oxford University Press, 2014.

8. J. Berndtsson and M. Stern, 'Private Security Guards', in R. Abrahamsen and A. Leander, eds, *Routledge Handbook of Private Security Studies*, Abingdon: Routledge, 2016.

9. Mark Sedwill, 'Afghanistan: The 2011–14 Campaign', speech to the Institute for International Affairs, Helsinki, 25 January 2011.

10. Michael Clarke, ed., 'The Afghan Papers: Committing Britain to War in Helmand, 2005–6', WHP 77, Royal United Services Institute, 8 November 2011, available at https://rusi.org/publication/white-hall-papers/afghan-papers-committing-britain-war-helmand-2005-06-whp-77.

11. Key Findings of the 2011 Progress Report on Kosovo, Memo/11/691, Brussels, 12 October 2011, available at http://europa.eu/rapid/press-ReleasesAction.do?reference=MEMO/11/691.

12. L. Tardelli, 'The (Eternal) Return of Liberal Interventionism', *Intervention Today*, LSE IDEAS (2013); N. Cooper, 'On the Crisis of the Liberal Peace', review article, *Conflict Security and Development* 7:4 (2007).

13. United Nations, *The Challenge of Sustaining Peace*, Report of the Advisory Group of Experts for the 2015 Review of the UN Peacebuilding Architecture, 2015.

14. D. Chandler, *Peacebuilding, the Twenty Years Crisis*.

15. 'What's Wrong with Corporate Social Responsibility?' Corporate Watch report, 28 June 2006.

16. Bob Diamond, inaugural BBC Today Business Lecture, 2011. Diamond was forced to resign a year later after the bank was caught rigging interest rates.

17. P. Polman, 'A Sustainable Business Model', Business for Peace speech, Oslo, 19 May 2015.

18. N. Stoop, M. Verpoorten and P. van der Windt, 'More Legislation, More Violence? The Impact of Dodd-Frank in the DRC', *PLoS ONE*

13:8 (2018): e0201783, https://doi.org/10.1371/journal.pone.020 1783.

3. NEW LEVIATHANS

1. M. Brito Vieira, 'Leviathan contra Leviathan', *Journal of the History of Ideas* 76:2 (2015), pp. 273, 282.
2. Thomas Hobbes, *Leviathan*, ed. N. Malcolm, Oxford: Oxford University Press, 2012; K. Hoekstra, 'The Clarendon Edition of Hobbes's *Leviathan*: Leviathan and its Intellectual Context', *Journal of the History of Ideas* 76:2 (2015).
3. Carl Schmitt, *The Concept of the Political*, Chicago: University of Chicago Press, 2008, p. 52.
4. O. Richmond, 'States, Capital, and Institutions vs. Positionality, Arbitrage, Mobility and Verticality', *Globalizations* 6:1 (2017).
5. A. Phillips, 'Company Sovereigns, Private Violence and Colonialism', in R. Abrahamsen and A. Leander, eds, *Routledge Handbook of Private Security Studies*, Abingdon: Routledge, 2016, p. 40.
6. Edmund Burke, speech, House of Commons, December 1783 in debate on East India bill, para. 4.5.17, available at http://www.econlib.org/library/LFBooks/Burke/brkSWv4c5.html#f81; speech on impeachment of Warren Hastings, House of Lords Select Committee 1788: *Edmund Burke, Miscellaneous Writings*, vol. 4, para. 4.F.12, in *Select Works of Edmund Burke*, 4 vols, Indianapolis: Liberty Fund, 1999.
7. Van Reybrouck, *Congo: The Epic History of a People*, London and New York: Fourth Estate/Ecco, 2015, pp. 37–8.
8. J. Micklethwait and A. Wooldridge, *The Company*, London: Weidenfeld & Nicolson, 2003.
9. J. Bakan, *The Corporation: The Pathological Pursuit of Profit and Power*, New York: Free Press, 2004.
10. K. N. Chaudhuri, 'The English East India Company in the 17th and 18th Centuries: A Pre-Modern Multinational Organization', in P. Tuck, ed., *The East India Company: 1600–1858*, London: Routledge, 1998, p. 86.
11. J. Phillips, 'A Successor to the Moguls: The Nawab of the Carnatic and the East India Company 1763–1785', in Tuck, ed., *The East India Company*.
12. N. Robins, *The Corporation that Changed the World*, London: Pluto Press, 2006.
13. D. Honeyman, 'Indian Trappers and the Hudson's Bay Company: Early Means of Negotiation in the Canadian Fur Trade', *Arizona Anthropologist* 15 (2003), pp. 33, 38; R. Ommer, ed., *Merchant Credit and Labour Strategies in Historical Perspective*, Fredericton: Acadiensis Press, 1990,

pp. 189, 196; M. P. Stopp, 'Eighteenth Century Labrador Inuit in England', *Arctic* 62:1 (March 2009); M. P. Stopp, 'Faceted Inuit–European Contact in Southern Labrador', *Études/Inuit/Studies* 39:1 (2015).

14. Jervis Babb, *The Human Relations Philosophy of William Hesketh Lever*, New York: Newcomen Society of North America, 1952, pp. 13–14.

15. Letter to H. R. Greenhalgh, 8 October 1908, Unilever Archives, UARM LBC 8104A.

16. B. Lewis, *'So Clean': Lord Leverhulme, Soap and Civilisation*, Manchester: Manchester University Press, 2008, p. 166.

17. M. Hardt and A. Negri, *Empire*, Cambridge, MA: Harvard University Press, 2001, p. 151.

18. The term used by Argentinian sociologist Guillermo O'Donnell in *Counterpoints: Selected Essays on Authoritarianism and Democratization*, Notre Dame, IN: Notre Dame University Press, 1999.

19. O'Donnell, *Counterpoints*; J. Pearce, 'Elites and Violence in Latin America: Logics of the Fragmented Security State', Violence, Security, and Peace Working Papers No. 1, LSE Latin American and Caribbean Centre, August 2018, pp. 5–6.

20. B. R. Schneider, *Business Politics and the State in Twentieth-Century Latin America*, Cambridge: Cambridge University Press, 2004, p. 131.

21. Edmund Dene Morel, letter to Emile Vandervelde, 29 March 1911, LSE Morel Papers F8, File 99.

22. A. G. Gardner, *Life of George Cadbury*, London: Cassell & Co., 1923, p. 73.

23. *Illustrated London News*, 1851, quoted in Lewis, *'So Clean'*, p. 98.

24. D. Della Porta, H. Kriesi et al., eds, *Social Movements in a Globalizing World*, Basingstoke: Macmillan, 1999, p. 214.

25. Susan Strange, in M. Griffiths et al., eds, *Fifty Key Thinkers in International Relations*, New York: Routledge, 1999, p. 45.

26. E. Grande and L. W. Pauly, eds, *Complex Sovereignty: Reconstituting Political Authority in the Twenty-First Century*, Toronto: University of Toronto Press, 2005, pp. 288, 293.

27. Ignacio Ramonet, *Le Monde Diplomatique*, March 1996, p. 1, quoted in J. C. Graz, 'How Powerful are Transnational Elite Clubs? The Social Myth of the World Economic Forum', *New Political Economy* 8:3 (2003).

28. M. Mann, 'Has Globalisation Ended the Rise and Rise of the Nation State?' *Review of International Political Economy* 4 (1997).

29. UNDP, *New Dimensions of Human Security*, Human Development Report 1994, available at http://hdr.undp.org/sites/default/files/reports/255/hdr_1994_en_complete_nostats.pdf.

30. P. W. Singer, *Corporate Warriors*, New York: Cornell University Press, 2008, Postscript: The Lessons of Iraq.

31. Niall McCarthy, 'Private Security Outnumbers the Police in Most Countries Worldwide', *Forbes*, online, 31 August 2017.

32. D. Avant, *The Market for Force*, Cambridge: Cambridge University Press, 2009.

33. Singer, *Corporate Warriors*, p. 56.

34. The question of whether corporate security consultants can carry arms is part of the controversy around their role. Many PMSCs who work for corporations stress that they are unarmed, although in practice they may have recourse to sub-contractors who are. In fragile environments they often lobby the UN and state authorities to be allowed to carry weapons in order to offer better protection against insurgents and criminals.

35. I have used the term transnational corporation rather than multinational, as these companies are defined by being able to operate across borders, not simply in multiple locations.

36. Pankaj Ghemawat and Thomas Hout, 'Can Chinese Companies Conquer the World? The Overlooked Importance of Corporate Power', *Foreign Affairs*, March/April 2016.

37. Aisha Dodwell, 'Corporations Running the World used to be Science Fiction—Now it's a Reality', *Global Justice Now*, 12 September 2016.

38. F. Halliday, 'The Romance of Non-State Actors', in D. Josselin and W. Wallace, eds. *Non-State Actors in World Politics*, London: Palgrave Macmillan, 2001, p. 27.

39. This power is not solely from private enterprises. The growing role of both Chinese state-owned and private companies in Africa and in the new industries such as communications technology is a piece in the expanding puzzle of corporate influence, where it is linked to Chinese state economic policies. See for example *Dance of the Lions and Dragons: How are Africa and China Engaging*, McKinsey, July 2017.

40. N. Klein, *No Logo*, London: Fourth Estate, 2010, p. xvii (emphasis in original).

41. Brett Forest, 'Shakhtar Fights to Survive in the UCL, but its Owner is in Even More Peril', *ESPN FC*, 18 October 2015, http://www.espnfc.co.uk/uefa-champions-league/2/blog/post/2664720/the-story-behind-shakhtar-donetsks-owner-rinat-akhmetov.

4. THE RESPONSIBILITY GAP

1. A notable exception was a foreign company, Unilever, which had strong personal connections with President Santos who had signed the

controversial agreement with FARC (interview with author, Bogotá, October 2017).

2. Bogotá Chamber of Commerce, *National Peace Business Survey*, 2017.
3. Brigard Urrutia, Business roundtable, Bogotá, 6 March 2019.
4. International Commission on State Sovereignty, *The Responsibility to Protect: Report of the International Commission on Intervention and State Sovereignty*, Ottawa: International Development Research Centre, 2001.
5. International Commission on State Sovereignty, *The Responsibility to Protect*.
6. The use of armed force by NATO against Libya in 2011, using an R2P justification, was particularly criticised as being a cover for Western interference.
7. J. Welby, *Can Companies Sin? 'Whether', 'How' and 'Who' in Company Accountability*, Nottingham: Grove Books, 1992, quoted in Andrew Brown, 'Justin Welby on BP, Deepwater Horizon and Corporate Sin', *The Guardian*, 18 November 2012, available at https://www.theguardian.com/commentisfree/andrewbrown/2012/nov/18/justin-welby-bp-deepwater-corporate-sin.
8. C. Tilly, 'War Making and State Making as Organized Crime', in P. B. Evans et al. (eds), *Bringing the State Back In*, Cambridge: Cambridge University Press, 1985, p. 160.
9. Karen Lund Petersen, 'Risk, Responsibility and Roles Redefined: Is Counterterrorism a Corporate Responsibility?' *Cambridge Review of International Affairs* 21:3 (2008).
10. W. Davies, 'Home Office Rules', *London Review of Books* 38:21, 3 November 2016.
11. M. Friedman, *Capitalism and Freedom*, Chicago: University of Chicago Press, 1962; M. Friedman, 'The Social Responsibility of Business is to Increase its Profits', *New York Times Magazine*, 13 September 1970.
12. T. Dodd, 'Private Sector and Conflict', address to Civil Society Dialogue Network Conference, European Peacebuilding Liaison Office, Brussels, 29 October 2012.
13. A. Scherer, G. Palazzo and D. Baumann, 'Global Rules and Private Actors: Towards a New Role of the Transnational Corporation in Global Governance', *Business Ethics Quarterly* 16:4 (2006), p. 508.
14. In 2015 Shell agreed a £55 million settlement with residents in Ogoniland regarding two oil spills in 2008 and 2009. A UN report of 2011 said the region would take 30 years to recover. Shell has vigorously denied claims in several reports by Amnesty International that the company colluded with Nigerian military in actions which led to crimes including killings and burning of villages. The case of Kiobel v Royal Dutch Shell brought by Nigerian refugees in the US claiming the company abetted human rights abuses was rejected by the US

Supreme Court in 2013 on the grounds that US law was not an applicable mechanism for victims to seek redress.

15. D. Smith, 'Wikileaks Cables: Shell's Grip on Nigerian State Revealed', *The Guardian*, 8 December 2010, available at http://www.guardian.co.uk/business/2010/dec/08/wikileaks-cables-shell-nigeria-spying; E. Hennchen and J. Lozano, 'Mind the Gap: Royal Dutch Shell's Sustainability Agenda in Nigeria', 2012, available at http://www.oikos-international.org/academic/case-collection. Hennchen and Lozano say the claim was in a confidential memo from the US embassy in Abuja on 20 October 2009, recording a meeting between US ambassador Robin Renee Sanders and Ann Pickard, Shell's vice president for sub-Saharan Africa.

16. Ben Amunwa, *Counting the Cost: Corporations and Human Rights Abuses in the Niger Delta*, Platform, October 2011, available at http://platform-london.org/nigeria/Counting_the_Cost.pdf.

17. Robert Bruce Davies, *Peacefully Working to Conquer the World: Singer Sewing Machines in Foreign Markets 1854–1920*, New York: Arno Press, 1976; W. T. Hutchinson, *Cyrus Hall McCormick: Harvest 1856–1884*, New York: Da Capo Press, 1935, p. 728.

18. Lord Leverhulme, address to the annual Port Sunlight Men's Meeting, 1903.

19. Quoted in Steve Hilton and Giles Gibbons, *Good Business: Your World Needs you*, New York: Texere Publishing, 2002, p. 238.

20. H. R. Bowen, *Social Responsibilities of the Businessman*, New York: Harper & Row, 1953, p. 6; for a concise history of the literature of CSR see A. B. Carroll, 'Corporate Social Responsibility: Evolution of a Definitional Construct', *Business and Society* 38:3 (September 1999).

21. Quoted in Carroll, 'Corporate Social Responsibility', p. 275.

22. Big Innovation Centre, The Purposeful Corporation, interim report, 2016, available at https://www.google.co.uk/url?sa=t&source=web&rct=j&url=http://www.biginnovationcentre.com/media/uploads/pdf/The%2520Purposeful%2520Company%2520Interim%2520Report.pdf&ved=0ahUKEwj54Z_hm-zPAhUDI8AKHZnhBX0QFggfMAA&usg=AFQjCNEpkNRYL9x5p4EIIxYCe02hF0e3-w.

23. See for example organisations such as the Ethical Corporation and the Responsible Business Alliance.

24. Jem Bendell, 'In Whose Name? The Accountability of Corporate Social Responsibility', *Development in Practice* 15:3–4 (2005).

25. J. Entine, 'The Myth of Social Investing: A Critique of its Practice and Consequences for Corporate Social Performance Research', *Organization and Environment* 16:3 (2003); M. Martin, 'Conflicted Corporates: Rethinking the Role of Business in Global Security', *Global Policy* 3:1 (February 2011).

26. John Morrison, *The Social License: How to Keep your Organization Legitimate*, Abingdon: Palgrave Macmillan, 2014.

27. M. Porter and M. Kramer, 'Creating Shared Value: How to Reinvent Capitalism—and Unleash a Wave of Innovation and Growth', *Harvard Business Review* 89:1–2 (January–February 2011), p. 64.

28. A. Scherer and G. Palazzo, 'Towards a Political Conception of Corporate Responsibility: Business and Society Seen from a Habermasian Perspective', *Academy of Management Review* 32 (2008).

29. T. Fort and C. Schipani, *The Role of Business in Fostering Peaceful Societies*, Cambridge: Cambridge University Press, 2004.

30. J. Makinen and E. Kasanen, 'Boundaries between Business and Politics: A Study on the Division of Moral Labor', *Journal of Business Ethics* 134 (2016).

31. Blackrock CEO Larry Fink, letter to investors, 2018.

32. Morrison, *The Social License*.

33. http://www.coca-cola.co.uk/stories/coca-cola-goals-for-2020-water-women-wellbeing.

34. Porter and Kramer, 'Creating Shared Value', p. 64.

35. M. Welker, *Enacting the Corporation: An American Mining Firm in Post-Authoritarian Indonesia*, Oakland: University of California Press, 2014.

36. A. Ong, *Neoliberalism as Exception: Mutations in Citizenship and Sovereignty*, Durham, NC: Duke University Press, 2006.

37. The UK Bribery and Corruption Act of 2011 attempted to make individual executives of companies registered in the UK liable for abuses in other countries.

38. Business and Sustainable Development Commission, 'Better Business, Better World', January 2017, p. 6, available at http://report.business-commission.org/.

39. UN deputy secretary general, remarks to ECOSOC Partnership Forum, New York, 11 April 2019.

5. CORPORATES, CARTELS AND A DIFFERENT KIND OF CONFLICT

1. C. Fuentes, *A New Time for Mexico*, Oakland: University of California Press, 1997.

2. Mexico Demographic Profile 2016: *Index Mundi*, available at http://www.indexmundi.com/mexico/demographics_profile.html.

3. US census bureau and INDEX, available at www.index.org.mx.

4. Gordon H. Hanson, 'What Has Happened to Wages in Mexico since NAFTA? Implications for Hemispheric Free Trade', University of California, February 2003, available at https://gps.ucsd.edu/_files/faculty/hanson/hanson_publication_it_NAFTA.pdf.

5. Source: Trading Economics, based on data 2000–16 from Secretariat of Labour and Social Welfare, Mexico.

6. Paul Gootenberg, 'Cocaine's "Blowback" North: A Commodity Chain Pre-History of the Mexican Drug Crisis', in J. Collins, ed., *Governing the Global Drug Wars*, LSE IDEAS Special Report, 2012, p. 41, available at http://www.lse.ac.uk/IDEAS/publications/reports/pdf/SR014/SR-014-FULL-Lo-Res.pdf.

7. US Department of Justice, National Drug Threat Assessment 2011, National Drug Intelligence Center, no. 2011-Q0317–001, available at https://www.justice.gov/archive/ndic/pubs44/44849/44849p.pdf.

8. For the methodology of reporting violence and a comparison of available sources see Cory Molzahn, Viridiana Ríos and David A. Shirk, 'Drug Violence in Mexico: Data and Analysis through 2011', Trans-Border Institute Special Report, March 2012, pp. 2–3.

9. Uppsala Conflict Data Program, Department of Peace and Conflict Research, available at www.ucdp.uu.se/#/country/70.

10. Autonomous University of Mexico, https://www.unam.mx/medidas-de-emergencia/secuestros-en-mexico.

11. Molzahn, Ríos and Shirk, 'Drug Violence in Mexico'.

12. Source: INEGI Survey of Public Security 2013.

13. A victim is abducted, held for up to twenty-four hours while a ransom is negotiated with their family, and then released if it is paid.

14. Tony Payan, 'Ciudad Juárez: A Perfect Storm on the US–Mexico Border', *Journal of Borderlands Studies* 29:4 (2014).

15. Ricardo Ainslie, *The Fight to Save Juárez*, Austin: University of Texas Press, 2013; Stephen Eisenhammer, 'Bare Life in Ciudad Juárez: Violence in a Space of Exclusion', *Latin American Perspectives* 41:2 (2014).

16. See George W. Grayson, 'Mexican Governors: The Nation's New Viceroys', in Courtney Hillebrecht, Tyler R. White and Patrice C. McMahon, eds, *State Responses to Human Security: At Home and Abroad*, Abingdon: Routledge, 2014. Grayson applies the term 'viceroys' to state leaders, arguing that decentralisation gave them political strength and embedded their links to drug cartels and their extravagant behaviour.

17. Source: Economics Ministry, foreign direct investment dataset 99–2019, available at https://datos.gob.mx/busca/dataset/informacion-estadistica-de-la-inversion-extranjera-directa.

18. David Barstow and Alejandra Xanic von Bertrab, 'The Bribery Aisle: How Wal-Mart got its Way in Mexico', *New York Times*, 17 December 2012.

19. Telephone interview with Eduardo Bollorguez, Transparency International, Mexico City, April 2012.

20. S. Sassen, *Deciphering the Global: Its Scales, Spaces, and Subjects*, New York and Abingdon: Routledge, 2007, pp. 213–14.

21. When China joined the World Trade Organization in 1990, the effect was to increase global wage competition, undermining Juárez's cheap wage advantage.

22. Not his real name. His identity has been changed to protect him.

23. K. Staudt and Z. Y. Mendez, *Courage, Resistance, and Women in Ciudad Juárez*, Austin: University of Texas Press, 2015.

24. M. Wright, 'National Security versus Public Safety', in Shelley Feldman, Charles Geisler and Gayatri A. Menon, eds, *Accumulating Insecurity*, Athens: University of Georgia Press, 2011.

25. Staudt and Mendez, *Courage, Resistance, and Women*.

26. N. Parrish Flannery, 'Big Businesses Boom in an Unlikely Mexican City', GlobalPost.com, 23 August 2012.

27. 'Los Templarios se adjudican los incendios contra Sabritas', *Informador. MX*, 1 June 2012.

28. These figures reflect 2012 rates.

29. Interview, Unilever, Mexico City, April 2012.

30. Government of Mexico, 'Informe de victimas de homicidio, secuestro y extorsion 2015', Secretaria do Ejecutivo, 20 September 2016.

31. Interview, Unilever, April 2012.

32. Interview, Unilever, April 2012.

33. Government of Mexico, 'Se Promueve en Ciudad Juárez Recuperacion de la Actividad Economica', press release, Economics Ministry 2010, available at http://www.economia.gob.mx/eventos-noticias/sala-de-prensa/comunicados/6417-se-promueve-en-ciudad-Juárez-recupera-cion-de-la-actividad-economica; F. Calderon, 'Todos Somos Juárez: An Innovative Strategy to Tackle Violence and Crime', *Latin America Journal*, 19 February 2013.

34. Lucy Conger, 'The Private Sector and Public Security: The Cases of Ciudad Juárez and Monterrey', Working Paper Series on Civic Engagement and Public Security in Mexico, Wilson Center and University of San Diego, March 2014.

35. Interview, Cemex, 5 December 2018.

6. GOING OFF THE RAILS IN JERUSALEM

1. F. Halliday, *The Middle East in International Relations*, Cambridge: Cambridge University Press, 2005, p. 111; K. Schulze, *The Arab–Israeli Conflict*, London: Longman, 1999.

2. R. Hinnebusch, *The International Politics of the Middle East*, Manchester: Manchester University Press, 2003, p. 184.

3. Hinnebusch, *The International Politics of the Middle East*.

4. Palestinian populations are also the majority in the Gaza Strip bordering Egypt. Under Menachem Begin, prime minister from 1977, the Israeli government refused to accept the legitimacy of the 1949 armistice lines and refused to return the Occupied Territories on the basis that they were part of the historical land of Israel.

5. Security Council Resolution 2334 (2016), 23 December 2016, available at www.un.org/press/en/2016/sc12657.doc.htm; UN Security Council Resolution 465, which states that 'all measures taken by Israel to change the physical character, demographic composition, institutional structure or status of the Palestinian and other Arab territories occupied since 1967, including Jerusalem, or any part thereof, have no legal validity'. See also R. Hollis, 'The Politics of Israeli–European Economic Relations', *Israel Affairs* 1 (1994); F. Bicchi and B. Voltolini, 'Europe, the Green Line and the Issue of the Israeli–Palestinian Border: Closing the Gap between Discourse and Practice?', *Geopolitics*, online, 17 April 2017.

6. A second line—named without apparent irony 'the Green Line'—was later proposed, intersecting Line 1 to the west of the centre of Jerusalem but also entering areas that Israel captured in the 1967 war.

7. Urban planning in East Jerusalem is an intensely political exercise, with geo-political ramifications, in which higher ranks of the Israeli government become involved. The award of tenders to foreign contractors is part of this politicisation. See D. Seidmann, 'A Layman's Guide to the Planning Process in Jerusalem', 2013, available at www.t-j.org.il/Publications.aspx.

8. Amina Nolte and Haim Yacobi, 'Politics, Infrastructure and Representation: The Case of Jerusalem's Light Rail', *Cities* 43 (2015).

9. Civic Coalition for Palestinian Rights in Jerusalem, 'The Jerusalem Light Rail Train, Consequences and Effects', December 2009, p. 8.

10. Nolte and Yacobi, 'Politics, Infrastructure and Representation'.

11. Interview, Jamal Juma, East Jerusalem, 18 May 2010.

12. O. Barghouti, 'Derailing Injustice: Palestinian Civil Resistance to the "Jerusalem Light Rail"', *Jerusalem Quarterly* 38 (2009), p. 48; Civic Coalition, 'The Jerusalem Light Rail Train', p. 13; Human Rights Watch, 'Occupation Inc.: How Settlement Businesses Contribute to Israel's Violations of Palestinian Rights', 19 January 2016.

13. UN Resolution 63/201 of 2009 called on Israel to cease dumping waste materials in the Occupied Palestinian Territory, because it gravely threatens Palestine's natural resources, and poses an environmental hazard and health threat to the civilian populations.

14. UN Human Rights Council (2016), quoting the Israeli Central Bureau of Statistics.

15. Peter Beaumont and Orlando Crowcroft, 'Bodies of Three Missing Israeli Teenagers Found in West Bank', *The Guardian*, 30 June 2014.

16. Quoted in Peter Beaumont, 'Huge New Israeli Settlement in West Bank Condemned by US and UK', *The Guardian*, 1 September 2014.

17. See http://www.dafka.org/news/index.php?pid=4&id=1120.

18. John Reed, 'Israel: A New Kind of War', *Financial Times*, 12 June 2015.

19. 2018 figures from https://www.veolia.com/en/veolia-group/profile.

20. www.verolia.com/en/veolia-group/profile/csr-performance.

21. www.unglobalcompact.org.

22. Veolia Waterforce Annual Report 2008, available at http://www.veolia.com/en/citizenship/foundation-veolia-environnement/.

23. Israel Ministry of Energy, press release, 11 February 2009.

24. 'Jerusalem Tramway: Exercising our Responsibility in a Difficult Context', available at http://www.sustainable-development.veolia.com/en/Articles/2008.

25. Diakonia, 'Jerusalem Light Rail: IHL Analysis', available at www.diakonia.se/en/IHL.

26. In 2017 the Jerusalem municipality attempted to attract other foreign companies, reluctant to become embroiled in the controversy of building the second rail line, by offering them sub-contracts rather than investment stakes in the project: Avi Bar Eli, 'Foreign Companies Wary of Operating Jerusalem's Light Rail', *Haaretz*, 18 July 2017.

27. See Diakonia press statement, Stockholm, 20 January 2009. The Swedish council said the €3.5 billion decision was based on commercial factors.

28. Hague Regulations, Arts. 46, 47, 52–6; Fourth Geneva Convention, Arts. 33, 43, 46, 53, 55 and 64.

29. For example, UN General Assembly Resolution 70/89, UN Security Council Resolution 465 (1980) and 2334 (2016); International Court of Justice, 'Consequences juridiques de l'édification d'un mur dans le territoire palestinien occupé' (Legal implications of the erection of a wall in the occupied Palestinian territory), Advisory Opinion, 19 July 2004.

30. Reply of the spokesman of the French Ministry of Foreign Affairs (Paris, 26 October 2005); website of the French Ministry of Foreign Affairs, quoted in M. Mendes-France, 'The Jerusalem Light Railway: Symbolic Issue or International Responsibility of the French State?', *Guild Practitioner* 63 (2006), p. 215 (emphasis added).

31. Mendes-France, 'The Jerusalem Light Railway', p. 222.

32. V. Azarova, 'Backtracking on Responsibility: French Court Absolves Veolia for Unlawful Railway Construction in Occupied Territory', 1 May 2013, available at www.rightsasusual.com?p=414.

33. Subsequent cases in the Netherlands and Canada have reached contradictory views on whether corporate liability can be judged by a foreign court: in the Dutch case, which concerned whether Shell (Netherlands domiciled) could be held liable for environmental and human rights abuses in Nigeria, the court ruled that any Dutch person and legal entity was responsible for ensuring that they did not in any way infringe international humanitarian law, with even minor incidents capable of triggering prosecution in the courts of the home country: see Lee James McConnell, 'Establishing Liability for Multinational Corporations: Lessons from Akpan', *International Journal of Law and Management* 56: 2 (2014), pp. 88–104; also VBDO (Dutch Association of Investors for Sustainable Development), 'Dutch Institutional Investors and Investments Related to the Occupation of the Palestinian Territories', research report, Section 3.2, February 2014, for other relevant cases.

34. In 2017 France began considering a bill to require companies to perform due diligence on their subsidiaries and sub-contractors overseas: Novethic, 'Une proposition de loi sur le devoir de vigilance pour les multi-nationales', 8 November 2013, available at http://www.novethic.fr/isr-et-rse/actualite-de-lisr/isr-rse/une-proposition-de-loi-sur-le-devoir-de-vigilance-pour-les-multinationales-141118.html. See also V. Azarova, 'The Bounds of (Il)legality: Rethinking the Regulation of Transnational Corporate Wrongs', in Ekaterina Yahyaoui Krivenko, ed., *Human Rights and Power in Times of Globalisation*, Leiden and Boston: Brill, 2017.

35. Reed, 'Israel: A New Kind of War'.

36. Amnesty International in France had issued a document warning Veolia's management not to get involved in the light rail project, because it risked breaching international law. Quoted in Barghouti, 'Derailing Injustice', p. 52; Diakonia, 'The Unsettling Business of Settlement Business', May 2015.

37. http://www.ohchr.org/Documents/Issues/Business/OCCUPIED TERRITORIESStatement6June2014.pdf.

38. UN Guiding Principles on Business and Human Rights, UN Human Rights Council Resolution A/HRC/17/31, Principle 11.

7. STATE BUILDING IN THE BALKANS

1. Interview, Ezio Barra, business development director, Fiat, 18 January 2010.

2. Interview, FAS management, Kragujevac, April 2014.

3. Bulletin of Public Finance of the Republic of Serbia, 2013.

4. M. Martin and V. Bojicic-Dzelilovic, '"It's Not Just the Economy, Stupid": The Multi-Directional Security Effects of the Private Sector in Post-Conflict Reconstruction', *Conflict, Security and Development* 43:2 (2017).

5. Marija Babovic et al., 'Workplace Violence Related to Privatization: SERBIA. Country Report on Research Findings Related to Structural Violence in Connection with Unlawful and Irresponsible Privatization in Serbia', *SECONS*, July 2014. The authors point out that privatization data are contested but they have used official figures as the most reliable.

6. There are claims that the use of depleted uranium during the NATO bombing of Serbia has led to a significant increase in cancer in areas around the bombsites: Marco Co, 'Depleted Uranium Used by NATO during Bombing of Serbia Takes its Toll', *In Serbia*, 29 March 2016; A. Kerekes, A. Capote-Cuellar and G. J. Köteles, 'Did NATO Attacks in Yugoslavia Cause a Detectable Environmental Effect in Hungary?', *Health Physics* 80:2 (2001).

7. inserbia.info/today/2014/09/serbia-fiat-temporary-closes-factory/.

8. Aleksandar Djordjevic and Milivoje Pantovic, '"Serbia's Detroit" Faces Return to Hunger Years', *Balkan Insight*, 20 June 2016.

9. Interview, Fiat management, Kragujevac, 28 April 2014.

10. Interview, citizens and workers, Kragujevac, 28 April 2014.

11. Fiat policy was to replace all expatriate managers from 2015 in favour of locals. One reason for favouring young workers was to promote them to management positions after training them in Fiat's Italian plants.

12. Babovic et al., 'Workplace Violence Related to Privatization'.

13. This is also based on conversations with citizen groups in 2014 as documented in the report by Babovic et al. ('Workplace Violence Related to Privatization').

14. There is no evidence as to whether this has proved detrimental to the improvement of public healthcare or, inversely, has taken some pressure from it.

15. Interview, FAS non-executive director, Belgrade, 29 April 2014.

16. Interview, Francesco Ciancia, plant director, Kragujevac, 28 April 2014.

17. See http://www.automobear.com/mergers/zastava-automobili-4-years-after-the-fiat-handover.html.

18. 'Balkan Legacy', *The Economist*, 2 November 2013.

19. http://www.automobear.com/mergers/zastava-automobili-4-years-after-the-fiat-handover.html.

20. Best 2013 Global Project award in the roads and highway category by *Engineering News Records* magazine.

21. Kosovo Agency of Statistics: results from the Labor Force Survey 2012 in Kosovo; Ministry of Labor and Social Welfare: Performance Report—Work and Employment, 2012; see http://www.institutigap. org/documents/73419_KEDS.pdf.

22. Foreign direct investment (FDI) 2009–13 amounted to £343 million, slightly higher than Bosnia-Herzegovina, less than one-third of the total invested in Albania; source: World Bank, http://data.worldbank.org/ indicator/BX.KLT.DINV.CD.WD.

23. While McDonald's has invited tenders to extend its franchise in Kosovo, failure to open a chain is proof to some critics of Kosovan politics of the Golden Arches Theory of Conflict Prevention. Advanced by economist Thomas Friedman, the theory adapts democratic peace theory to claim that countries with McDonald's restaurants within their borders will not go to war with each other.

24. Source: UK Highways Agency. Motorway construction figures vary widely depending on the difficulty of the terrain and the cost of land purchase.

25. Paul Lewis, Lawrence Marzouk, Petrit Collaku and Erjona Rusi, 'US Ambassador to Kosovo Hired by Construction Firm he Lobbied for', The Guardian, 14 April 2014.

26. In an interview, the American Chamber of Commerce, seen as the mouthpiece of the US embassy, said that the appointment of the former ambassador did not infringe protocols.

27. GAP Institute, 8 July 2014, available at http://www.institutigap.org/ news/589.

28. Interview, American Chamber of Commerce, 10 October 2014.

29. Jeta në Kosovë (Kosovo news website), 2012.

30. Centre for Research, Documentation and Publication, 'Occupational Safety in the Construction Industry', in Country Report on Human Security: Kosovo, November 2014.

31. Law No. 04/L-161 on Safety and Health at Work, June 2013.

32. ENKA's construction sites are audited by the British Standards Institute on a random basis twice a year, but none of these reports is published or available externally. Any allegations of safety breaches by employees are dealt with by the company's legal department.

33. Quoted in Centre for Research, Documentation and Publication, 'Occupational Safety in the Construction Industry'.

34. This is however lower than comparable projects elsewhere in the region. Source: ENKA Overview 2014.

35. The EU Special Representative in Kosovo told a meeting of business leaders that the highway would be good for Kosovan traders and producers, giving them 'improved access to materials and markets': 'The Business Horizon', American Chamber of Commerce, August 2014.

36. A. Capussella, 'Kosovo's Pyramidal Highway and Remarkable Generosity', LSE blog, 19 February 2015, available at https://blogs. lse.ac.uk/lsee/2015/02/19/kosovos-pyramidal-highway-and-remark-able-generosity/; see also A. Capussella, *State-building in Kosovo: Democracy, EU Interests and US Influence in the Balkans*, London: I. B. Tauris, 2015.

8. BEYOND THE PIPELINE: REPUTATION RECOVERY IN GEORGIA

1. Caspian Development Advisory Panel, Final Report and Conclusions, January 2007, available at http://www.bp.com/.../CDAP_final_report_conclusions_jan2007.pdf.

2. \BP annual report and accounts 2018.

3. Friends of the Earth UK conducted a campaign examining the impact of the Georgia pipeline on the basis that BP was a British company building it.

4. Jonathan Prynn and Lucy Tobin, 'Protesters Storm Stage at BP Annual Meeting', *London Evening Standard*, 14 April 2011.

5. J. Stempel and P. Bansal, 'BP Sues Transocean for $40 Billion over Oil Spill', Reuters (online), 21 April 2011; 'BP Shareholders Call for Sell-off', Australian Network News (online), 18 April 2011.

6. Deep Horizon Study Group, *Final Report on the Investigation of the Macondo Well Blowout Disaster*, 1 March 2011, available at http://ccrm. berkeley.edu/pdfs_papers/bea_pdfs/DHSGFinalReport-March2011-tag.pdf.

7. Christian Oliver, 'EU Strengthens Resilience to Russian Gas Supply Threats', *Financial Times*, 16 February 2016.

8. OPEC is the oil-producing countries' cartel.

9. Quoted in T. de Waal, 'Reinventing the Caucasus', Institute of War and Peace Reporting, 2002, available at https://iwpr.net.

10. Interview, Liana Jervalidze, Tbilisi University, 16 March 2011.

11. M. Kaldor, 'Oil and Conflict: The Case of Nagorno Karabakh', in M. Kaldor, T. L. Karl and Y. Said, eds, *Oil Wars*, London: Pluto Press, 2007.

12. See e.g. P. Collier and A. Hoeffler, *Greed and Grievance in Civil War*, Washington, DC: World Bank, 2001.

13. N. Killick, *Conflict Prevention in Azerbaijan*, London: International Alert, 2002.

14. J. Pearce, 'Oil and Armed Conflict in Casanare Colombia: Complex Contexts and Contingent Moments', in M. Kaldor, T. L. Karl and Y. Said, eds, *Oil Wars*.

15. M. Vardiashvili, 'Georgia Tourism Push Marred by Land Disputes',

Institute for War and Peace Reporting (online), 22 April 2011, available at https://iwpr.net/report-news/georgia-tourism-push-marred-land-disputes.

16. 'Oil Pipeline has the Power to Change Lives', *Financial Times*, 14 February 2003.

17. Interview, Gardabani District, Georgia, 17 March 2011.

18. Interview, Kvemo Kapanakhchi district, 17 March 2011.

19. Interview, Ketevan Vashakidze, Eurasia Partnership Foundation, Tbilisi, 15 March 2011.

20. Interview, Irina Pruidze, Tbilisi, 16 March 2011.

21. In partnership with the publicly funded European Bank for Reconstruction and Development, which committed $1 million.

22. See https://www.thecornerhouse.org.uk/resource/environmental-and-social-impact-assessment-btc-pipeline.

23. Terry McAlister, 'Amnesty Calls for Action on Caspian', *The Guardian*, 20 May 2003.

24. Interview, Ketevan Vashakidze, Tbilisi, 15 March 2011.

25. BP's contract with the Georgian government had followed EU rather than local law.

26. For example, it sponsored the introduction of a food-safety label.

27. Interview, Ekaterine Popkhadze, Georgian Young Lawyers' Association, 16 March, 2011; interview, Liana Jervalidze, Tbilisi University, 16 March 2011.

28. In the same year the government decided to ban NGOs from entering schools without specific prior approval.

29. Debra Sequeira, Richard Wyness, Ted Pollett and Rachel Kyte, *The Baku–Tbilisi–Ceyhan (BTC) Pipeline Project*, International Finance Corporation (IFC), Lessons of Experience, No. 2, September 2006, available at https://www.ifc.org/wps/wcm/connect/227f116b-f504-4d64-92c4-415edd461d2d/BTC_LOE_Final.pdf?MOD=AJPERES&CACHEID=ROOTWORKSPACE-227f116b-f504-4d64-92c4-415edd461d2d-jqeJ4q9.

30. H. Lax, *States and Companies: Political Risks in the International Oil Industry*, New York: Praeger, 1988.

31. Interview, Gia Gvaladze, Tbilisi, March 2011.

32. Caspian Development Advisory Panel, Final Report and Conclusions, January 2007; see also response by BP: https://www.bp.com/content/dam/bp-country/en_az/pdf/CDAP-reports/CDAP_Final_Report_Response_Letter_en.pdf.

33. See https://www.bp.com/en/global/corporate/sustainability/value-to-society/case-studies/building-community-relations-in-iraq.html.

9. THE POWER OF PROTECTION IN LIBERIA

1. Interview, Alan Knight, London, 21 July 2017.
2. World Health Organization, 'Ebola Situation Report 17 June 2015', WHO, 2015, available at http://apps.who.int/ebola/current-situation/ebo-la-situation-report-17-june-2015, p. 4.
3. Interview, Alan Knight, London, 21 July 2017.
4. Suzanne Beukes, 'Finding Ebola's "Patient Zero"', *The Guardian*, 28 October 2014.
5. Marc Dubois, Caitlin Wake, Scarlett Sturridge and Christina Bennett, 'The Ebola Response in West Africa', Humanitarian Policy Group working paper, October 2015, available at https://www.odi.org/sites/odi.org.uk/files/odi-assets/publications-opinion-files/9903.pdf.
6. The HPG report citing the final report of the Ebola Interim Assessment Panel in July 2015 (Dubois et al., 'The Ebola Response in West Africa', p. 16) notes that the WHO did not want to anger governments in the countries at the heart of the outbreak by declaring an emergency. 'MSF's early appeals for help went largely unheeded, and most organisations continued to distance themselves from Ebola even after it became more evidently a crisis.' Moreover, interviews for the HPG study revealed that many international agencies and NGOs already present in West Africa stayed silent out of deference to the WHO, which was assumed to have superior technical expertise and designated authority.
7. World Health Organization, 'Ebola Response Roadmap Situation Report 1', 29 August 2014, available at http://apps.who.int/iris/bitstream/10665/131974/1/roadmapsitrep1_eng.pdf?ua=1.
8. Centers for Disease Control and Prevention (CDC), 'Estimating the Future Number of Cases in the Ebola Epidemic: Liberia and Sierra Leone, 2014–2015', *Morbidity and Mortality Weekly Report (MMWR)* 63:3 (2014).
9. WHO Ebola Response Team, 'Ebola Virus Disease in West Africa: The First 9 Months of the Epidemic and Forward Projections', *New England Journal of Medicine* 371 (16 October 2014).
10. Telephone interview, 27 June 2017.
11. World Bank figures for 2013, published 2014.
12. World Food Programme 2016 figures.
13. Amended agreements in 2005 and 2008 included new requirements for the company to provide housing, drinking water and bathrooms to employees.
14. Review of 2005 Concession Agreement, TLC Africa.com, available at http://tlcafrica.com/Firestone_Agreement_Comparison_2005–02007.pdf.

15. World Bank, 'Citizens' Engagement in Concession Management in Liberia', unpublished report, 2016.

16. For example, between 2006 and 2016 mining companies contributed more than $40 million to community projects.

17. Liberia Extractive Industries Transparency Initiative, available at http://www.leiti.org.lr/uploads/2/1/5/6/21569928/leiti_report_7th____8th_summary_final_for_printing.pdf.

18. John Aglionby, 'Miners Dig in to Weather Storm in Liberia', *Financial Times*, 8 April 2016.

19. An Australian government report in 2014 noted that concession sites, especially in mining and agriculture, were 'mired' in abuses of workers, poor working conditions and conflicts over land. It noted that while iron-ore mining in particular had the potential to pull Liberia out of its post-war, post-crisis poverty, the business model chosen by the state to exploit this valuable national asset was 'unfavourable': Silas Kpanan Ayoung Siakor and Ismaail Qaiyim, 'Poverty in the Midst of Plenty', Sustainable Development Institute, 2014.

20. 2016 profits before interest, tax and dividends. Source: Press release, 2016 financial results March 2017, available at http://corporate.arcelormittal.com/~/media/Files/A/ArcelorMittal/investors/results/previous-results/2016/ER2016Q4_en.pdf.

21. Graham Greene's account of a four-week journey through Sierra Leone and Liberia in 1935, *Journey without Maps*, claimed that secret societies are more embedded in Liberia than anywhere else in West Africa. Greene gave lurid accounts of human sacrifices by animalist societies—the Terrapin Society for women and the Snake Society for men. This is echoed in journalist Tim Butcher's account of his own journey following Greene's footsteps more than seventy years later in 2014, where he describes what is known of the Poro and Mano societies in northern Liberia. See T. Butcher, *Chasing the Devil*, New York: Vintage, 2011, p. 247.

22. 'Shots Fired as Liberia Police Quell ArcelorMittal Mine Protest', Reuters, 5 July 2014, available at http://www.reuters.com/article/us-liberia-arcelormittal-sa-idUSKBN0F924020140704.

23. Claire Zillman, 'In Africa, Foreign Corporations Protect their Own from Ebola', *Fortune*, 8 August 2014.

24. Interview, Alan Knight, London, 21 July 2017.

25. Telephone interview, Ewa Gebala, 17 July 2017.

26. Interview, Rio Tinto, London, 20 September 2017.

27. See http://www.imedpub.com/integrative-journal-of-global-health/.

28. Telephone interview, Jessi Hanson, University of Pittsburgh.

29. J. Hanson, P. S. Faley and M. Quinn, 'Analysis of the Liberian Ebola

Survivors Support System (ESSS)', *Integrative Journal of Global Health* 1:2 (2017).

30. Telephone interview, Ewa Gebala, 17 July 2017.
31. Telephone interview, Ewa Gebala, 17 July 2017.
32. Rio Tinto, for example, established strict guidelines including designating which government ministry in Guinea it would liaise with, primarily in order to avoid confusion and duplication.
33. Anna Hood, 'Ebola: A Threat to the Parameters of a Threat to the Peace?' *Melbourne Journal of International Law* 16 (2015).
34. Dubois et al., 'The Ebola Response in West Africa', p. 16.
35. Telephone interview, Ewa Gebala, 17 July 2017.

10. FINDING NEW GROUND

1. For more examples of business actions in conflict zones see D. Sweetman, *Business, Conflict Resolution and Peacebuilding*, Abingdon: Routledge, 2009, particularly pp. 41–7.
2. The UN's Guiding Principles on Business and Human Rights, for example, are seen by some as emphasising the separateness of business and failing to encourage companies, governments and civil society groups to develop a combined duty of care towards individuals, which also builds community resilience and mends broken societies. See D. Bilchitz, 'A Chasm between "Is" and "Ought"? A Critique of the Normative Foundations of the SRSG's Framework and Guiding Principles', in S. Deva and D. Bilchitz, *The Human Rights Obligations of Business: Beyond the Corporate Responsibility to Respect?* Cambridge: Cambridge University Press, 2013, p. 119.
3. T. Borzel and T. Risse, 'Public–Private Partnerships: Effective and Legitimate Tools of Transnational Governance', in E. Grande and L. W. Pauly, eds, *Complex Sovereignty: Reconstituting Political Authority in the Twenty-First Century*, Toronto: University of Toronto Press, 2005; G. Schuppert, 'Von Ko-produktion von Staatlichkeit zur Co-Performance of Governance', SFB Governance Working Paper Series no. 12, 2008; N. Deitelhoff and K. D. Wolf, *Corporate Security Responsibility? Corporate Governance Contributions to Peace and Security in Zones of Conflict*, Basingstoke: Palgrave Macmillan, 2010.
4. See the study of Danish companies by Karen Lund Petersen ('Risk, Responsibility and Roles Redefined', *Cambridge Review of International Affairs* 21:3 (2008).); S. Levin, 'Tech Giants Team up to Fight Extremism Following Cries that they Allow Terrorism', *The Guardian*, 26 June 2017.
5. J. Webb, 'The Shared Value of Corporate Social Responsibility', *Financial*

Times, 11 February 2016. The idea of shared value was put forward by Harvard Business School professors Michael Porter and Michael Kramer in their article 'The Big Idea: Creating Shared Value', *Harvard Business Review*, available at https://philoma.org/wp-content/uploads/docs/2013_2014_Valeur_actionnariale_a_partagee/Porter__Kramer_-_The_Big_Idea_Creating_Shared_Value_HBR.pdf.

6. Interview, Diageo, 16 August 2017.

7. Interview, Peter Harvey, Rio Tinto, London, 20 September 2017.

8. D. Avant, 'NGOs, Corporations and Security Transformation in Africa', *International Relations* 21:2 (2007), quoted in M. Feill, *Global Governance and Corporate Responsibility in Conflict Zones*, Basingstoke: Palgrave Macmillan, 2011, p. 29.

9. H. Banks, 'The Business of Peace: Coca-Cola's Contribution to Stability, Growth and Optimism', *Business Horizons* 59(2016).

10. Interview, Anglo-American, London, 8 December 2016.

11. Interview, CSR representative, Ecopetrol, Bogotá, 19 October 2017.

12. Colombian communities have the right under the constitution to hold local plebiscites on whether they want the continued presence of mining companies. In a number of recent cases these so-called popular consultations have led to companies being asked to leave.

13. Interview, CEO of Cerrejon, Bogotá, 8 March 2019.

14. Private-sector initiatives to organise security in Ciudad Juárez in Mexico, discussed in Chapter 4, included two bar and two employer associations, business chambers, restaurant owners and a local economic development organization.

15. See C. J. Bond, 'Positive Peace and Sustainability in the Mining Context: Beyond the Triple Bottom Line', *Journal of Cleaner Production* 84 (2014) on how mining companies face different conditions from other companies in considering how to contribute to a 'triple bottom line' that includes promoting peace.

16. D. B. Subedi, '"Pro-Peace Entrepreneur" or "Conflict Profiteer"? Critical Perspective on the Private Sector and Peacebuilding in Nepal', *Peace and Change* 38:2 (April 2013).

17. A. Rettberg, 'Need, Creed and Greed: Understanding why Business Leaders Focus on Peace', *Business Horizons* 59:5 (2016); Feill, *Global Governance and Corporate Responsibility*.

18. J. P. Lederach, *Building Peace: Sustainable Reconciliation in Divided Societies*, Washington, DC: United States Institute for Peace, 1997.

INDEX

INDEX

INDEX

INDEX